Message a

We are inviting you to become a Charter Member of our recently launched zagat.com subscription service for a special introductory price of only $9.95 (a 33% discount off the normal membership charge).

The benefits of membership include:

- **Ratings and Reviews:** Our trademark restaurant ratings and reviews for 45 cities worldwide. By year-end, our coverage will expand to 70 cities.
- **New Restaurants:** A look at restaurants as they open throughout the year.
- **ZagatWire:** Our monthly e-mail newsletter covering the latest restaurant openings, closings, chef changes, special offers, events, promotions and more.
- **Advanced Search:** With 50+ criteria, you'll find the perfect place for any occasion.
- **Discounts:** Up to 25% off at our online Shop.
- **Dining Diary:** An online record of your restaurant experiences, both positive and negative.

Given all these benefits, we believe that your zagat.com membership is sure to pay for itself many times over – each time you have a good meal or avoid a bad one.

To redeem this special offer, go to zagat.com and enter promotional code BOST2003 when you subscribe.

Please join us.

Nina and Tim
Nina and Tim Zagat

P.S. Voting at zagat.com will continue to be free of charge.

Offer expires 12/31/03. Cannot be combined with any other offer.

ZAGATSURVEY®

2003/04

BOSTON RESTAURANTS

Local Editor: Carolyn B. Heller
Local Coordinator: Maryanne Muller
Editor: Sinting Lai

Published and distributed by
ZAGAT SURVEY, LLC
4 Columbus Circle
New York, New York 10019
Tel: 212 977 6000
E-mail: boston@zagat.com
Web site: www.zagat.com

Acknowledgments

We gratefully acknowledge the assistance of the following people and organizations: Alan, Michaela and Talia Albert, Kimberly Barrett, Lynn Bryant, Nancy Civetta, Culinary Guild of New England, Bill DeSousa, Glenn Faria, Randy Hammer, Anne Hanyen, Chris Haynes, Audrey and Ken Heller, Sue Jensen, Kit and Michael Krugman, Michelle Langlois, Sarah Leaf-Herrmann, Chris Lyons, Martha's Vineyard Chamber of Commerce, Nantucket Chamber of Commerce, Lisa O'Neill, Carol Pankin, Andrea Pyenson, Joy Rotondi, Marji Smith, Martha Sullivan and Jennifer Yogel.

This guide would not have been possible without the hard work of our staff, especially Reni Chin, Anna Chlumsky, Schuyler Frazier, Shelley Gallagher, Katherine Harris, Natalie Lebert, Mike Liao, Dave Makulec, Rob Poole, Robert Seixas and Sharon Yates.

The reviews published in this guide are based on public opinion surveys, with numerical ratings reflecting the average scores given by all survey participants who voted on each establishment and text based on direct quotes from, or fair paraphrasings of, participants' comments. Phone numbers, addresses and other factual information were correct to the best of our knowledge when published in this guide; any subsequent changes may not be reflected.

© 2003 Zagat Survey, LLC
ISBN 1-57006-493-8
Printed in the United States of America

Contents

About This Survey	5
What's New	6
Key to Ratings & Symbols	7
TOP RATINGS	
• Most Popular Places	9
• Food; Cuisines, Features, Locations	10
• Decor; Outdoors, Romance, Rooms, Views	14
• Service	15
• Best Buys	16
RESTAURANT DIRECTORY	
Names, Addresses, Phone Numbers, Web Sites, Ratings and Reviews	
• Boston	18
• Cape Cod	158
• Martha's Vineyard	173
• Nantucket	179
INDEXES	
Cuisines	188
Locations	199
Special Features	
Breakfast	208
Brunch	208
Buffet Served	209
Business Dining	209
BYO	210
Catering	210
Child-Friendly	212
Critic-Proof	214
Dancing	214
Delivery/Takeout	214
Dining Alone	216
Entertainment	217
Fireplaces	218
Game in Season	218
Historic Places	219
Hotel Dining	220
"In" Places	221
Jacket Required	221
Late Dining	221
Meet for a Drink	222
Noteworthy Newcomers	222
Offbeat	223
Outdoor Dining	223
Parking	225
People-Watching	227
Power Scenes	227
Private Rooms	228
Quiet Conversation	230

Raw Bars	230
Reserve Ahead	231
Romantic Places	232
Singles Scenes	232
Sleepers	232
Tasting Menus	233
Theme Restaurants	233
Views	233
Waterside	234
Winning Wine Lists	234
Worth a Trip	235
Wine Chart	236

About This Survey

For 24 years, Zagat Survey has reported on the shared experiences of diners like you. Here are the results of our *2003/04 Boston Restaurant Survey,* covering more than 900 restaurants. This marks the 17th year we have covered restaurants in Boston.

By regularly surveying large numbers of avid local restaurant-goers, we hope to have achieved a uniquely current and reliable guide. For this book, more than 4,900 people participated. Since they dined out an average of three times per week, this *Survey* is based on roughly 774,000 meals annually. We sincerely thank each of these surveyors; this book is really "theirs."

Of our surveyors, 55% are women, 45% men; the breakdown by age is 29% in their 20s, 26% in their 30s, 19% in their 40s, 17% in their 50s and 9% in their 60s or above.

Of course, we are especially grateful to our editor, Carolyn B. Heller, a Cambridge-based food and travel writer, and our coordinator, Maryanne Muller, a personal chef and cooking instructor in Boston.

To help guide our readers to Boston's best meals and best buys, we have prepared a number of lists. See Top Ratings, including Most Popular (pages 9–15), and Best Buys (page 16). To help the user find just the right restaurant for any occasion, we have also provided 41 handy indexes and have tried to be concise. Finally, it should be noted that our editors have synopsized our surveyors' opinions, with their comments shown in quotation marks.

As companions to this guide, we also publish *Cape Cod & The Islands Restaurants, America's Top Restaurants* and *Top U.S. Hotels, Resorts & Spas,* as well as maps and guides to 70 other world markets. Most of these guides are also available on mobile devices and at **zagat.com,** where you can vote and shop as well.

To join our next **Boston Survey** or any of our other upcoming *Surveys,* just register at **zagat.com.** Each participant will receive a free copy of the resulting guide when it is published.

Your comments and even criticisms of this guide are also solicited. There is always room for improvement with your help. You can contact us at boston@zagat.com or by mail at Zagat Survey, 4 Columbus Circle, New York, NY 10019. We look forward to hearing from you.

New York, NY
April 29, 2003

Nina and Tim Zagat

What's New

Despite the sluggish local economy and the uncertain international scene, Boston's restaurants, from the latest and greatest to the humble and enduring, seem to be thriving. Plenty of the city's big-name toques launched new ventures this year, thumbing their noses at the sluggish local economy. Here's the scoop:

Who's on First: The owners of the former UpStairs at the Pudding assembled an all-star team to premiere UpStairs on the Square in a dramatic Harvard Square setting. Jamie Mammano (Mistral) turned up the lights on Teatro, a Northern Italian stunner in the Theater District, while Robert Fathman (ex Federalist) conceived a seafood-slanted menu for the Lenox Hotel's Azure. Daniel Bruce revamped the dining room at the Boston Harbor Hotel on the waterfront, renaming it Meritage and making it an oenophile's delight, and to the thrill of local raw-fish fans, Ken Oringer added a sashimi bar, Uni, on the premises of Clio. After debuting the Italian hot spot Via Matta, the crew from Radius sets its sights on seafood with Great Bay, slated to open in the Hotel Commonwealth as we go to press. At about the same time, Lydia Shire (Locke-Ober) will turn her former Biba space into Excelsior.

What's the Word? The big news at a number of this year's trendy newcomers is the lounge concept, where the ambiance is at least as important as the food. Oh-so-chic Saint even bills itself as a nitery and features a cocktail-friendly menu of Eclectic small plates designed by Rene Michelena (ex Centro, Vault). At 33 Restaurant & Lounge, the French-Italian menu takes a back seat to the over-the-top decor, while Epiphany charged into the Leather District with its sleek Asian Fusion style. Ethnic eateries too are going the stylish route, from the Moroccan Argana in Inman Square to the upscale Indian Bhindi Bazaar in the Back Bay to the smartly outfitted Malaysian Pinang at Faneuil Hall.

Where's the Beef? Among our surveyors, 45% feel that the Back Bay and South End boast the best restaurants. Only enhancing that reputation are such additions to these neighborhoods as Caffe Umbra, Nightingale and Rouge, along with the opulently restored Ritz-Carlton Dining Room. Other areas, though, are holding their own, with the introduction of Craigie Street Bistrot to the Harvard Square vicinity, and Carmen in the North End. The proprietors of Aspasia bring their Mediterranean-influenced New American cooking to Newtonville with Ariadne, while Ten Tables offers its own New American interpretations in the former Perdix space in Jamaica Plain.

When and How: Bostonians eat out an average of three meals per week, so it's good news that costs have remained quite reasonable, with the average check running $27.50.

Boston, MA
April 29, 2003

Carolyn B. Heller

Key to Ratings/Symbols

Name, Address, Phone Number & Web Site

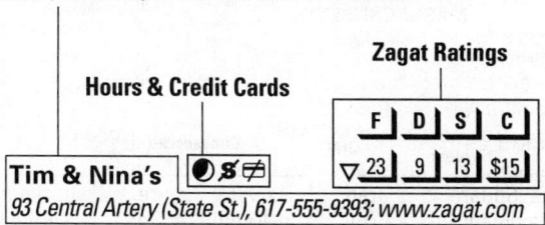

Zagat Ratings

Hours & Credit Cards

F	D	S	C
▽ 23	9	13	$15

Tim & Nina's ☾ ✗ ⊄
93 Central Artery (State St.), 617-555-9393; www.zagat.com

☒ The first restaurant to open directly atop the now-underground Central Artery, this "shaking" supper club "hums at all hours"; the signature cocktails (especially the "No Exit" and the "Tunnel of Love") really "get things moving", while the "speedy" staff "whizzes by" "faster than rush-hour traffic"; if only the traditional New England menu, including such aptly named constructions as "Fender-Bender Franks" and "Side-Swiping Scrod", weren't "so middle-of-the-road."

Review, with surveyors' comments in quotes

Restaurants with the highest overall ratings and greatest popularity and importance are printed in CAPITAL LETTERS.

Before reviews a symbol indicates whether responses were uniform ■ or mixed ☒.

Hours: ☾ serves after 11 PM
✗ not open on Sunday

Credit Cards: ⊄ no credit cards accepted

Ratings: Food, Decor and Service are rated on a scale of **0** to **30**. The Cost (C) column reflects our surveyors' estimate of the price of dinner including one drink and tip.

F Food	D Decor	S Service	C Cost
23	9	13	$15

0–9 poor to fair **20–25** very good to excellent
10–15 fair to good **26–30** extraordinary to perfection
16–19 good to very good ▽ low response/less reliable

For places listed without ratings or a numerical cost estimate, such as an important newcomer or a popular write-in, the price range is indicated by the following symbols.

I $15 and below **E** $31 to $50
M $16 to $30 **VE** $51 or more

get updates at zagat.com

Most Popular

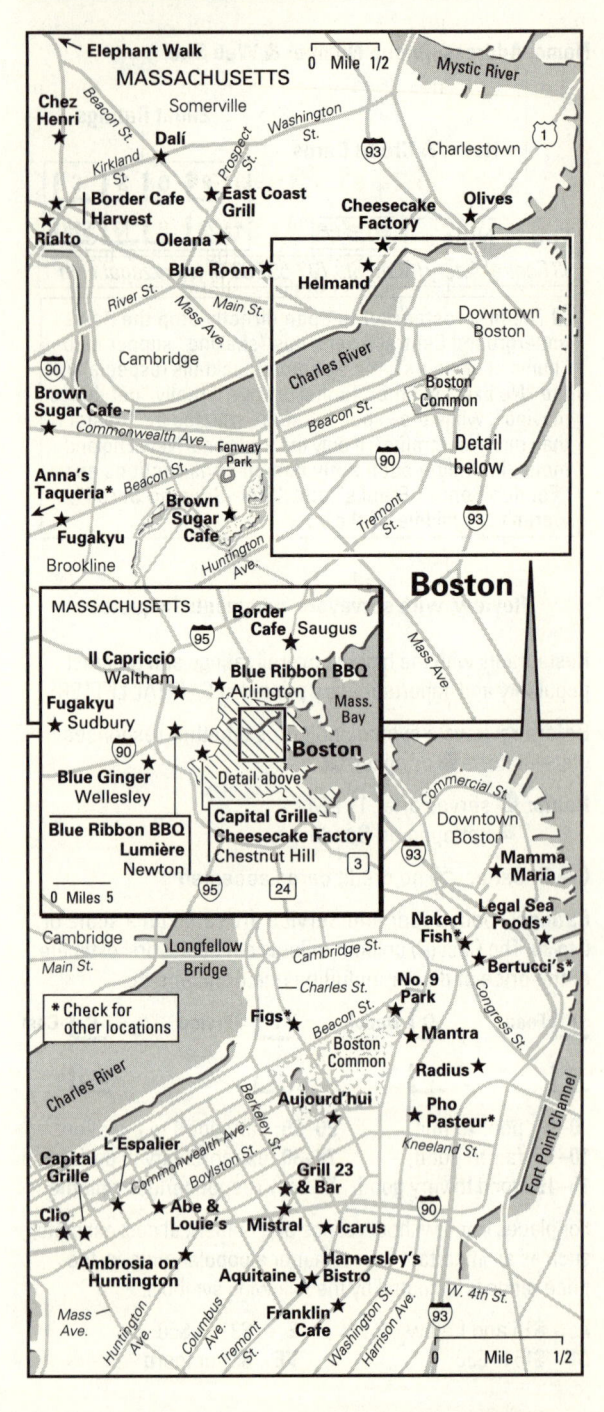

Top Ratings

Top lists exclude restaurants with low voting and restaurants in Cape Cod, the Vineyard and Nantucket. An asterisk indicates the restaurant is tied with the one directly above it.

Most Popular

Each of our reviewers has been asked to name his or her five favorite Boston restaurants. The places most frequently named, in order of their popularity, are:

1. Legal Sea Foods
2. Blue Ginger
3. Aujourd'hui
4. Hamersley's Bistro
5. L'Espalier
6. Radius
7. Capital Grille
8. Olives
9. Mistral
10. Clio
11. Pho Pasteur
12. Elephant Walk
13. No. 9 Park
14. Lumière
15. Grill 23 & Bar
16. Blue Room
17. Figs
18. Dalí
19. East Coast Grill*
20. Fugakyu*
21. Rialto
22. Abe & Louie's
23. Icarus
24. Oleana*
25. Ambrosia on Huntington
26. Anna's Taqueria
27. Brown Sugar Cafe
28. Helmand*
29. Chez Henri
30. Naked Fish
31. Il Capriccio
32. Aquitaine
33. Border Cafe
34. Bertucci's
35. Blue Ribbon BBQ
36. Cheesecake Factory
37. Mamma Maria
38. Harvest
39. Mantra
40. Franklin Cafe

It's obvious that many of the restaurants on the above list are among the Boston area's most expensive, but if popularity were calibrated to price, we suspect that a number of other restaurants would join the above ranks. Given the fact that both our surveyors and readers love to discover dining bargains, we have added a list of 80 Best Buys on page 16. These are restaurants that give real quality at extremely reasonable prices.

get updates at zagat.com

Top Food

Top 40 Food

- **29** Oishii
- **28** L'Espalier
- **27** Aujourd'hui
  Il Capriccio
  Olio
  Lumière
  Hamersley's Bistro
  Salts
  Coriander
  Caffe Bella
- **26** Terramia
  Blue Ginger
  No. 9 Park
  Trattoria a Scalinatella
  Le Soir
  Troquet
  Radius
  Clio
  Mistral
  Rialto
  Grill 23 & Bar
  Saporito's
  La Campania
  Julien
  Helmand
  Oleana
  Sage
  Bistro 5
  Mamma Maria
  Sweet Basil
  Blue Room
  Prezza
  Icarus
  Grapevine
  Pigalle
- **25** Barker Tavern
  Fugakyu
  Oak Room
  Silks
  Franklin Cafe

By Cuisine

American (New)
- **27** Aujourd'hui
  Olio
  Salts
- **26** Icarus
  Grapevine

American (Traditional)
- **25** Barker Tavern
  Oak Room
  Yanks
- **22** eat
- **20** Silvertone B&G

Barbecue
- **25** Uncle Pete's
  East Coast Grill
- **24** Blue Ribbon BBQ
- **23** Redbones BBQ
- **22** New Bridge Cafe

Cambodian/Vietnamese
- **23** Elephant Walk
  Pho Pasteur
- **22** Wonder Spice Cafe
  Carambola
  Lam's

Chinese
- **24** Jumbo Seafood
  Taiwan Cafe
  Grand Chau Chow
- **23** East Ocean City
  New Shanghai

Delis
- **19** Zaftigs
- **18** Rubin's
  Milk Street Cafe
- **17** S&S
- **15** B & D Deli

Eclectic
- **26** Blue Room
- **24** EVOO
- **22** Metropolis Cafe
  Claremont Cafe
- **21** Dish

French
- **26** No. 9 Park
  Le Soir
  Mistral
  Pigalle
- **25** Silks

French (Bistro)
- **27** Hamersley's Bistro
  Coriander
- **26** Troquet
- **24** Sel de la Terre
  Chez Henri

French (New)
- **28** L'Espalier
- **27** Lumière
- **26** Radius
  Clio
  Julien

10 subscribe to zagat.com

Top Food

Hamburgers
- **23** Mr. & Mrs. Bartley's
- **21** Audubon Circle
- **20** Tim's Tavern
- **18** Sunset Grill
- **17** Miracle of Science

Indian
- **24** India Quality
- Punjab
- Rangoli
- Kashmir
- **23** Tanjore

Italian
- **26** Terramia
- Trattoria a Scalinatella
- La Campania
- Sweet Basil
- Prezza

Italian (Northern)
- **27** Il Capriccio
- **26** Saporito's
- Sage
- Bistro 5
- Mamma Maria

Japanese
- **29** Oishii
- **25** Fugakyu
- Oga
- **24** Ginza
- Shabu-Zen

Mediterranean
- **27** Caffe Bella
- **26** Rialto
- Oleana
- **25** Olives
- Aspasia

Mexican
- **24** El Sarape
- **23** Taqueria la Mexicana
- **22** El Pelón Taqueria
- La Paloma
- Cilantro

Middle Eastern
- **26** Helmand
- **24** Sultan's Kitchen
- **23** Lala Rokh
- Istanbul Cafe
- **21** Sepal

New England
- **25** Harvest
- **21** Fireplace
- Henrietta's Table
- **19** Jasper White's
- **18** Tom Shea's

Pan-Asian
- **26** Blue Ginger
- **22** Bernard's
- Billy Tse
- **20** Jae's
- Soya's

Pizza
- **24** Emma's Pizzeria
- Pizzeria Regina
- Galleria Umberto
- **23** Santarpio's Pizza
- Veggie Planet

Seafood (American)
- **26** Grill 23 & Bar
- **25** Clam Box
- East Coast Grill
- **23** Back Eddy
- **22** Legal Sea Foods

Seafood (Ethnic)
- **24** Jumbo Seafood
- Grand Chau Chow
- **23** Out of the Blue
- Giacomo's
- East Ocean City

Spanish/Portuguese
- **25** Dalí
- **24** Tasca
- **23** Tapeo
- Atasca
- **22** Casa Portugal

Steakhouses
- **26** Grill 23 & Bar
- **25** Oak Room
- Capital Grille
- Morton's of Chicago
- **24** Abe & Louie's

Thai
- **25** Brown Sugar Cafe
- **24** House of Siam
- **23** Rod Dee
- Khao Sarn
- Bamboo

Top Food

By Special Feature

Brunch
- 26 Blue Room
- 25 East Coast Grill
  - Harvest
- 24 Sel de la Terre
- 22 Tremont 647

Child-Friendly
- 22 Anna's Taqueria
- 21 Figs
- 19 Jasper White's
- 18 Full Moon
  - Johnny's Luncheonette

Chowder
- 22 Legal Sea Foods
- 21 KingFish Hall
- 20 McCormick & Schmick's
  - Atlantic Fish Co.
- – Turner Fisheries

Dessert
- 26 flour bakery & café
- 25 Finale
- 24 Bristol Lounge
  - Hi-Rise Bread Co.
- 21 Cafe Fleuri

Dim Sum
- 22 China Pearl
  - Chau Chow City
- 20 Imperial Seafood∇
- 15 Dynasty
- – Emperor's Garden

Hotel Dining
- 27 Aujourd'hui
  - Four Seasons Hotel
- 26 Clio
  - Eliot Suite Hotel
  - Rialto
  - Charles Hotel
  - Julien
  - Le Méridien Hotel
- 25 Oak Room
  - Fairmont Copley Plaza

Landmarks
- 23 Maison Robert
- 21 Locke-Ober
- 18 Union Oyster House
- 16 Durgin Park
  - Wayside Inn

Late Dining
- 25 Fugakyu
  - Franklin Cafe
  - Finale
- 24 Ginza
  - Jumbo Seafood

Newcomers (Rated)
- 25 Carmen
- 23 Caffe Umbra
- 22 Via Matta
- 21 Nightingale
- 20 Spire

Newcomers (Unrated)
- Ariadne
- Meritage
- Ritz-Carlton Din. Rm.
- Rouge
- UpStairs on the Square

People-Watching
- 26 Mistral
- 25 Café Louis
- 23 Mantra
- 22 Via Matta
- 19 Sonsie

Power Lunch
- 27 Aujourd'hui
- 26 No. 9 Park
  - Radius
- 25 Federalist
- 21 Locke-Ober

Winning Wine List
- 27 Il Capriccio
  - Lumière
- 26 No. 9 Park
  - Troquet
- 25 Federalist

By Location

Back Bay
- 28 L'Espalier
- 27 Aujourd'hui
- 26 Clio
  - Grill 23 & Bar
- 25 Oak Room

Beacon Hill
- 26 No. 9 Park
- 25 Federalist
- 23 Lala Rokh
  - Antonio's
  - Istanbul Cafe

12   subscribe to zagat.com

Top Food

Brookline/Chestnut Hill
- **29** Oishii
- **25** Fugakyu
   Capital Grille
- **24** Ginza
- **23** Washington Square

Central/Inman/Kendall Squares
- **27** Salts
- **26** Helmand
   Oleana
   Blue Room
- **25** East Coast Grill

Chinatown
- **24** Ginza
   Jumbo Seafood
   Shabu-Zen
   Taiwan Cafe
   Grand Chau Chow

Downtown/Financial District
- **26** Radius
   Julien
- **24** Sultan's Kitchen
- **23** Mantra
   Sakurabana

Harvard Square/Fresh Pond
- **26** Rialto
- **25** Harvest
   Aspasia
- **24** Chez Henri
- **23** Tanjore

Newton/Needham
- **27** Lumière
- **26** Le Soir
   Sweet Basil
- **25** Fava
- **24** Blue Ribbon BBQ

North End
- **26** Terramia
   Trattoria a Scalinatella
   Sage
   Mamma Maria
   Prezza

Somerville/Medford
- **26** Bistro 5
- **25** Dalí
- **24** Gargoyles
   EVOO
   Vinny's at Night

South End
- **27** Hamersley's Bistro
- **26** Mistral
   Icarus
- **25** Franklin Cafe
- **24** House of Siam

Suburbs (Outlying)
- **29** Oishii
- **27** Olio
   Coriander
   Caffe Bella
- **26** Blue Ginger

Theater District
- **26** Troquet
   Pigalle
- **24** blu
- **22** Legal Sea Foods
- **21** Montien

Waltham/Watertown
- **27** Il Capriccio
- **26** La Campania
- **24** Tuscan Grill
- **23** New Ginza
   La Casa de Pedro

Cape Cod
- **27** Regatta of Cotuit
   Chester
   Bramble Inn
- **26** Chillingsworth
   Abba

Martha's Vineyard
- **26** L'Etoile
   Jimmy Seas
- **25** Atria
- **24** Le Grenier
   Ice House

Nantucket
- **28** Topper's
- **26** Òran Mór
   Pearl*
   West Creek Cafe
   Chanticleer

get updates at zagat.com

Top 40 Decor

27 Aujourd'hui
Julien
Oak Room
L'Espalier
Bristol Lounge
26 Bay Tower
Top of the Hub
Atlantica
Tangierino
25 Mistral
Mantra
Federalist
Silks
Clio
Radius
Yanks
Rialto
24 Dalí
Hungry i
Icarus

Locke-Ober
Grill 23 & Bar
Ambrosia on Huntington
Bar 10
33 Restaurant & Lounge
Cuchi Cuchi
Maison Robert
Hamersley's Bistro
75 Chestnut
23 Tosca
Mamma Maria
Andover Inn
Barker Tavern
Le Soir*
Capital Grille
Wayside Inn
Trattoria a Scalinatella
Cafe Fleuri
Lumière
Harvest

Outdoors

Armani Cafe
Back Eddy
Barking Crab
Casa Romero
Finz
Grapevine

Hamersley's Bistro
Harvest
Maison Robert
Oleana
Stephanie's on Newbury
Via Matta

Romance

Casa Romero
Clio
Craigie Street Bistrot
Dalí
Hungry i
Julien

Lala Rokh
L'Espalier
Maison Robert
Tangierino
Trattoria a Scalinatella
Truc

Rooms

Aquitaine
Ariadne
Azure
Bomboa
Epiphany
Fugakyu
Jer-Ne

KingFish Hall
Mantra
No. 9 Park
Ritz-Carlton Din. Rm.
Saint
Sel de la Terre
UpStairs on the Square

Views

Anthony's Pier 4
Aujourd'hui
Bay Tower
Davio's (Cambridge)
Jimmy's Harborside

Landing
Meritage
Red Rock Bistro
Spinnaker
Top of the Hub

Top 40 Service

- **27** Aujourd'hui
  - Julien
  - L'Espalier
- **26** Jasmine Bistro
  - Bristol Lounge
  - Silks
  - Oak Room
- **25** No. 9 Park
  - Coriander
  - Il Capriccio
  - Salts
  - Trattoria a Scalinatella
  - Radius
  - Troquet
  - Federalist
  - Rialto
  - Grill 23 & Bar
- **24** Icarus
  - Lumière
  - Le Soir

- Hamersley's Bistro
- Clio
- Pigalle
- Capital Grille
- Taranta
- Blue Ginger
- Tosca
- Maison Robert
- Lala Rokh
- **23** blu
  - Mamma Maria
  - Prezza
  - La Campania
  - Jer-Ne
  - Harvest
  - Mistral
  - Caffe Bella
  - Seasons*
  - Morton's of Chicago
  - Grapevine

get updates at zagat.com

Best Buys

Top 40 Bangs for the Buck

List derived by dividing the cost of a meal into its ratings.

1. 1369 Coffee House
2. Anna's Taqueria
3. Baja Betty's Burritos
4. Taqueria la Mexicana
5. flour bakery & café
6. Cafe Pamplona
7. Galleria Umberto
8. Purple Cactus
9. Boca Grande
10. Mr. Crepe
11. El Pelón Taqueria
12. Sound Bites
13. Mr. & Mrs. Bartley's
14. Charlie's Sandwich Shoppe
15. Mike's City Diner
16. Punjabi Dhaba
17. Blue Ribbon BBQ
18. Caffe Vittoria
19. Picante Mexican Grill
20. Upper Crust
21. Hi-Rise Bread Co.
22. Other Side Cosmic Cafe
23. Blue Plate Express
24. House of Tibet Kitchen
25. Rod Dee
26. Sorella's
27. Deluxe Town Diner
28. Sultan's Kitchen
29. Rosebud Diner
30. Milk Street Cafe
31. Bamboo
32. Veggie Planet
33. Taqueria Mexico
34. Skewers
35. Cafe Belo
36. Caffe Paradiso
37. Cambridge, 1.
38. Emma's Pizzeria
39. Uncle Pete's
40. Neighborhood

Other Good Values

Addis Red Sea
Ajanta
Atasca
Audubon Circle
Baraka Cafe
Brown Sugar Cafe
B-Side Lounge
Cafe Brazil
Cafe Polonia
Carlo's Cucina Italiana
Delux Cafe
Dish
El Oriental de Cuba
Enormous Room
House of Siam
India Quality
Istanbul Cafe
JP Seafood Cafe
Jumbo Seafood
Kebab Factory
Khao Sarn
Lam's
Matt Murphy's Pub
Merengue
Pho Pasteur
Punjab
Rangoli
Seoul Food
Sepal
Shabu-Zen
Taiwan Cafe
Tango
Tanjore
Tantawan
Tasca
Tim's Tavern
Tu y Yo
Viet's Café
Wonder Spice Cafe
Zaftigs Delicatessen

Restaurant Directory

Boston

F	D	S	C

Abbondanza   ▽ 21 | 13 | 19 | $23
Ristorante Italiano *S*
195 Main St. (Broadway), Everett, 617-387-8422
■ A "great find" for "authentic", "homestyle" Italian cooking, this "hidden gem" "tucked away" in Everett is a sweet little neighborhood place worked by friendly folks who always aim to please; "while the decor isn't much to celebrate, the food is worth" cheering about, since it's "wonderful", plentiful and affordable.

ABE & LOUIE'S   24 | 22 | 22 | $49
793 Boylston St. (bet. Exeter & Fairfield Sts.), 617-536-6300; www.abeandlouies.com
■ "Can a steakhouse be sexy?" – sure can according to the "expense-account crowd" that frequents this "classy", "lively" ode to "carnivorous gluttony" in the Back Bay, whose "dark wood interior" just "oozes testosterone"; nestle into a Hollywood-style booth under the "beautiful" gold-leaf ceiling and let the "knowledgeable" staff ("no attitude at all here") bring you a martini ("second to none") and a "phenomenal" bone-in fillet; not only is it ideal for a "power lunch" due to its "great location", but it's a "real favorite for dinner any night."

Addis Red Sea   21 | 20 | 19 | $22
544 Tremont St. (bet. Clarendon & E. Berkeley Sts.), 617-426-8727; www.addisredsea.com
■ "Indiana Jones would feel right at home" among the "adventurous eaters" who patronize this "exotic" African "dream" known for its "rich, flavorful" and "authentic" Ethiopian food; "bring a big group", as the "obliging" staff serves meals "family-style" on communal platters lined with spongy injera bread ("eat with your fingers"); it makes for a "cheap and delicious" dinner in the "usually pricey" South End – just "be prepared to sit on a hard stool."

Aegean   19 | 16 | 19 | $20
47 Beacon St. (Rte. 30), Framingham, 508-879-8424
640 Arsenal St. (Coolidge Ave.), Watertown, 617-923-7771
www.aegeanrestaurant.com
◪ Though this "traditional" Watertown Hellenic is "not glitzy" or "gourmet", it is a "wonderful family spot" for an "extensive" roster of "quite good" "home cooking" where the "portions are more than satisfying" and the "price is right"; the fact that there's usually a "wait" attests to its popularity, even if those who huff "nothing special" quip

Boston | F | D | S | C |

"this is a Greek bearing no gifts"; P.S. also a "great value" is the original site in Framingham.

Aigo Bistro ⓢ | 21 | 17 | 18 | $42 |
84 Thoreau St. (Main St.), Concord, 978-371-1333
◪ Moncef Meddeb (ex L'Espalier) "cooks like an angel" swoon satisfied suburbanites about the chef-owner of this Mediterranean bistro housed above the Concord train station, where he creates dishes that are "inventive and delightful" yet "unfussy"; dissenters, though, warn that the food and service can be "aggravatingly inconsistent", while the "tables are very close" together.

Ajanta | 23 | 14 | 19 | $20 |
145 First St. (bet. Bent & Binney Sts.), Cambridge, 617-491-0075
■ "Tired of the same old Indian food?" – then head to this "real" deal "tucked away" in East Cambridge that's always "filled with people from South Asia" sampling their way through the "interesting" menu of "regional" Northern and Southern "treats" (particularly the "outstanding vegetarian dishes"); "come hungry" at midday, as the "good-value" lunch buffet goes way beyond the "run-of-the-mill" – and don't mind the "impersonal" service.

Akbar India | ▽ 16 | 11 | 15 | $17 |
1248-1250 Cambridge St. (Prospect St.), Cambridge, 617-497-6548
◪ "Respectable" Indian fare at "budget prices" and "speedy" service keep business steady at this Inman Square standby, but "what really separates it from the rest" of the competition is its parking lot (rare in this part of town); even so, since the menu is "predictable" and the "outdated" atmosphere "leaves everything to be desired", critics ask "why go here when there are better options" around?

Al Dente | 20 | 15 | 20 | $26 |
109 Salem St. (Parmenter St.), 617-523-0990; www.aldenteboston.com
◪ "One of those reliable places that make the North End what it is", this "family-type" Italian fixture "gets all the basics right"; though it may be "tight on space, it's easy on the wallet", and the "accommodating" staff is "very sweet", but those who are "not impressed" advise "there are better" choices in this restaurant-dense neighborhood.

Alloro | ▽ 24 | 12 | 19 | $35 |
351 Hanover St. (bet. Fleet & Prince Sts.), 617-523-9268
◪ "Every item is tasty" at this "quaint", "intimate" North End Italian mainstay where the "delicious" cooking is "dependably" a "cut above the usual"; note, though, that it can be "difficult to get a seat" in the "tiny" room, and once you're finally shown to a table you better be prepared to "be friendly with the other patrons", since "you'll be listening to their conversations and they'll be listening to yours."

get updates at zagat.com

Boston | F | D | S | C |

Amarin of Thailand | 22 | 18 | 20 | $23 |
287 Centre St. (Galen St.), Newton, 617-527-5255
27 Grove St. (Spring St.), Wellesley, 781-239-1350
◪ Admirers insist that "some of the best Thai food in the suburbs" comes out of the kitchens at these "surefire standbys" in Newton Corner and Wellesley that satisfy with "fresh and flavorful" (if "Americanized") fare; the quarters are "pleasant" and the staff "goes out of its way to make you comfortable", so while the chow "may not blow your socks off", at least there are "no unpleasant surprises."

AMBROSIA ON HUNTINGTON | 24 | 24 | 23 | $52 |
116 Huntington Ave. (bet. Exeter & W. Newton Sts.), 617-247-2400;
www.ambrosiaonhuntington.com
◪ "Tony Ambrose is one of the most inventive chefs in Boston" fawn followers awed by his "imaginative" French–Asian Fusion dishes that are "dressed to kill" (each plate "looks as good as the customers"); even if "some combos seem done for shock value" and thus "miss the mark", most maintain that this "buzz-worthy", "impress-your-guest type of restaurant" prepares "food fit for the gods", while the "hip servers play against type by actually being attentive" as they work the "gorgeous" Back Bay room.

Amelia's Trattoria ⌀ | 20 | 18 | 20 | $28 |
111 Harvard St. (Portland St.), Cambridge, 617-868-7600;
www.ameliastrattoria.com
■ The "menu is short and sweet" at this "casual" Kendall Square "sleeper", a teeny trattoria that comforts with "homey, down-to-earth" Italian food native to the region of Abruzzo; regulars recommend the "delicious daily specials" and "nice selection of wines by the glass", but caution that it "gets packed at lunch, so go early or late"; though it "may not be worth going out of your way", it's a "treasure" for those in the neighborhood.

Amrheins | 15 | 13 | 15 | $21 |
80 W. Broadway (A St.), South Boston, 617-268-6189
◪ Still dishing up "regular fare for regular folks", this South Boston "institution" is a "throwback to an earlier time", a "classic" "family restaurant" that's "been around for generations" (since 1890, in fact); a "friendly" crew delivers "large portions" of New England "comfort food" amid surroundings full of "local color", but dissenters who deem it all "ordinary" frown "no frills, not a lot of thrills."

Anam Chara | 19 | 18 | 17 | $22 |
1648 Beacon St. (Washington St.), Brookline, 617-277-2880
◪ Brookline barflies cheer about this "swell addition to the neighborhood", a "casual" bar-cum-restaurant with "lots of Gaelic charm"; the "limited but decent menu" of "hearty" Eclectic eats is "surprisingly good for an Irish-style pub", though "you have to be pushy" to get served, since the

Boston F | D | S | C

"seat-yourself policy makes for table vultures" and the staff can be "clueless"; locals who feel it's "still working out the kinks" "go for the live music and a beer" instead.

Anchovies ● 18 | 13 | 16 | $18
433 Columbus Ave. (bet. Braddock Park & Holyoke St.), 617-266-5088
☑ A late-night "stop for carb-lovers and lushes alike", this "dive bar" may well be the "*Cheers* of the South End"; it's "not fancy" and it's "usually packed" "like a can" of "smelly oily fish", but you get "generous portions" of "decent" "red-sauce" "grub" at a "reasonable price"; while even regulars admit that "you could cook" this "basic" Italian "comfort food" "at home", "it wouldn't be nearly as fun."

Andover Inn 19 | 23 | 22 | $50
Andover Inn, Phillips Academy, 4 Chapel Ave. (Rte. 28), Andover, 978-475-5903; www.andoverinn.com
☑ "Men wear jackets and women wear jewels" at this "genteel" dining room on the campus of Phillips Academy, which serves as an "old-fashioned" reminder of "pure elegance"; loyalists continue to recommend the "well-prepared", "traditional items" from the Continental-American menu, brought to table by an "accommodating" staff, but skeptics sniff "stodgy" and "tired"; P.S. "don't miss the Indonesian rijsttafel" extravaganza on Sundays.

Angelo's ⑤ 24 | 12 | 20 | $37
237 Main St. (William St.), Stoneham, 781-279-9035
■ "When great food is more important than atmosphere", Italophiles head to this "well-kept secret" in Stoneham for "North End quality in the suburbs"; the facade may make it look like a "pizza joint" ("time for a makeover"), but inside awaits "fantastic" food (notably the "wonderful" pastas) and "good wine values", making it definitely "worth the visit."

ANNA'S TAQUERIA ⌿ 22 | 9 | 17 | $8
1412 Beacon St. (Summit Ave.), Brookline, 617-739-7300
446 Harvard St. (Thorndike St.), Brookline, 617-277-7111
822 Somerville Ave. (White St.), Cambridge, 617-661-8500
236 Elm St. (Grove St.), Somerville, 617-666-3900
☑ Ask any local college student "where they would want to eat their last meal" and the answer is likely to be this Tex-Mex quartet that has a "cult following" with the "under-25 set"; the "lightning-fast" team works with "assembly-line efficiency", so the queues "out the door" "move through quickly"; it's "hard not to be besotted" with the "stomach-stuffing meals" you can buy here with "change found in the couch", even if purists wonder "what's all the fuss about?"

Anthony's Pier 4 15 | 16 | 16 | $40
140 Northern Ave. (Pier 4), 617-423-6363; www.pier4.com
☑ "Take your cousin from Peoria" to this "ultimate tourist trap" on the waterfront for its "beautiful view" of the harbor

Boston F | D | S | C

and the skyline beyond; otherwise, though it may have been a "special night out when your parents were courting", the experience is too "dated" for many – from the "old-fashioned" New England seafood dishes (the "awesome popovers" are the "best part of the meal") to the "stuffy" ambiance to the "age-challenged" clientele.

Antico Forno   22 | 14 | 18 | $26
93 Salem St. (bet. Cross & Parmenter Sts.), 617-723-6733; www.anticofornoboston.com

■ "Though the North End is saturated with so-called rustic Italian eateries", the "homestyle comfort" provided by this "welcoming" trattoria makes it the "real deal" (like "Napoli in Boston"); the "wood-fired oven" lends the "fantastic pizzas" ("they know how to toss a pie" here) and other "yummy" dishes "great flavor" (most "everything is baked, as the name suggests"), the service is "warm" and the prices "quite reasonable", making it a "cozy" "gem."

Antonia's ⌀   ∇ 21 | 13 | 16 | $20
37 Davis Sq. (College Ave.), Somerville, 617-623-6700

■ "Why drive to the North End when you can get a taste of Italy in Davis Square?" ask Somerville residents who've discovered this "adorable spot", a "satisfying" trattoria that brings a bit of "romance to the neighborhood"; the "space is tiny", but the kitchen turns out Italian "basics" that are "well executed" and "filling", while its sidewalk tables provide for "great people-watching."

Antonio's Cucina Italiana ⌇   23 | 12 | 19 | $22
288 Cambridge St. (bet. Anderson & Grove Sts.), 617-367-3310

◪ "Good prices, especially by Beacon Hill standards", pack in plenty of penny-pinchers at this "tiny hole-in-the-wall", an "exuberant" "red-sauce joint" that's "nothing fancy but just delightful" nonetheless; regulars "never open the menu", "always" opting instead for one of the "fantastic specials" ("you can't go wrong with any of them") served by "cheerful" folks in a "great neighborhood" atmosphere; even if a few dissenters deem it "nothing to write home about", most cheer "*molto bene!*"

Apollo Grill & Sushi ☾   21 | 13 | 16 | $23
84-86 Harrison Ave. (Kneeland St.), 617-423-3888

◪ "After a night of clubbing and drinking", a "young, hip crowd" descends upon this "after-hours" (open till 4 AM) Asian "gathering place" in Chinatown for "excellent" Korean barbecue "with all the fixings" and "quite good" sushi; as expected, it can get "noisy", but it's "worth" a try "if you're in the area" and need to fuel up.

Appetito   19 | 17 | 18 | $32
761 Beacon St. (Langley Rd.), Newton, 617-244-9881

◪ "If you don't mind the long wait to get in", this "popular" pick in Newton Centre will reward patient patrons with a

Boston | F | D | S | C |

"something-for-everyone" Italian menu filled with "tasty" selections; those in-the-know, however, advise don't plan a "private conversation" in the very "close quarters", while foes warn about "uninspired", "hit-or-miss" fare; P.S. check out the brunch, which offers just the "right mix of interesting and comforting" choices.

Aqua ⑤ | 15 | 19 | 14 | $29 |
120 Water St. (Broad St.), 617-720-4900; www.aquaboston.com
■ "It looks like Miami Beach in Boston" at this "trendy" new Downtown bar that draws a "noisy" "after-work crowd"; yuppies into "cool" ambiance "meet up with friends" during the "boisterous happy hour", but gourmands caution that the "forgettable" New American menu doesn't offer much more than "standard pub fare", making it "more of a place to go for drinks than a meal."

AQUITAINE | 23 | 22 | 20 | $43 |
569 Tremont St. (bet. Clarendon & Dartmouth Sts.), 617-424-8577
■ "One of the best of the South End's great little places", this "chic", "lively" French "scene" is a sheer "slice of Parisian heaven"; a "citywide crowd" of "beautiful patrons" frequents it for "expertly executed" bistro classics, from "out-of-this-world steak frites" to "must-have mussels" to "wonderful" apple tart; despite some reports of "spotty" (if not "rude") service, habitués "would go back in a second", even if the "portions are a tad small for the semi-hefty tabs."

Aquitaine Bis | 21 | 20 | 19 | $39 |
The Mall at Chestnut Hill, 11 Boylston St. (Hammond Pond Pkwy.), Chestnut Hill, 617-734-8400; www.aquitainebis.com
■ "If you aren't glam enough for the South End" cousin of this Chestnut Hill French bistro, then just "relish" your "suburban" status and dine instead at this "sophisticated" "alternative"; while the ambiance is still "*très élégant*" and the traditional dishes will leave "your taste buds smiling", here the "pace is more relaxing" and there's "free parking"; doubters, however, lament that this spin-off lacks the original's "charm and romance."

Argana | 20 | 22 | 16 | $30 |
1287 Cambridge St. (bet. Oakland & Prospect Sts.), Cambridge, 617-868-1247
■ Boasting a "fantastic" ambiance, "great visuals" and a "roaming belly dancer" on the weekends, this "festive" Moroccan newcomer in Inman Square "transports you to a scene out of *Casablanca*"; "after stuffing yourself" on "hearty" North African specialties, "recline" on a "big loungey pillow" and "try something from the surprising drink menu"; early admirers predict that they'll be "repeat customers", but those who deem it a "bit disappointing" caution that it's "still working to find its place."

Boston

| F | D | S | C |

Ariadne ⌀
— | — | — | E

344 Walnut St. (Washington Park), Newton, 617-332-4653
The husband-and-wife team that owns Aspasia have taken their show on the road – across town, that is, to Newtonville, where Christos Tsardounis mans the stove and Kathleen Malloy runs the front of the house at their sumptuously decorated new bistro; as at their original eatery, they offer a small but imaginative New American menu accented with the flavors of the Mediterranean.

Armani Cafe
— | — | — | E

214 Newbury St. (bet. Exeter & Fairfield Sts.), 617-437-0909
"Sport your trendiest outfit" to mingle among the "pretty people" (whose "arms must be tired from all that posing with their drinks") at this "fashionable" Back Bay cafe in the "heart of it all" on Newbury Street, where chef-partner Seth Woods (Aquitaine) has taken over the kitchen and updated the Italian menu; if you can nab a coveted "sidewalk table", just try to ignore the sea of "ringing, buzzing, singing cell phones."

Artichokes Ristorante Trattoria ⌀ ▽
21 | 18 | 19 | $27

2 Florence St. (Pleasant St.), Malden, 781-397-8338
■ "Bring your appetite" to this "lovely little place" in Malden, where the "large portions" of "terrific", "rich" Italian cooking are "aimed at a ravenous crowd"; sure, it's "off the beaten track", but at least you can avoid the "hassle of looking for parking in the North End", though "be prepared to wait" for a table (and there's "no waiting area to speak of").

Artu
20 | 14 | 17 | $25

89 Charles St. (bet. Mt. Vernon & Pinckney Sts.), 617-227-9023
6 Prince St. (bet. Hanover St. & North Sq.), 617-742-4336
◪ "Great home cooking" that "never fails to wow" beckons at these "charming little trattorias" on Beacon Hill and in the North End, where the "simple" Italian fare is "reliably delicious", "filling" (particularly the "gorgeously seductive mounds of antipasti") and "one of the best values" around; though the digs are "not fancy", the staff is as "down-to-earth" as the tabs.

Asgard ●
15 | 19 | 18 | $20

350 Mass Ave. (Sidney St.), Cambridge, 617-577-9100; www.classicirish.com
◪ Quartered in a "cavernous space" that resembles a "Viking-themed" "Disneyland", this "lively" Irish-American pub near Central Square is a "funky" "after-work meeting place for high-tech and biotech" types; it also does a steady trade dishing up "quick business lunches", even if "finding the good items on the menu" can be a "chore", but sophisticates sneer about the "generic" eats and "ersatz" Celtic production.

Boston | F | D | S | C |

Asmara | 21 | 12 | 19 | $19 |
739 Mass Ave. (bet. Inman & Prospect Sts.), Cambridge, 617-864-7447
■ "Even if you can't find Eritrea [or Ethiopia] on a map", the "gracious" staff at this "family-owned" African storefront in Central Square will "make you feel right at home" while feeding you "something out of the ordinary"; the kitchen's "deliciously" "spiced stews" are served "traditional-style" atop injera flatbread (so "you get to eat your plate"), but "don't be in a rush", because service can be "slow."

Aspasia ⚡ | 25 | 19 | 22 | $44 |
377 Walden St. (Concord Ave.), Cambridge, 617-864-4745
◪ "Dinner is a delight" at this "intimate", "hideaway" between Harvard Square and Fresh Pond that has "all the refinement of an urban star"; the "warm, stylish" setting and "charming owners" make it a "wonderfully romantic, individual" "jewel", while the "big-time" Mediterranean-inflected New American menu is "creative" and "fabulous"; even so, a minority isn't "sure what all the shouting is about", especially given the "cramped space."

Assaggio ◐ | 24 | 20 | 22 | $29 |
29 Prince St. (Hanover St.), 617-227-7380
◪ "Ask to sit downstairs amid all the grapevines and candlelight" advise amorous admirers of this North End "darling" that provides a "perfect setting" for a "romantic" meal; the decor may be a "little kitschy" for some, but the "superb" "traditional" Italian food, servers who "know their stuff" ("you're never rushed") and "reasonable prices" make it a "favorite" among many; P.S. with "80 choices by the glass", the wine bar is a "hidden treasure."

Atasca | 23 | 21 | 21 | $27 |
279 Broadway (bet. Columbia & Prospect Sts.), Cambridge, 617-354-4355
50 Hampshire St. (Cardinal Medeiros Ave.), Cambridge, 617-621-6991
www.atasca.com
■ You "feel like you're among family" at this "old-world" duo that prepares the "best Portuguese food in Cambridge"; "each location has its own merits" – the "unassuming" original, a storefront near Central Square, is "homey", while the Kendall Square branch is a bit more "refined" – but at both sites it's a good idea to bring a group and "share many small plates" of "robust", "authentic" Iberian "standards" served by "kind, down-to-earth people."

ATLANTICA | 16 | 26 | 17 | $39 |
Cohasset Harbor Inn, 44 Border St. (Summer St.), Cohasset, 781-383-0900; www.atlanticadining.com
◪ Overlooking a fleet of lobster boats, this "stunning" Cohasset seafood house with a "million-dollar harbor

get updates at zagat.com

Boston

view" is a "big hit" with the South Shore "yacht set"; beyond the "beautiful location", however, the "mediocre", "unimaginative" and "overpriced" menu, along with "just fair" service, means you "might as well eat at home."

Atlantic Fish Co. | 20 | 18 | 19 | $33 |
761 Boylston St. (Fairfield St.), 617-267-4000; www.atlanticfish-restaurant.com

☑ There are "tons to choose from" on the "diverse menu" at this seafood house blessed with an "ideal location" in the Back Bay; "attractively" appointed like a classic cruise ship, replete with detailed woodwork and murals of the sea, it provides an appropriately "nautical" backdrop for what fin fanatics laud as "flapping-fresh" fish; critics, though, who carp about "middle-of-the-road" fare (and quip that "during the long wait for a table", you "could catch your own dinner") snipe "tourists only need apply."

Audubon Circle | 21 | 19 | 16 | $20 |
838 Beacon St. (Arundel St.), 617-421-1910

■ Bringing a "cool vibe" to the Kenmore Square area, this "chichi" yet "low-key" "neighborhood hangout" with "more than a touch of class" pulls in an "after-work crowd" of "25- to 35-year-olds" with its "freshly prepared" "gourmet" American "bar food", including one of the "best burgers in town"; "everyone – from meat lovers to vegans – can find something tasty to nosh on", and it's "easy on the wallet", making it a "good bet if you don't want to deal with the BC, BU crowd."

AUJOURD'HUI | 27 | 27 | 27 | $72 |
Four Seasons Hotel, 200 Boylston St. (bet. Arlington & S. Charles Sts.), 617-351-2071; www.fourseasons.com

■ "Luxe to the max", this "special-occasion" destination at the Four Seasons Hotel is a "serenely" "transcendent experience"; voted No. 1 for both Decor and Service in Boston, it's "worth the mortgage on the house" to indulge in chef Edward Gannon's "imaginative", "flawless" French-influenced New American creations, accompanied by a "sublime" wine list and proffered with "unmatched" "refinement" amid "gorgeous" surroundings; "could life get any better?"

Aura | 20 | 17 | 20 | $45 |
Seaport Hotel, 1 Seaport Ln. (bet. Congress St. & Northern Ave.), 617-385-4300; www.seaporthotel.com

☑ "If you're near the World Trade Center", this Seaport Hotel dining room is a "pleasant" place to partake of "nicely prepared and presented" New American fare; supporters say that the "attentive" service makes it suitable for a "business lunch", but naysayers nix the "unremarkable" menu and "strange" setting ("it feels like you're eating in the lobby"), advising "there are better choices" around.

Boston　　　　　　　　　　　　　　F | D | S | C |

Azafran　　　　　　　　　　　　18 | 19 | 21 | $33 |
34 Church St. (Main St.), Winchester, 781-729-7722
☛ "Terrific" "aromas waft from the open kitchen" at this saffron-hued storefront in "suburban" Winchester, where the "charming" proprietors (who also own Taberna de Haro) have created a "warm, arty" haven; the menu offers the "real tastes of Spain", from the "great tapas" to the "excellent paella" to the "yummy" flan, and it's paired with a "good selection of wines"; a few frugal sorts find it "pricey", but aficionados embrace it as a "little gem."

Azure　　　　　　　　　　　　　– | – | – | VE |
Lenox Hotel, 61 Exeter St. (Boylston St.), 617-933-4800; www.lenoxhotel.com
Chef Robert Fathman (ex Federalist and Trio) has taken charge of the "sleek", stylishly revamped main dining room at the Lenox Hotel, renamed for the vivid blue accents that offset the pale yellow walls; his "creative", "artistically presented" seafood-centric New American menu roams the world for inspiration, dabbling in the flavors of Asia, the Mediterranean and Latin America, and early reports are that these "unusual combinations of tastes" are "all delicious."

Bacco　　　　　　　　　　　　　18 | 19 | 17 | $30 |
107 Salem St. (Parmenter St.), 617-624-0454
☛ A "far cry from the quaint mom-and-pop" eateries more "typical of the North End", this "trendy", "upscale" Italian scene features a "big", "lively" bar and "beautiful windows" that "open onto the street"; though the food is "nothing special", it's a "decent place to go for a drink and some appetizers" (the fried calamari is "not to be believed").

Back Eddy　　　　　　　　　　　23 | 20 | 17 | $36 |
1 Bridge Rd. (Rte. 88), Westport, 508-636-6500
☛ Though Chris Schlesinger is no longer the owner, loyalists say that this "laid-back" fish house is still a "perfect place for a summer meal"; boasting a "gorgeous view" of Westport Harbor and "paradisiacal" outdoor dining ("sunsets on the deck" can't be beat), it appeals with "first-rate" "fresh seafood" and "even fresher local produce"; the impatient whine about "endless waits on weekends" and occasionally "sluggish" service, but fin fans just want to know "why can't there be a place like this in Boston?"

Baja Betty's Burritos ⊄　　　　20 | 12 | 19 | $9 |
3 Harvard Sq. (bet. Harvard & Washington Sts.), Brookline, 617-277-8900
■ "Have it your way" at this "brightly colored" Mexican taqueria in Brookline known for its "delicious", "inventive" "California-style" burritos, "customized" to order yet served up "fast"; not only are the portions "huge" ("you'll never leave hungry") but everything is "cheap" and "pretty healthy"; "run by the nicest guys", aficionados say it adds

get updates at zagat.com　　　　　　　　　　　　　　27

Boston F | D | S | C |

up to a "great neighborhood place – we only wish it were in our neighborhood."

Baja Mexican Cantina   15 | 13 | 15 | $20
111 Dartmouth St. (Columbus Ave.), 617-262-7575
◪ "Popular with the younger crowd", this "loud", "kitschy" cantina situated where the Back Bay meets the South End gets some nods for its "fun" vibe and "decent" drinks; though its "simple" south-of-the-border "standards" may be "nondescript", tequila-fueled revelers shrug "enough margaritas and anything will taste good", but skeptics scoff about "Boston's idea of California's idea of Mexican food" ("we're never awed by the service" either).

Baker's Best Cafe   23 | 15 | 17 | $23
27 Lincoln St. (Walnut St.), Newton, 617-332-4588
◪ "Clamoring hordes" of Newton Highlands neighbors descend upon this little "gem" for "high-quality" New American "comfort food" "galore"; the surroundings are "utilitarian" (despite a recent "remodeling") and the wait can be "excruciating" (though insiders tip that dinners are more "peaceful" than the "hectic" lunches and weekend brunches), but the "imaginative" dishes and "helpful" service certainly compensate.

Bamboo   23 | 17 | 20 | $18
1616 Commonwealth Ave. (Washington St.), Brighton, 617-734-8192
■ "Mouthwatering aromas" pull in plenty of fans at this "cozy", "unassuming" "neighborhood" "jewel" in Brighton, praised for its "generous portions" of "spicy, sophisticated" Thai dishes (including "some unique ones that aren't found at every other place") distinguished by "wonderful flavors"; not only is the service "gracious" and the atmosphere "pleasant", but you "can't beat the prices", so "what's not to love" (aside from the "hassle" of "searching for a parking space")?

B & D Deli   15 | 8 | 12 | $14
1653 Beacon St. (Washington St.), Brookline, 617-232-3727
◪ Homesick New Yorkers pack into this "old-style" Jewish deli in Brookline that's been drawing "crazed crowds" since it opened in 1924; supporters swear that its "great corned beef", "real matzo ball soup" and smoked fish platters are "as good as it gets without hopping the train" to the Big Apple, but mavens who kvetch about the "so-so" "basic" eats, "shabby" space and "surly" service sum it up in one word: "*feh!*"

Bangkok Basil   ∇ 16 | 11 | 17 | $18
1374 Beacon St. (Centre St.), Brookline, 617-739-1236
◪ No, it's "not the best", but this bare-bones Thai "joint" in Coolidge Corner turns out "acceptable" food "fast" and "cheaply", making it a "take-out savior" for many Brookline

Boston | F | D | S | C |

residents; detractors, however, who conclude that "you get what you pay for", advise you "can do much better at several other places within a short distance."

Bangkok Bistro | 18 | 12 | 16 | $18 |
1952 Beacon St. (Chestnut Hill Ave.), Brighton, 617-739-7270

◪ "Better-than-average" Thai food is what you can expect at this Cleveland Circle "hole-in-the-wall", while some "select items" are quite "excellent", such as the massaman curry; it "lacks atmosphere", but the portions are "plentiful" and a "good value", and the service "quick", making it "fine for local carryout"; dissatisfied customers, however, frown "bland, bland, bland" and suggest "entertaining your taste buds elsewhere."

Bangkok Blue | 21 | 15 | 18 | $21 |
651 Boylston St. (bet. Dartmouth & Exeter Sts.), 617-266-1010

◪ People-watching is prime when dining "alfresco" at this "nice" Thai option "perfectly located" in the "busy" Copley Square area; inside, the "ambiance is zip", but the "delicious" food and "courteous" service make it a suitable place for a "quick" bite; though it may "not be worth going out of your way", it's a "reliable" choice if you're working or shopping in the Back Bay.

Bangkok City | ∇ 20 | 17 | 19 | $23 |
167 Mass Ave. (bet. Boylston St. & Huntington Ave.), 617-266-8884

■ Ticket-holders "always enjoy" a pre-concert meal at this "wonderful place to dine in the Symphony" neighborhood; a "respectable alternative to Bangkok Cuisine" just down the street, it earns applause with its "consistently" "great" Thai food, "nice room" and "fine" service, and it can "seat large groups in its private room."

Bangkok Cuisine | ∇ 24 | 15 | 19 | $24 |
177A Mass Ave. (bet. Boylston St. & Huntington Ave.), 617-262-5377

■ The "first and still among the best" of Boston's Thai establishments, this enduring "favorite" continues to attract the "Huntington Theatre and Symphony crowd" "before and after" an event; the "terrific" dishes, "fairly priced", are always "well prepared" and they "seem more authentic than most", making it a "great place" for novices to "learn" about the cuisine.

Baraka Cafe ⊄ | 25 | 16 | 18 | $22 |
80½ Pearl St. (bet. Auburn & Williams Sts.), Cambridge, 617-868-3951

■ For "a whole new aromatic experience", adventurous appetites seek out this "bohemian" haunt near Central Square for "exotic (yet comforting)", "fantastic" North

Boston

| F | D | S | C |

African "dishes you won't find elsewhere" in Boston; the "genuine" Tunisian specialties are "prepared with care and love", so who minds that the pace can be "slow" or that the tables in this "cramped" storefront aren't much bigger than a "grain of couscous"?

BARCODE
14 | 19 | 14 | $31
955 Boylston St. (bet. Hereford St. & Mass Ave.), 617-421-1818

☑ "Wear black" and make a martini your drink of choice if you want to fit in with the "young, professional crowd" at this "cool" Back Bay watering hole, where the "scene" is so "noisy" it can "make even the hard of hearing long for earplugs"; brace yourself for a sea of "Prada shoes and plastic people" and "less-than-thrilling" American grub – clearly, this "place is about satisfying other appetites."

Barker Tavern
25 | 23 | 23 | $40
21 Barker Rd. (Jericho Rd.), Scituate, 781-545-6533; www.barker-tavern.com

■ Overlooking "picturesque" Scituate Harbor, this "quaint old tavern" is graced with a location that "couldn't be more perfect"; quartered in a "charming" building that "dates back a few centuries" (to 1634, in fact), it's a "classy", "romantic" destination where patrons "dress up and enjoy the ambiance" while partaking of "top-notch" "classic" American fare ("don't go and not get the swordfish") brought to table by a "delightful" staff; it's among the "best the South Shore has to offer."

Barking Crab
14 | 14 | 13 | $23
88 Sleeper St. (Northern Ave.), 617-426-2722

☑ "Oh, just give me the fresh sea air, a cheap beer" and some "messy seafood" sigh those hooked on this "rustic" fish "shack", a "bustling" "dive with a great waterfront location" "overlooking Fort Point Channel"; the "simple" menu is "decent", if "boring", and the room "isn't beautiful" (though fans say the "rough edges add to the atmosphere"), but groupies, who "wouldn't change a thing" here, insist "you can't help but have a good time at a place called the Barking Crab."

Bar 10 ◐
17 | 24 | 18 | $29
Westin Copley Place, 10 Huntington Ave. (bet. Dartmouth & Stuart Sts.), 617-424-7446; www.westin.com

☑ A "hip" late-night "oasis of youth amid a desert of three-piece suits", this "posh", "Manhattan-esque" lounge at the "staid" Westin Copley Place is "comfortably" appointed with "way-cool couches and chairs" (the "perfect place to rest your weary feet"); the bartenders mix "unbelievable cocktails" and the kitchen's "interesting" Mediterranean munchies are definitely a "step up from the average hotel bar fare", but thrifty types warn it costs "too much money for what you get."

Boston F | D | S | C

BAY TOWER ⑤   20 | 26 | 22 | $54
60 State St. (Congress St.), 617-723-1666;
www.baytower.com
◪ Without a doubt, the "spectacular" panoramic view of Boston Harbor from the 33rd floor of this office tower high above Faneuil Hall will "take your breath away"; the New American menu may not offer the "latest in cutting-edge cuisine" (if the "food were as good" as the setting, "we'd be in heaven"), but the "pampering" service will ensure a "swanky", "special-occasion" experience that's sure to "impress a client or a date."

Beacon Hill Bistro   19 | 19 | 18 | $39
Beacon Hill Hotel, 25 Charles St. (bet. Branch & Chestnut Sts.),
617-723-1133; www.beaconhillbistro.com
◪ "Ooh-la-la" purr devotees of this "relaxing" French bistro on Beacon Hill whose "reasonably priced" menu and "great-value" wine list keep them "coming back" again and again; though the "tables are too close together" and the service can be "discombobulated", the dining room is a "statement of simplicity and style"; "if only the food were a touch better, it'd be a real find."

Bella's   20 | 16 | 18 | $30
933 Hingham St. (Rte. 3), Rockland, 781-871-5789
◪ "Go early" to this long-standing Rockland "favorite", because there's frequently a "long wait" "after 6 PM" advise partisans who praise its "good-sized portions" of "delicious" (if "basic") Italian-American fare; an "old reliable", it's always "pleasant" and "sometimes even shines", though the disappointed declare that it's getting "tired", with food that's "just fair" these days and decor that "needs some tweaking."

Bernard's   22 | 15 | 19 | $27
The Mall at Chestnut Hill, 199 Boylston St.
(Hammond Pond Pkwy.), Chestnut Hill, 617-969-3388
◪ "East meets West" at this Chestnut Hill Pan-Asian where the "gourmet" fare "pleases the palates" of patrons who brave the "long wait" to take a dining break in "between shopping sprees"; owner Bernard Leung (a "perfect gentleman") oversees an "accommodating" staff, and even if opponents opine that the menu "caters to mall rats" with "Americanized flavors", the majority insists it's far "better than your average suburban" Chinese chow.

BERTUCCI'S   17 | 13 | 15 | $19
Faneuil Hall Mktpl., 22 Merchants Row (State St.),
617-227-7889
39-45 Stanhope St. (bet. Berkeley & Clarendon Sts.),
617-247-6161 ⑤
412 Franklin St. (Five Corners), Braintree, 781-849-3066
(continued)

Boston | F | D | S | C |

(continued)
BERTUCCI'S
4 Brookline Pl. (bet. Brookline Ave. & Rte. 9), Brookline, 617-731-2300
21 Brattle St. (Harvard Sq.), Cambridge, 617-864-4748
799 Main St. (Windsor St.), Cambridge, 617-661-8356
Atrium Mall, 300 Boylston St. (Florence St.), Chestnut Hill, 617-965-0022
4054 Mystic Valley Pkwy. (Rte. 28), Medford, 781-396-9933
275 Centre St. (Pearl St.), Newton, 617-244-4900
475 Winter St. (Rte. 128), Waltham, 781-684-0650
www.bertuccis.com
Additional locations throughout the Boston area

◪ "Chain or no chain", "they know how" to make a brick-oven pizza at these "dependable" franchises where you can "take the kids" for a sit-down meal "without burning a hole in your pocket"; the "addictive" hot rolls alone make it "worth the visit", though regulars recommend "sticking to the basics" on the "growing menu" of Italian entrees; be warned, however, that it can get "noisy as all get out" and service "varies widely."

Betty's Wok & Noodle Diner | 17 | 15 | 15 | $22 |
250 Huntington Ave. (Mass Ave.), 617-424-1950

◪ "Mix and match" "your own noodles, toppings and sauces" to come up with a customized bowl at this "funky" diner where Pan-Asian cuisine meets Nuevo Latino; it's a "fun concept" that "adds a creative element" to a meal "before the theater or Symphony", and design divas defend the "cool retro-chic" decor (think '50s LA), but dissenters dismiss the "generic" eats as "all gimmick" while wondering "where, oh, where is the staff?"

Bhindi Bazaar | - | - | - | M |
95 Mass Ave. (Newbury St.), 617-450-0660; www.bhindibazaar.com

Samir Majmudar, whose local restaurant empire includes Bombay Bistro, Rangoli and Tanjore, has just opened his latest venture in the Back Bay, a more-upscale-than-average Indian dining room with smart appointments; the ambitious kitchen specializes in the cuisines of five regions of the Subcontinent, including Bengal, Goa and Kashmir.

Big Fish Seafood ◐ | ▽ 18 | 7 | 15 | $19 |
18-20 Tyler St. (bet. Beach & Kneeland Sts.), 617-423-3288

◪ Find plenty of Asian patrons, "instead of just the tourists", at this "nothing fancy" Chinatown hole-in-the-wall that's a solid choice for "good, fresh seafood" (you can even "pick your own" from the tanks); despite the occasional language barrier, the servers are "pretty friendly" and they bring forth "real" Chinese food.

Boston F | D | S | C

Billy Tse
22 | 14 | 19 | $24

240 Commercial St. (Atlantic Ave.), 617-227-9990
441 Revere St. (Pierce St.), Revere, 781-286-2882 ◐

☑ "Lots of regulars" frequent this pair of "neighborhood meeting places" in the North End and Revere because the "great variety" of "excellent", "always fresh" Pan-Asian cooking is "sure to make them happy" (the "sushi is just a bonus" at the Boston branch); even if the digs "leave something to be desired", the food satisfies most surveyors' "cravings" and the service is "efficient", but still, detractors who deem it "overrated" shrug "nothing unique."

Bison County BBQ
17 | 13 | 15 | $19

275 Moody St. (Crescent St.), Waltham, 781-642-9720

☑ "You won't go home hungry" after strapping on the feedbag at this "haven for meat eaters" in Waltham that serves up "good, straight", "finger-licking" Southern-style barbecue at "rock-bottom prices" ("and that's no bull!"); adding to the "fun" atmosphere is the "campy" "Western saloon" decor and "friendly" service, but naysayers who find it "so average" warn "avoid this buffalo."

Bistro 5 ⌀
26 | 21 | 21 | $38

5 Playstead Rd. (High St.), West Medford, 781-395-7464

■ An "oasis of creative fine dining" in a "town better known for subs", this "charming" "little" bistro (now, thankfully, doubled in space) in West Medford has made a niche for itself with its "fabulous", "Downtown quality" Northern Italian fare, "artful presentations" and "personal care"; admirers are easily "won over" by "inventive" chef-owner Vittorio Ettore, who pays "attention to every detail" and provides for a "pampering evening."

Bisuteki
17 | 15 | 19 | $29

Radisson Hotel, 777 Memorial Dr. (Pleasant St.), Cambridge, 617-492-7777
Howard Johnson Hotel, 407 Squire Rd. (Rte. 60 W.), Revere, 781-284-7200

☑ "Watching them cook is almost as much fun as eating" say boosters of these "novelty" Japanese steakhouses in Central Square and Revere; while "kids who like the Iron Chef" will "go wild here", critics pan the "super-cheesy" production, citing "nothing spectacular" food and "tacky" decor, and caution that the "canned routine" "falls flat when the chef isn't enthusiastic" about performing that night.

Black Cow Tap & Grill
19 | 19 | 17 | $34

16 Bay Rd. (Rte. 1A), South Hamilton, 978-468-1166
54R Merrimac St. (Green St.), Newburyport, 978-499-8811

☑ Set right "on the water", the Newburyport offshoot boasts a "pretty" "view" of the Merrimack River (get a table on the "fabulous deck"), while the South Hamilton flagship features "clubbier" environs, but both of these "suburban

get updates at zagat.com 33

Boston　　　　　　　　　　　F | D | S | C

havens" on the North Shore are "respectable" places to relax over "upscale" American "pub grub" and "great brews"; despite "mixed reviews" for dishes that "aren't very creative", the service is "pleasant", making them "good" standbys for locals.

Black Sheep Cafe　　　　　　　　－ | － | － | M
Kendall Hotel, 350 Main St. (Ames St.), Cambridge, 617-577-1300; www.kendallhotel.com
If you've ever wanted to chow down at a fire station, this new Kendall Square cafe may be the next best thing; set in the lobby of the Kendall Hotel, a modern boutique lodging built around an 1894 Victorian firehouse, it dishes up Traditional American breakfasts hearty enough to nourish a firefighter, while later in the day it offers a limited menu of updated classics; N.B. no dinner on weekends.

blu　　　　　　　　　　　　24 | 21 | 23 | $53
Millennium Complex, 4 Avery St. (bet. Tremont & Washington Sts.), 617-375-8550; www.blurestaurant.com
☑ "Movers and shakers" flock to this "trendy" Theater District table (run by the Rialto team) where "talented" chef Dante de Magistris masterminds "sensational" New American fare; the "sweeping" "urban views" from the "glass-walled room" and the "attentive" service enhance the experience, which, by the way, is "less pretentious than you might expect"; just "don't be intimidated" by its "strange location" – to enter, you "have to walk through the health club's juice bar", past all the "sweaty people fresh from a workout."

Blue Cat Cafe　　　　　　　　16 | 20 | 16 | $27
94 Mass Ave. (Newbury St.), 617-247-9922
☑ "Cool cats" "chill" at this "spirited" "see-and-be-seen" "scene" in the Back Bay, a "jazzy" haunt where a "DJ spins nightly"; "break out the black pants", order an "excellent martini" (perhaps the "best in the city") and ogle the "beautiful" servers, but be forewarned that the American menu of light bites is no better than "mediocre"; bottom line: "stick with the drinks and dine elsewhere."

Blue Fin　　　　　　　　　　20 | 11 | 17 | $20
Porter Exchange Bldg., 1815 Mass Ave. (Roseland St.), Cambridge, 617-497-8022
■ "Quality" "sushi at insanely cheap prices" keeps this modest "neighborhood favorite" in Porter Square "always humming" with an Asian twentysomething clientele; the menu also offers traditional "homestyle" Japanese cooking, including some dishes "not seen in other local" eateries, but most fin fanatics are reeled in by the raw fish (you "can't beat the deals" here, which make many other restaurants "seem guilty of extortion"); P.S. "expect a long wait on weekends."

Boston

| F | D | S | C |

BLUE GINGER ⌀   26 | 22 | 24 | $47
583 Washington St. (Rte. 16), Wellesley, 781-283-5790;
www.ming.com

■ "Actually surpassing all the hype", "celebrity" chef-owner Ming Tsai's "bustling" Pan-Asian "winner" in Wellesley "wittily blends East-West cuisines" into "inspired" dishes that taste "even better than they look on the Food Network"; his "delectable fusion offerings bring joy to the foodie in all of us", while the "cosmopolitan" ambiance and feng shui–correct layout provide a "refreshing break from the dime-a-dozen bistros" around town; the "only problem": "getting a reservation is torture", but you'll (eventually) be rewarded with a "wow" of an experience.

Blue Plate Express   20 | 12 | 14 | $13
315 Broadway (Mass Ave.), Arlington, 781-646-4545;
www.blueplateexpress.com

■ "Like mom used to make", the all-American "comfort food" "prepared to order" at this Arlington time-saver makes for a "consistently good", "well-balanced" "family meal"; though there are "no culinary adventures" to be had here, the "home cooking" is "fresh", "tasty" and "affordable" ("love the mac 'n' cheese" and caramelized balsamic chicken), and a "wonderful alternative to pizza or burgers"; "plan on getting takeout", however, since there's "not much room to sit."

BLUE RIBBON BBQ   24 | 11 | 18 | $13
908 Mass Ave. (Highland Ave.), Arlington, 781-648-7427
1375 Washington St. (Elm St.), Newton, 617-332-2583
www.blueribbonbbq.com

■ "Stuff yourself silly" with "A-1 barbecue" at these "down-home" "hog heavens" in Arlington and West Newton, where "diners' big bellies and smiling faces testify" that "from the cornbread to the ribs, there are no misses" at these "little slices of the South"; the "funky", "bare-bones" quarters hold only a few seats, but the "snappy" service makes it a "favorite" pick for "pig-out takeout"; moonshiners only "wonder where do they keep the still?"

BLUE ROOM   26 | 21 | 22 | $38
1 Kendall Sq. (bet. Broadway & Portland St.), Cambridge, 617-494-9034

■ "High-class" "enough to make you feel special" yet sufficiently "relaxed" that you can "wear jeans", this "perennial favorite" in Kendall Square appeals with "vibrant" cooking that's "gourmet without any pretense"; chef-partner Steve Johnson's "innovative" Eclectic menu (so "interesting" it's "always hard to choose", but it's "all good"), based on "lots of local produce and fish", is presented by an "efficient" team that knows how to take care of its "intellectual" clientele, making this a "must on any diner's list."

get updates at zagat.com

Boston F | D | S | C

Bluestone Bistro 19 | 12 | 15 | $17
1799 Commonwealth Ave. (Chiswick Rd.), Brighton, 617-254-8309

■ "Arty" and "casual", this "old standby" is a "good place to fill up on a budget", which explains why "hungry" students as well as "loyal locals of all ages" drop by for "terrific gourmet pizzas", "fantastic calzones" and other "appetizing" Italian items; just "leave the car at home – you'll never find parking" in the jam-packed Cleveland Circle neighborhood; P.S. "check out the all-you-can-eat pizza night on Tuesdays."

Bob the Chef's 20 | 16 | 18 | $23
604 Columbus Ave. (Mass Ave.), 617-536-6204; www.bobthechefs.com

☑ "God bless Bob" profess acolytes who worship this "wonderfully" offbeat "institution" in the South End that dishes out "heaping portions" of "divine" Southern (and Cajun) vittles; the "convivial", "diverse" congregation knows that the "down-home cooking" prepared with "panache" will "brighten any dark day", particularly when accompanied by "live jazz" (Thursday–Saturday), even if nonbelievers complain that the fare "sounds better than it tastes."

Boca Grande 16 | 9 | 13 | $8
1294 Beacon St. (bet. Harvard & Pleasant Sts.), Brookline, 617-739-3900
149 First St. (Bent St.), Cambridge, 617-354-5550
1728 Mass Ave. (Linnaean St.), Cambridge, 617-354-7400

☑ "Get a ton" of "fresh" Tex-Mex grub at this trio of "student meccas" that are "nothing fancy" but deliver the "best value for the peso"; "if you come in with low expectations, you may be pleasantly surprised" by the "flavorful", "filling" food, not to mention the "best lemonade", served by a "lightning fast" staff that makes the "long line" move quickly; while it's "nothing spectacular", it "does what it does better than many" others of its ilk, making it a "burrito heaven" for aficionados.

Bocelli's – | – | – | M
374 Main St. (Harvard St.), Medford, 781-396-7070

Old-timer De Pasquale's may have closed its doors in Medford, but another traditional ristorante has recently taken its place, ready to satisfy neighbors' cravings for classic Italian fare; all the familiar crowd-pleasers are on the expansive menu – from pastas to pizzas to parmigianas – dished up in comfortable, family-friendly quarters.

Bombay Bistro 22 | 15 | 20 | $21
1353 Beacon St. (bet. Harvard & Winchester Sts.), Brookline, 617-734-2879; www.bombaybistroboston.com

■ For "consistently" "well-prepared" renditions of "classic" Indian dishes, Brookline denizens depend upon this

Boston   F | D | S | C

"popular" "neighborhood" bistro that offers "all the standards" (the "chicken tikka masala is awesome", with "just the right kick of spice"); though the decor "won't do much to enhance your meal", the "pleasant" staff will get you out "quickly", particularly if you're "catching a film at the nearby Coolidge Corner Theatre"; P.S. the Sunday lunch buffet is "terrific and a great value."

Bombay Classic   ▽ 23 | 17 | 22 | $19
9 Medford St. (bet. Mass Ave. & Park Terrace), Arlington, 781-648-7557; www.bombayclassic.com

■ The few surveyors who've discovered this "underrated" "gem" next door to the Regent Theatre in Arlington laud its "delicious" dishes from the Northern, Southern and Western regions of India; "consistently excellent", it "beats many of its fancier and more crowded competition in quality and service", making it "wonderful to have in the neighborhood."

Bombay Club   21 | 17 | 16 | $23
57 JFK St. (Winthrop St.), Cambridge, 617-661-8100

✍ "Snag a window seat" at this second-floor Indian mainstay to take in a "bird's-eye view of the action in Harvard Square" while partaking of "flavorful", "authentic" fare; some respondents report that the dining experience is "tarnished" by "lax" service that's "at best impersonal and at worst dismissive", though they concede that the "generous" lunch and weekend brunch buffets make it "well worth a visit."

Bomboa ●   22 | 22 | 20 | $41
35 Stanhope St. (bet. Berkeley & Clarendon Sts.), 617-236-6363; www.bomboa.com

■ "Totally sassy", this "sleek" and "sexy" Back Bay haunt really "gets going late at night", attracting a "très chic" clientele that congregates for "awesome cocktails" and a "unique", almost "daring" menu that mixes New French flavors with "hip" Nuevo Latino "flair"; the "snappy" scene ensures a "fun night out" (there's "nothing else even remotely like it in Boston"), and besides, the combination of "cold mojitos and hot halter tops" "makes you feel young."

Bonfire   18 | 22 | 17 | $48
Park Plaza Hotel, 50 Park Plaza (St. James St.), 617-262-3473; www.toddenglish.com

✍ At this "meat-eater's heaven" in the Back Bay, the "real showstopper" is the "striking" setting whose "soft red glow" gives the "beautiful interior" an "early bordello" feel; though the menu is an "interesting concept" – spanning all the cattle-ranging regions of the world – detractors feel it "doesn't measure up to Todd English's other stars", not to mention that it's "ridiculously expensive"; the "shaky" service can be "out of sync" too, leading foes to charge "this place couldn't light my fire with a book of matches."

get updates at zagat.com

Boston   F | D | S | C

BORDER CAFE   17 | 16 | 16 | $19
32 Church St. (Palmer St.), Cambridge, 617-864-6100
817 Broadway/Rte. 1 (Lynn Fells Pkwy.), Saugus, 781-233-5308
◪ It's "packed to the gills" with "Harvard undergrads" (at least at the Cambridge branch), "but you don't need an Ivy League education to love the fajitas" sizzled up at this "cheap", cigar-friendly Tex-Mex twosome; "despite the insane lines", amigos dig the "cheese-smothered" dishes and "frat party" vibe (the Saugus offshoot, meanwhile, is "terrific fun" for kids), but the older demographic gives a failing grade to the "forgettable" grub.

Boston Beer Works   15 | 15 | 16 | $19
61 Brookline Ave. (Lansdowne St.), 617-536-2337 ◐
112 Canal St. (bet. Causeway & Market Sts.), 617-896-2337
◪ A handy place to "hang out before a game" – or to "drown your sorrows after another Red Sox collapse" – this cavernous, neo-industrial microbrewery across the street from Fenway Park is known for its "quality handcrafted ales"; note, though, that the "high ceilings and copper vats make for a cacophonous environment", while the Traditional American pub grub scores "no more than a single"; N.B. there's also a sibling near the Fleet Center.

Boston Sail Loft   16 | 14 | 15 | $24
80 Atlantic Ave. (Lewis Wharf), 617-227-7280
◪ "One of the only affordable restaurants on the waterfront", this sometimes "raucous" "local hangout" is a "perfect summer spot" for "after-work drinks and appetizers" or a "basic" fish dinner (expect the "typical New England fried foods"); nautical types "love" chowing down while "looking out at the harbor", but prepare for "slow" service.

Brasserie Jo ◐   19 | 19 | 19 | $38
The Colonnade, 120 Huntington Ave. (W. Newton St.),
617-425-3240; www.colonnadehotel.com
◪ "Before the Symphony" or a show at the Huntington Theatre, ticket-holders stop by this "bustling" "gathering spot" at the Back Bay's Colonnade for a "classic" French brasserie meal that's "tasty", if "not remarkable" (but "save room" for those "amazing profiteroles"); the ambiance is "unintimidating", the "savvy" staff "knows how to serve the pre-performance crowds" and it's a "surprising value", but critics pan the "sketchy" production.

Brenden Crocker's   ▽ 24 | 23 | 20 | $41
Wild Horse Cafe
392 Cabot St. (Bennett St.), Beverly, 978-922-6868;
www.wildhorsecafe.com
■ "So many martinis, so little time" sighs the "hip crowd" that "fills" the "lively" cigar bar at this "atmospheric" "local favorite" in Beverly; whether you settle into a "comfy" "soft sofa" in the "more formal main dining room" or pull up a

Boston   F | D | S | C |

stool in the "festive" lounge (where "interesting" light bites are available), you'll be "graciously" served "superb" American fare from the open kitchen's wood-fired grill.

Bricco   22 | 20 | 19 | $40 |
241 Hanover St. (bet. Cross & Richmond Sts.), 617-248-6800

☑ The "tasty" "tapas-style" Italian antipasti and "good bar scene" "beg you to come with friends" to this ristorante/enoteca in the North End, where the "modern" decor makes it a "pleasant alternative" to all the "red-sauce" throwbacks; though the "tab adds up quickly" and service ranges from "excellent" to "disappointing", overheated singles insist it's a "great date place", with "food that's the equivalent of sex."

Bridgeman's   24 | 21 | 22 | $34 |
145 Nantasket Ave. (bet. Berkley Rd. & Park Ave.), Hull, 781-925-6336

■ On the South Shore, the "action" is at the latest New Kid on the Block in Hull, a casually "chic" "up-and-comer" where some fans "love sitting downstairs and watching the chef" (Paul Wahlberg, Donnie and Mark's brother) at work as much as others prefer to dine upstairs to take in the "amazing view" of Nantasket Beach; the "innovative", "consistently good" Northern Italian fare and "wonderful" service combine to make this a "great find."

BRISTOL LOUNGE ◐   24 | 27 | 26 | $43 |
Four Seasons Hotel, 200 Boylston St. (bet. Arlington & S. Charles St.), 617-351-2053; www.fourseasons.com

■ "Nothing beats a window table looking out on the Public Garden" – "unless it's something delicious" from the Viennese "dessert buffet" – declare devotees of this "civilized" Back Bay "haven"; it's also a "lovely spot for tea" and "perfect" for "entertaining business clients" at lunch or dinner, as the New American menu is "top-shelf" and the service team a "class act" ("every restaurant should train its staff this well"); in sum, you get "all of the opulence" of the Four Seasons "without defaulting on the mortgage."

BROWN SUGAR CAFE   25 | 17 | 19 | $20 |
1033 Commonwealth Ave. (Babcock St.), 617-787-4242
129 Jersey St. (Boylston St.), 617-266-2928
www.brownsugarcafe.com

■ "Like Thailand – minus the elephant rides" rhapsodize respondents about this "true gem" that's renowned for preparing the "best Thai food in Boston"; given a menu that may be "bigger" than nearby Fenway Park, there's definitely "something to please everyone" here, particularly when all the dishes are "fresh and delicious" (akin to a "colorful party for your mouth"); granted, the "tables are crammed" into the "intimate" quarters, but the service is "quick" and the tabs "cheap"; all in all, it's a "sweet choice"; N.B. there's a larger branch near BU.

get updates at zagat.com

Boston   F | D | S | C

B-Side Lounge ◐   20 | 16 | 18 | $26
92 Hampshire St. (Windsor St.), Cambridge, 617-354-0766
■ "Go to b-seen" at this "super-cool" hangout "for grown-ups" near Kendall Square, where the "quirky", "retro-style" setting lures an "eclectic mix of people"; "for a bar", the New American food is "inventive" and "pleasing" (and a "bang for the buck" too), and the "with it" staff has "surprisingly little attitude", but it can be "a mob scene" that's "just too loud for conversation"; "if your eardrums can take it", "this place rocks."

Buddha's Delight   18 | 9 | 15 | $16
3 Beach St. (Washington St.), 617-451-2395
404 Harvard St. (bet. Beacon St. & Commonwealth Ave.), Brookline, 617-739-8830
■ "Where tofu goes when it wants to taste like beef", this pair of animal-free Asian options in Chinatown and Brookline is "pure heaven for vegetarians"; the "freshly prepared" Chinese and Vietnamese dishes are "healthy", "accessible" and "cheap", though the service in the "dreary" digs can be as "slow as molasses"; cynical carnivores, meanwhile, carp "while the fake meats come close, they sure aren't the real thing."

Bugaboo Creek Steak House   14 | 16 | 16 | $22
551 John Mahar Hwy. (Pearl St.), Braintree, 781-848-0002
345 Cochituate Rd. (bet. Rtes. 9 & 30), Framingham, 508-370-9001
Northshore Mall, 210 Andover St./Rte. 114 (Rte. 128), Peabody, 978-538-0100
Arsenal Mall, 617 Arsenal St. (Arlington St.), Watertown, 617-924-9000
www.bugaboocreeksteakhouse.com
■ "If you want to listen to talking moose heads" "mounted on the wall", "bring the kids – or anyone with a sense of humor" – to this "corny" chain where the "steaks aren't bad" (at least a "step up from fast food") and the atmosphere is "fun and friendly"; foes, however, beef about a "truly tacky" scene with a "theme-park" setting that "feels like Frontierland" at Disney World.

Bukhara   22 | 19 | 19 | $22
701 Centre St. (Burroughs St.), Jamaica Plain, 617-522-2195; www.bukharabistro.com
■ "Even Gandhi would salivate" over the "fragrant" aromas produced by this "pretty" "neighborhood" mainstay in Jamaica Plain that's "not your dime-store Indian place"; the menu is "standard", but the dishes are "authentic" and "delicious" ("great vegetarian options" too), with the breads the "stars of the show"; the "helpful" waiters are "prompt" and "courteous", making savvy sahibs happy to "spend monsoon season bingeing" here, but detractors deem the entire experience "erratic."

40   subscribe to zagat.com

Boston F | D | S | C

Burren   15 | 18 | 15 | $17
247 Elm St. (Chester St.), Somerville, 617-776-6896; www.burren.com
■ Expect "lots of character – and characters" at this Somerville "joint", a "dark", "traditional pub" that "could easily be in Dublin"; the menu runs to "homey, filling favorites" like fish 'n' chips and shepherd's pie, but with "real Guinness on tap" poured by "efficient" folks and live Celtic music featured nightly, regulars who just "while away the time with a pint" ask "who needs to eat?"

Buteco   ▽ 23 | 11 | 20 | $18
130 Jersey St. (Park Dr.), 617-247-9508
■ For "large portions" of "excellent" Brazilian cuisine ("heavy on the meat"), satisfied surveyors samba over to this tiny Fenway "hole-in-the-wall" where the "feijoada is out of this world" and the "rice and beans are amazing"; though the room's "not much to look at", the servers are "friendly", and as it has "been around for so long" (since '84) it's "dependably good."

Cactus Club   16 | 15 | 15 | $23
939 Boylston St. (Hereford St.), 617-236-0200
■ "No one over 25 need apply" to this "hot happy-hour" haunt, a "young" "singles joint" in the Back Bay that's a "major pickup scene" for the "college" and "post-college crowd"; "they make pretty darn good margaritas", but naysayers nix the "hit-or-miss" Tex-Mex menu (the signature "fajitas might sizzle, but other options fizzle"); P.S. "earplugs recommended" for sensitive sorts.

Cafe Barada   – | – | – | I
2269 Mass Ave. (Dover St.), Cambridge, 617-354-2112
Long an Arlington standby, this low-key Middle Eastern cafe has reopened in small but smart new digs north of Porter Square; the inexpensive menu remains about the same, featuring Lebanese maza, salads and kebabs, along with more substantial plates; it's also a pleasant spot to have afternoon tea and baklava while listening to tunes from the region play softly in the background.

Cafe Belo   18 | 7 | 14 | $12
636 Beacon St. (Raleigh St.), 617-236-8666
Brooks Plaza, 181 Brighton Ave. (Harvard Ave.), Allston, 617-783-4858
254 Bennington St. (Prescott St.), East Boston, 617-561-0833
94 Union Ave. (bet. Main St. & Mt. Wayte Ave.), Framingham, 508-620-9354
120 Washington St. (Broadway), Somerville, 617-623-3696
■ "Popular" with expats and "international students on a budget", this "cafeteria-style" mini-chain is "perfect for what it is"; get a "quick", "fresh" taste of Brazil by loading

Boston   F | D | S | C

up your plate from the rodizio grill, adding on "yummy sides" and "paying by the pound" at the register; there's "not much ambiance", but you get "plenty to eat for under $10", so it's "definitely worth a visit" to enter "carnivore heaven."

Café Brazil   20 | 13 | 21 | $19
421 Cambridge St. (Harvard Ave.), Allston, 617-789-5980; www.cafebrazilrestaurant.com

■ The "accommodating owner" "treats you like family" and the staff seems "really glad you're here" at this "warm" "neighborhood hangout", which brings a slice of Brazil to Allston; not only can you enjoy "good", "authentic" "homestyle cooking", "without breaking the bank", you can watch *futbol* on the TV and on weekends do the "bossa nova"; any wonder that it remains such a "favorite"?

Café China   ∇ 19 | 13 | 18 | $22
1245 Cambridge St. (Prospect St.), Cambridge, 617-868-4300; www.cafechina.com

◪ Sample an "interesting" "twist" on the standard Asian theme at this "consistently good" alternative that "holds its own among the plethora of restaurants in Inman Square"; with one Chinese owner and one Swiss owner, the result is "gourmet" Far Eastern fare teamed with a European approach to the decor and service; regulars recommend "get the specials and you won't regret it", but "don't bother with the traditional dishes" – if you want the "real thing", "drive the extra distance" to Chinatown.

Cafe Escadrille ⌇   17 | 17 | 17 | $40
26 Cambridge St. (Rte. 128, exit 33A), Burlington, 781-273-1916; www.cafeescadrille.com

◪ "If you're not looking for anything new or exciting", you can "get a good meal" at this Continental "constant" in Burlington that's a "decent" choice for a "night out" with "your spouse"; the staff, which prepares some dishes tableside in the Gourmet Room, is "efficient", but detractors who dismiss the "pricey", "boring" menu and "fern bar" decor insist its "time has passed."

Cafe Fleuri   21 | 23 | 22 | $41
Le Méridien Hotel, 250 Franklin St. (Oliver St.), 617-451-1900; www.lemeridienboston.com

◪ "Decadence on this scale hasn't been seen since the fall of Rome" sigh sated surveyors who've splurged on one of "Boston's best Sunday brunches" (live jazz included) or the "dream-come-true Saturday chocolate bar" extravaganza (September–May) presented at Le Méridien; after these weekend indulgences, this "airy" "atrium"-like cafe goes back to work as a "reliable, pleasant" place for a "power breakfast" or "business lunch" Downtown, even if a few feel the traditional French-American dishes "don't live up" to the "elegant" setting.

Boston | F | D | S | C |

Cafe Jaffa | 19 | 10 | 16 | $16 |
48 Gloucester St. (bet. Boylston & Newbury Sts.), 617-536-0230
■ "To recharge the batteries after a long day of shopping", mavens march to this "unpretentious" "everyday standby" for "authentic" Middle Eastern fare (with an Israeli bent) that may be the "best bargain in the Back Bay"; from hummus unrivaled "west of Tel Aviv" to "killer falafel" to "out-of-this-world schwarma", the portions are "large enough to feed a family"; the quarters are "plain", but at least "there's never a wait and you never feel rushed."

Café Louis ⍟ | 25 | 19 | 21 | $49 |
Louis Boston, 234 Berkeley St. (Newbury St.), 617-266-4680; www.louisboston.com
☑ "Every bit as lovely as the clothes down the hall" – and "nearly as expensive" – this "hip, stylish" cafe in the upscale Louis Boston store showcases an "extraordinary" "modern" Italian menu tweaked with some influences from chef David Reynoso's native Mexico; the result is "way cool", "delicious" dining, despite "tight seating" and service with a "healthy dose of *Vogue* attitude"; N.B. the folks from Providence's Al Forno are no longer involved.

Cafe Marliave ⍟ | 16 | 14 | 18 | $27 |
10 Bosworth St. (bet. Tremont & Washington Sts.), 617-423-6340
☑ "Considered an Italian version of *Cheers*" with food, this "reliable, comfortable oasis" in Downtown Crossing is the "kind of place you keep going back to"; long a "quaint" Boston "institution", it provides a "step back in time" with its "solid", "hefty" "red-sauce" eats, served with "lots of old-world charm" ("think the staff has been here for decades"); nostalgists cherish it as a "sentimental favorite", but others sum it up in one word: "tired."

Cafe of India | 22 | 19 | 18 | $23 |
52A Brattle St. (Hilliard St.), Cambridge, 617-661-0683
☑ A "cut above many local Indian places", this "refined" "favorite" boasts particularly "good people-watching" when its French doors "open onto the street" ("almost like dining alfresco"); "if you're not crowded out by all the Harvard kids", get in on the lunch buffet – a "spicy, flavorful and fast" feast and one of the "best buys around the Square"; the "diverse", "traditional" dinner menu is equally "satisfying" (the chicken tikka masala is "awesome"), presented by a "polite", "competent" staff.

Cafe Pamplona ⊘ | 17 | 15 | 15 | $10 |
12 Bow St. (Mass Ave.), Cambridge, 617-547-2763
☑ "One of the last places on earth" to find "honest-to-goodness beatniks", this "arty, bohemian" cafe evokes "Harvard Square in the '60s"; it's a "proverbial hole-in-the-

Boston F | D | S | C |

wall" where you can "grab a coffee" and "hang out with the intellectual crowd" in "claustrophobic" (at least the "eavesdropping is good") "basement" digs that make you "feel like there's something underground going on."

Cafe Polonia   – | – | – | I |
611 Dorchester Ave. (Southampton St.), South Boston, 617-269-0110
When you've tired of Nouvelle cuisine, consider dining at Boston's only Polish restaurant, a tiny, cheerful storefront cafe near Andrew Square that unapologetically serves its bread with a ramekin of (very tasty) pork fat; after that substantial beginning, you can tuck into stick-to-the-ribs specialties from pierogi to stuffed cabbage to kielbasa, and still leave with change from a 10-spot.

Cafe St. Petersburg   21 | 19 | 21 | $30 |
236 Washington St. (Harvard St.), Brookline, 617-277-7100
■ You'll "feel like you're in *Dr. Zhivago*" at this "romantic" Brookline cafe where comrades start with a "cranberry vodka (they make it themselves)" before moving on to a "hearty", "authentic" Russian meal "just like your Eastern European grandparents used to eat"; though it may be "quicker to fly to St. Petersburg than be served dinner here", at least the staff is "charming" and a pianist plays on the weekends.

Café Suisse   ∇ 18 | 15 | 19 | $36 |
Swissôtel Boston, 1 Ave. de Lafayette (bet. Chauncy & Washington Sts.), 617-451-2600; www.swissotel-boston.com
■ "Treat yourself" to the "out-of-this-world fondues" featured seasonally at the Swissôtel's 'winter festival' and "you'll think you're in the Alps" instead of a Downtown "high-rise"; the other items on the Swiss-American menu may be "better than you'd expect", while the "calm, professional" service is "as precise as a Swiss watch", but the lukewarm yodel "unless there's a blizzard keeping you here, take a short walk to a better restaurant."

Cafe Sushi   18 | 10 | 18 | $22 |
1105 Mass Ave. (Putnam Ave.), Cambridge, 617-492-0434
■ In Harvard Square and have a yen for raw fish? – "fill your craving" at this Japanese cafe that has been slicing and dicing "decent sushi" since 1984; it's "nothing exotic", but the selections are "competently" prepared and the "bento box lunch" comes at a "nice price"; the service is quite "attentive", though despite the too-bright lights, the environs are very "bleak."

CAFFE BELLA ⑤   27 | 19 | 23 | $39 |
19 Warren St. (Main St.), Randolph, 781-961-7729
■ "Wow!" exclaim enthusiasts of this Mediterranean "jewel" set in ("surprise!") a Randolph strip mall; it's a "consistent winner" thanks to chef-owner Patrick Barnes'

Boston F | D | S | C |

"fabulous", "absolutely tops" cooking ("complex without being fussy" and "innovative without straying from its true roots"), brought to table in a "rustic" room by a staff that "knows its business"; the only downsides: the "inevitable wait" to get seated and the "noise level."

Caffe Paradiso 19 | 14 | 14 | $14 |
255 Hanover St. (bet. Cross & Richmond Sts.), 617-742-1768
1 Eliot Sq. (Winthrop St.), Cambridge, 617-868-3240 ◐
www.caffeparadiso.com

☒ "Sit next to gaggles of godfathers arguing in Italian" (at the North End branch) or join the "mobs of students" (at the Harvard Square offshoot) at this pair of "quintessential European cafes", an "excellent" "hangout" for the "coffee and cannoli" crowd (it's primarily a "dessert shop") as well as those looking for some "real food" (panini, pizzettes, tortas); though the disappointed decree it's "far from paradise", acolytes praise the sweet treats as "heavenly."

Caffe Umbra 23 | 21 | 22 | $43 |
1395 Washington St. (bet. W. Dedham St. & Union Park), 617-867-0707

■ Plenty of "imagination" is evident at this "great addition" to the South End, where the "ambitious" kitchen "combines the best of the French and Italian countryside" to produce a "sophisticated", "inventive" lineup of dishes; with a "beautiful location" "in the shadow" of the Cathedral of the Holy Cross, the brick-walled environs soothe with a "wonderfully relaxing" ambiance, while the servers are "professional yet witty"; in short, this comer has "everything going for it."

Caffe Vittoria ◐ 19 | 18 | 13 | $13 |
294 Hanover St. (Prince St.), 617-227-7606

☒ "Just the place for coffee and dessert" "after a date" in the North End, this "charming", late-night "neighborhood" "institution" will make "you feel like you're in Italy"; "sit and watch the world go by" while soaking up the "old-world atmosphere" and satisfying your "sweet tooth"; though the staff "can be a little testy" (and "slow"), it's worth putting up with for the tiramisu alone.

California Pizza Kitchen 16 | 13 | 15 | $19 |
City Place, 137 Stuart St. (bet. S. Charles & Tremont Sts.), 617-720-0999
Prudential Ctr., 800 Boylston St. (Ring Rd.), 617-247-0888
Cambridgeside Galleria, 100 Cambridgeside Pl. (bet. 1st St. & Land Blvd.), Cambridge, 617-225-2772
Natick Mall, 1245 Worcester Rd. (Speen St.), Natick, 508-651-1506
www.cpk.com

☒ "Don't come here if you're a pepperoni-and-cheese kind of guy" (though you can indeed order that), because this

Boston F | D | S | C

Californian-style chain "thinks outside the pizza box"; a "haven for mall shoppers", it features an "eclectic menu" of "gourmet" pies topped with "something for every taste (no matter how weird)", from BBQ chicken to Peking duck to Jamaican jerk (the "salads are surprisingly tasty" too); still, the jaded jeer "once a novelty, twice a bore."

Caliterra Bar & Grille 17 | 19 | 19 | $36
Wyndham Hotel, 89 Broad St. (Franklin St.), 617-556-0006
◘ "For a business lunch" "or dinner with clients" in the Financial District, this art deco–style grill at the Wyndham Hotel is a "convenient" choice; it caters to a corporate clientele with its "subdued" room with plenty of "open space", "efficient" service and an "interesting" mix of Californian and Italian dishes; the bottom line: "don't go out of your way, but it's pretty good if you're in the area."

Cambridge Common ◐ 15 | 12 | 15 | $16
1667 Mass Ave. (Wendell St.), Cambridge, 617-547-1228
◘ Dishing up "basic" all-American eats "just like mom used to cook", this "burger-and-beer joint" is at least a "couple of steps up from a diner"; it's a "happy neighborhood hangout" near Harvard Square (prepare for lots of "law school" types) that'll do for "large quantities" of grub at "decent prices" – just don't mind the "dark, slightly seedy" digs.

Cambridge, 1. ◐ 22 | 20 | 18 | $18
27 Church St. (Palmer St.), Cambridge, 617-576-1111
■ "All they do" at this renovated firehouse in Harvard Square are "gourmet" pizzas with "pizzazz" and "simple, delicious salads", but they "do both extremely well"; the limited menu is presented in a "minimalist" setting (exposed brick, cement floors) that gives off a "cool yet unpretentious" vibe, making for a "perfectly light", "satisfying meal."

Cantina Italiana 24 | 16 | 22 | $34
346 Hanover St. (Fleet St.), 617-723-4577;
www.cantinaitaliana.com
■ "Delicious", "homey" food "like your Italian grandmother used to make" earns oodles of kudos for this "nostalgic favorite" in the North End; it may seem "cheesy from the outside", but "don't let the looks scare you", as they "belie the well-prepared, traditional offerings" awaiting within; "bucking the neighborhood's move to trendier, pricier restaurants", this "old-school" ristorante continues to please with its "tried-and-true dishes."

CAPITAL GRILLE 25 | 23 | 24 | $52
359 Newbury St. (bet. Hereford St. & Mass Ave.), 617-262-8900
250 Boylston St. (bet. Hammond Pond Pkwy. & Langley Rd.), Chestnut Hill, 617-928-1400
www.thecapitalgrille.com
■ "Well-dressed high rollers" and "budding masters of the universe" stake out this pair of "cosmopolitan" steakhouses

Boston F D S C

in the Back Bay and Chestnut Hill for just about the "top cow in town"; "lots of dark wood and cushy leather banquettes" give it an "old boys' club" feel, but it's also suitable "for a night out with your significant other"; not only are patrons ensured an "unbelievably good" porterhouse, but they're "treated like royalty", so though it's part of a "chain" it's also a "serious carnivore's" "dream."

Captain's Wharf 16 | 12 | 16 | $20
356 Harvard St. (Shailer St.), Brookline, 617-566-5590
◪ "Basic" seafood dishes at "reasonable prices" reel in a "loyal clientele" of frugal fin fans at this "neighborhood" "fallback" in Brookline; while it's "nothing special", the "consistently fresh fish" is "cooked right", but keep in mind that as it's a "senior citizen hangout" ("if you're over 70, this is the place for you") it "rolls up the welcome mat early."

Carambola 22 | 16 | 18 | $26
663 Main St. (Moody St.), Waltham, 781-899-2244; www.carambola.com
◪ "If variety is the spice of life", then this "cousin of the Elephant Walk" is "one of the spiciest around"; from the kitchen emerge "intriguing" Cambodian specialties that "delight the curious palate" with "incredible" flavors (insiders "recommend anything on the menu", but urge "don't miss the spring rolls"); though some habitués suggest that occasional menu "updates would be welcome", most have no quibbles about this "perfect example" of Waltham's "terrific", if "underrated", "restaurant scene."

Carlo's Cucina Italiana 25 | 12 | 20 | $23
131 Brighton Ave. (bet. Harvard Ave. & Linden St.), Allston, 617-254-9759
■ "Eat your heart out, North End" – this "family-run" "gem" in Allston is like a "little bit of heaven sprinkled with Parmesan cheese"; embraced as "one of the best homestyle Italian restaurants in Greater Boston", it's a "great find" for "authentic", "absolutely fabulous" cooking, though it may be "easier to squeeze into a two-year-old pair of jeans" than to get into this "tiny, cramped" storefront (no reservations are taken).

Carmen 25 | 21 | 20 | $38
33 North Sq. (Richmond St.), 617-742-6421
■ "Among the best new attractions in the North End", this "adorable" Italian "charmer" next door to the Paul Revere House is "not to be missed"; its "major league" cooking is "inventive" and "seductive", and it's served by a staff that "makes guests feel welcome" in a room made "warm and cozy" by the exposed brick walls and soft candlelight; just "plan on waiting", even "after your reservation time", and "stay away if you're claustrophobic"; N.B. the post-*Survey* departure of Bill Bradley may impact the above Food score.

Boston F | D | S | C |

Casablanca 21 | 20 | 18 | $32 |
40 Brattle St. (Harvard Sq.), Cambridge, 617-876-0999; www.casablanca-restaurant.com

☑ "Bogey would love" the atmosphere at this "funky joint" in Harvard Square that's "still going strong" after nearly a half-century; "hit the Brattle" Theatre (in the same building) to watch an art film, "then dine here" on "interesting, well-presented" Mediterranean dishes ("order a bunch of appetizers" "or have a full meal"); though a few feel that the "only impressive thing about this place" is the murals depicting scenes from *Casablanca*, fans just want to play it again at this "lively" "favorite."

Casa del Rey ▽ 13 | 13 | 16 | $19 |
15 North St. (bet. Cottage St. & Rte. 3A), Hingham, 781-740-9400; www.eatwellinc.com

☑ On the site of the former FireKing Bistro in Hingham, this new casa brings an "interesting" south-of-the-border twist to the South Shore with its "creative" Mexican menu; though amigos say it's a "great summertime outdoor spot", foes are adamant that its "only saving grace" is its "lovely patio", "but even that can't make up" for the "flavorless, boring" grub.

Casa Mexico 19 | 17 | 19 | $22 |
75 Winthrop St. (JFK St.), Cambridge, 617-491-4552

☑ "Hidden" in a "cramped basement" in Harvard Square, this "standby" seems "unchanged" "since it opened in the '60s"; it still attracts aficionados with its "great margaritas" and "tasty" Mexican food (regulars advise order "anything with mole"), while the "cozy space" and "reasonable prices" make it a "big date place" among students; the unimpressed, however, find it "disappointing", especially the "subterranean location" that "leaves much to be desired."

Casa Portugal 22 | 16 | 22 | $25 |
1200 Cambridge St. (bet. Prospect & Tremont Sts.), Cambridge, 617-491-8880; www.restaurantcasaportugal.com

■ Offering a taste of Lisbon in Inman Square, this "old-world" dining room has been feeding guests "satisfying", "traditional" Portuguese food since 1971; come hungry, because you'll be served generous helpings of "hearty" "home cooking" by folks who "couldn't be more solicitous"; the "simple" decor notwithstanding, you gets "lots of value for the money here."

Casa Romero 22 | 22 | 20 | $32 |
30 Gloucester St. (bet. Commonwealth Ave. & Newbury St.), 617-536-4341; www.casaromero.com

☑ "One of the most romantic spots" in town, this "charming" Mexican "hideaway" secreted in an "alley off Gloucester Street" delivers the "real stuff" – "authentic" dishes that are "consistently good year after year"; the starry-eyed recommend "dining alfresco" on the "romantic" patio, an

Boston F | D | S | C

"oasis in the Back Bay's urban jungle", but wherever you sit, you'll be taken care of by a "competent", *muy amable* staff; detractors, though, declare "lacks zing."

Cassis ⑤ ▽ 28 | 20 | 25 | $49
16 Post Office Ave. (Main St.), Andover, 978-474-8788
■ "Wow" – this "delightful" little "gem" in Andover is "as good as any city restaurant, and without the attitude"; those lucky enough to know about it "hate to give away the secret", but this "authentic" French bistro is "a labor of family love", appealing with "wonderfully" "delicious" cooking and "personalized" service; "what a find!"

Central Kitchen 22 | 20 | 18 | $32
567 Mass Ave. (Pearl St.), Cambridge, 617-491-5599
◪ With its "mix of urban funkiness and interesting cuisine", this "very un-Boston" bistro in Central Square is a "loud happening" hangout with a "great vibe"; the "eclectic" Mediterranean–New American menu is "enticing" (the "mussels in particular are excellent"), while the "beautiful blue-tiled bar" is quite the "after-work scene"; even if some wallet-watchers gripe that it's a "tad" "overpriced for what you get", most laud this "solidly upscale neighborhood place in what used to be a solidly downscale neighborhood."

Centre Street Café 22 | 12 | 18 | $19
669A Centre St. (bet. Burroughs & Myrtle Sts.), Jamaica Plain, 617-524-9217
■ "You can't help but leave with a grateful stomach" at this offbeat Eclectic "neighborhood institution" known for its "huge helpings" of "upscale hippie food" with plenty of "scrumptious", "healthy choices" for "both carnivores and herbivores"; feeding "artists, yuppies and activists together", it "captures the essence of Jamaica Plain", but better "line up early", since it's "itsy-bitsy."

Centro 24 | 19 | 21 | $37
720 Mass Ave. (bet. Inman & Prospect Sts.), Cambridge, 617-868-2405; www.centrocambridge.com
■ "Don't be put off by the peculiar entrance" through the Good Life bar next door, because this "small" Central Square trattoria is a "secret" "oasis" of "divine" Italian food; the menu changes every month or two, with each one focusing on a different region of The Boot, but the dishes always "burst with the flavors of the old world" and they're delivered by a "well-versed" staff in rustic environs.

Changsho 21 | 20 | 18 | $24
1712 Mass Ave. (bet. Linnaean & Martin Sts.), Cambridge, 617-547-6565; www.changsho.com
◪ Surveyors give "extra points for the breathing room between the tables" at this "lovely, upscale" "alternative to Chinatown" that accompanies "fancy" Chinese food with "quick" service to create a "welcome change from the

Boston   F | D | S | C |

hordes of indistinguishable take-out places"; while "never transcendent", it's "always reliable" and it "even has a parking lot" (a definite plus around Porter Square), but purists who dismiss the "bland, Americanized" chow just "say Chang-no."

Charley's   15 | 14 | 14 | $23 |
(fka Charley's Saloon)
284 Newbury St. (Gloucester St.), 617-266-3000
The Mall at Chestnut Hill, 199 Boylston St. (Hammond Pond Pkwy.), Chestnut Hill, 617-964-1200
www.backbayrestaurantgroup.com

☑ "Convenience is the major draw" at this pair of saloons that's handy for a "shopping break" when you're looking to "escape from Newbury Street's trendiness" or from the "chichi" Chestnut Hill mall; the "great burgers" lead off the "relatively inexpensive" menu of "basic" American eats, served in a "relaxing" atmosphere that almost makes it feel like "*Cheers*", but critics complain about "nothing special" "pub grub" and a "chain feel."

Charlie's Sandwich Shoppe ⓢ ∅   22 | 11 | 18 | $13 |
429 Columbus Ave. (bet. Dartmouth & W. Newton Sts.), 617-536-7669

■ "Sit side by side with strangers and share the sugar" at this "classic Boston greasy spoon", a "neighborhood institution" (circa 1927) in the South End that draws a "great mix of customers"; it's "justifiably famous" for its "solid", "down-home" American "comfort food" (don't miss the "best turkey hash around"), slung by a "friendly" staff that "makes everyone feel welcome", and it's a "bang for the buck"; N.B. no dinner.

Chart House   21 | 21 | 18 | $37 |
60 Long Wharf (Atlantic Ave.), 617-227-1576;
www.chart-house.com

☑ While "primarily for the tourists", easygoing "yachties and landlubbers" also "appreciate" this "dependable" chain link's "beautiful" "view of the waterfront" and its "nautical" ambiance; foodwise, "you know what you'll get" – "good fish" and other "basic" Traditional American food – and while it "won't let you down", it's "not too remarkable either", which explains why the piscatorial cognoscenti just keep paddling by ("there are too many superior seafood restaurants in Boston" to disembark here).

Chau Chow City ⓓ   22 | 10 | 15 | $19 |
83 Essex St. (bet. Chauncy & Oxford Sts.), 617-338-8158

■ "Yum yum dim sum" packs them in at this spare, multilevel Chinatown "experience" where the "carts brought round and round" deliver a "large selection" of "authentic" "Hong Kong–style" morsels that are virtually the "best in the city" (at "good prices" too); it's pure "madness" on the weekends,

Boston   F | D | S | C |

and you "could get lost in the cavernous" space, but at least "you can meet a zillion friends and still be accommodated", and it's open late for night owls who need a 3 or 4 AM snack.

Cheers   12 | 16 | 14 | $23 |
(fka Bull & Finch Pub)
*84 Beacon St. (bet. Arlington & Charles Sts.),
617-227-9605* ●
Faneuil Hall Mktpl., Quincy Mkt. (bet. Commercial & Congress Sts.), 617-227-0150
www.cheersboston.com

◪ It may be a "must-do for classic-TV fans", but at this Beacon Hill bar that "inspired *Cheers*", "if you're not a tourist, you're in the minority"; locals warn that "no one cares about your name here, only how many souvenirs you're going to buy", so just skip the "mediocre" American pub fare, "save your money and have your picture taken outside"; N.B. there's also a spin-off at Faneuil Hall.

Cheesecake Factory   18 | 17 | 16 | $24 |
Cambridgeside Galleria, 100 Cambridgeside Pl. (bet. 1st St. & Land Blvd.), Cambridge, 617-252-3810
Atrium Mall, 300 Boylston St. (Florence St.), Chestnut Hill, 617-964-3001
www.thecheesecakefactory.com

◪ Better "wear loose pants" before you "pig out" at these "raucous" franchises at the Cambridgeside Galleria and in Chestnut Hill, where "even finicky Aunt Selma will appreciate" the "*War & Peace*–sized menu"; prepare for "mounds and mounds" of American food, so unless you want "three days of leftovers", the sweet of tooth suggest "go straight to" the "indulgent cheesecakes", even if critics can't comprehend why the "lines are so absurd" given such "ho-hum", "glorified fast food."

Chef Chang's House   20 | 13 | 19 | $20 |
1004 Beacon St. (St. Mary's St.), Brookline, 617-277-4226

◪ "Why drive Downtown and fight for parking?" ask Brookline denizens who are pleased that this "mainstay" right in the neighborhood continues to serve "high-quality" Chinese food (you can even get "amazing" Peking duck, "carved tableside") at "reasonable prices"; though it has been "popular with families" for more than 20 years, purists deem the chow "Americanized" and urge "go to Chinatown for the real deal."

Chef Chow's House   18 | 15 | 17 | $19 |
230 Harvard St. (Coolidge Corner), Brookline, 617-739-2469;
www.chefchows.com

◪ Coolidge Corner customers patronize this "reliable neighborhood place" when they're looking for "well-prepared" Chinese food in a "comfortable" setting; the menu offers a "good variety" of "tasty", "cheap" dishes (the

get updates at zagat.com   51

Boston

F | D | S | C

"Hunan crispy beef is not to be missed"), and the "friendly" service is always "fast", so though it may not be the "best in Brookline", at least there are "no unpleasant surprises."

CHEZ HENRI
24 | 20 | 21 | $39

1 Shepard St. (Mass Ave.), Cambridge, 617-354-8980

☑ The "vibrant" "blend" of French and Cuban cuisines "brings a dash of spice" and "Latin flair" to this "romantic" storefront bistro near Harvard Square that's worked by "kind, attentive" people; insiders confide that "nothing beats" a Cubano sandwich "at the bar" ("one of Cambridge's best-kept secrets"), as the "laid-back" "dining room is a bit frumpy", but perhaps that suits the "academic crowd"; dissenters, however, complain the experience "doesn't live up to expectations."

China Pearl
22 | 11 | 15 | $18

9 Tyler St. (Beach St.), 617-426-4338
188 Mishawum Rd. (Ryan Rd.), Woburn, 781-932-0031

☑ "Arrive early" at this "legendary", "warehouse-sized" Chinatown "institution" for the "best dim sum in Boston"; though the joint resembles a "tacky function hall", it's "well worth the wait and chaos" to dine on "extraordinarily tasty" Cantonese specialties (the "enormous weekend crowds prove" that a meal is like a "visit to Hong Kong without the jet lag"), even if a "disappointed" few declare "this pearl has lost its luster"; P.S. the much smaller Woburn spin-off "isn't bad, if you don't want to drive Downtown."

Chinatown Seafood ◐
18 | 14 | 16 | $21

1306 Beacon St. (Harvard St.), Brookline, 617-232-9580

☑ "You know the fish is going to be good when you can see the waiter carrying it live across the room" to the kitchen say admirers of this "authentic Cantonese-style" addition to Brookline; "these guys can cook" and they "expertly prepare" a "variety" of seafood "straight from the tanks"; naysayers, however, carp "nothing exceptional" and wish the staff would learn "how to stay awake."

Christopher's ◐
17 | 15 | 17 | $20

1920 Mass Ave. (Porter Rd.), Cambridge, 617-876-9180

☑ A "great place to bring a vegetarian when what you really want is a burger", this "homey" Porter Square "hangout" has virtually "something for everyone" on its Eclectic menu of "upscale pub food"; the "Cambridge intelligentsia" appreciates the "extensive array of beers on tap", "friendly" service and "fair prices", but foes shrug "nothing dazzling."

Ciao Bella
18 | 16 | 17 | $33

240A Newbury St. (Fairfield St.), 617-536-2626;
www.ciaobella.com

☑ "Everyone is dressed in black" at this "trendy" haunt that boasts "one of the best people-watching locations" in the Back Bay; as "stylish" as the "sleek" surroundings

Boston F | D | S | C

are the Italian plates and "gorgeous" servers, but savvy sorts suggest that given the "run-of-the-mill" food, "save the \$30 and buy another lipstick."

Cilantro 22 | 17 | 18 | \$30
282 Derby St. (bet. Hawthorne Blvd. & Lafayette St.), Salem, 978-745-9436

☒ "If mole is your passion", then your "best bet on the North Shore" may be this "unexpected oasis" in Salem, where the "gourmet" Mexican fare is "truly authentic"; quench the "fire on your tongue" with a selection from the "great" "tequila list that could baffle even a connoisseur"; it certainly provides a welcome "break from Tex-Mex monotony", though peso-pinchers opine "overpriced."

Circolo – | – | – | E
7 Beach St. (bet. School & Summer Sts.), Manchester-by-the-Sea, 978-525-2400; www.circolo.biz

Upscale Northern Italian cuisine comes to the North Shore courtesy of this stylish addition to Manchester-by-the-Sea; though located not far from the beach, the sleek, taupe-hued dining room is definitely not a bathing-suit type of place, while the seasonal menu (inspired by the region of Venetia) is remote from the North End in both style and distance.

Clam Box of Ipswich ≠ 25 | 9 | 14 | \$17
246 High St. (bet. Haverhill St. & Mile Ln.), Ipswich, 978-356-9707

■ Hands down, the "best clams on the North Shore" come out of the fry-o-laters at this "whimsically shaped" shack that "really does look like an open box" of crispy bivalves; "if you're looking for fried seafood" of any sort, it "doesn't get much better" than at this "sentimental" New England "favorite" in Ipswich, to which fans make a "pilgrimage" to "eat in the rough"; note, though, that it's totally "no frills."

Claremont Cafe 22 | 16 | 19 | \$34
535 Columbus Ave. (Claremont Park), 617-247-9001; www.claremontcafe.com

☒ "You're treated like family" at this "convivial" "place where everyone knows your name", a "tiny" South End cafe that "attracts a huge following" with its "great weekend brunch"; "equally good for dinner", the Mediterranean-accented Eclectic fare is "lusty" and "enticing", though the "tight quarters" ensure that you'll be "rubbing elbows with your neighbors"; a minority maintains that it's "living on its reputation", but most only "wish it were on their block."

Clio 26 | 25 | 24 | \$66
Eliot Suite Hotel, 370A Commonwealth Ave. (Mass Ave.), 617-536-7200; www.cliorestaurant.com

■ "World-class" chef-owner Ken Oringer is a "god" in the "food laboratory" (aka "the kitchen"), where he "invents"

Boston   F | D | S | C

"absolutely divine" "ways to delight the palate"; the result is "Boston's most cutting-edge cuisine", an "extraordinary combination of taste sensations" that's "amazing from beginning to end"; despite portions so "skimpy" you may need to "have a sandwich" afterward, his New French–New American creations are "served with class" by a "knowledgeable" staff in a "chic" Back Bay room; N.B. raw fish finatics are flipping for its new Uni sashimi bar.

Club Cafe ◐   14 | 15 | 15 | $30
209 Columbus Ave. (Berkeley St.), 617-536-0966

A "must-stop on the South End gay scene", this nightspot can be "fun" for "meeting friends and people-watching", despite decor that the stylish shriek is "like cosmetic surgery gone wrong"; if you must eat, "stick with the appetizers" and "don't try anything fancy" on the "only passable" New American menu – "there are good reasons to come here, but unfortunately the food isn't one of them."

Colonial Inn   14 | 21 | 17 | $33
48 Monument Sq. (Rte. 62), Concord, 978-369-2373; www.concordscolonialinn.com

"Looking for historic New England?" – look no further than this "quaint colonial" inn, a "comfortable", rambling "throwback to yesteryear"; it's "all about atmosphere" here, though, since there's "nothing special" about the Traditional American grub that in "Concord of minuteman fame, takes too many minutes to be served."

Coolidge Corner Clubhouse ◐   16 | 12 | 16 | $17
307A-309 Harvard St. (bet. Babcock & Beacon Sts.), Brookline, 617-566-4948

To fuel a "steady diet of sports served up with their chow" and wash down "more beers than they can shake a mug at", fans head to this Brookline "haven" to "hang out and watch the game" on "TVs everywhere" (22, in fact); the American menu is "dependably" "solid", but "isn't there some way to reduce the din?"

Copley's Grand Café   ▽ 24 | 23 | 24 | $47
Fairmont Copley Plaza, 138 St. James Ave. (bet. Dartmouth St. & Trinity Pl.), 617-267-5300; www.fairmont.com

■ Providing a "touch of old Boston", this "splendid" cafe at the "grand" Fairmont Copley Plaza exudes plenty of "charm", "pampering" patrons with "excellent" Traditional American and New England fine dining; though it's often overlooked, stalwarts praise it as "perfect for a special occasion"; N.B. no dinner.

CORIANDER ⌀   27 | 21 | 25 | $45
5 Post Office Sq. (bet. Billings & S. Main Sts.), Sharon, 781-784-5450

■ In the vast wasteland of the southern suburbs, this "jewel" set in a Sharon storefront stands out as a "lovely oasis";

Boston F D S C

chef-owner Kevin Crawley is "one of the most talented chefs" in the Boston area, which is evident after one bite of his "fantastic", "imaginative" French bistro dishes, and along with his spouse and co-owner Jill, "they make you feel like a million bucks"; the "wine list deserves kudos" too, as well as the "intelligent and warm" service, so though it may seem "pricey by neighborhood standards, if it were in the city it'd be a steal."

Cornwall's ●𝒮 16 | 16 | 16 | $18
654 Beacon St. (Commonwealth Ave.), 617-262-3749
◪ "Fun without being rowdy", this "low-key", late-night tavern in Kenmore Square is a "great place" to "hang out" before or "after a game at Fenway"; sample a "wide variety" of ales while choosing from an "awesome selection" of "board games", and if you insist on eating, "really nice" folks will bring you some "typical" English pub grub; most regulars, however, "don't come here for the food."

Cottonwood Cafe ● 18 | 17 | 17 | $29
222 Berkeley St. (St. James St.), 617-247-2225
◪ Especially "hopping" "after work", this "casual" cafe has long been a Back Bay "favorite" thanks to its "cool vibe" and "hot and spicy" Southwestern bites; though the eats are "always decent, if never memorable", the margaritas are "super", but scenesters declare that this "overpriced" "watering hole for weary office workers" is getting as "tired" as its clientele.

Country Life Vegetarian 17 | 8 | 13 | $13
200 High St. (Broad St.), 617-951-2534;
www.countrylifeboston.com
◪ Part of an international chain, this Financial District option pulls in an "eclectic crowd" of healthy-minded "suits" dining "elbow-to-elbow with skateboarders", all digging into a "bottomless well" of Vegetarian "comfort food" served "on the cheap"; the fare is a "blessing" for herbivores, though the "spartan" "cafeteria" digs have an "assembly-line feel."

Court House Seafood 𝒮 ▽ 19 | 3 | 14 | $13
498 Cambridge St. (6th St.), Cambridge, 617-491-1213;
www.courthouseseafood.com
◪ "Basic seafood done well" lures fin fans to this (really) bare-bones "joint" in East Cambridge, where the "simple", "tasty" fare is "really fresh" because it comes straight from the owners' market next door; you always get a "good piece of fish at a good price", but note that there's "no decor" and "they close quite early."

Craigie Street Bistrot ▽ 24 | 20 | 22 | $35
5 Craigie Circle (bet. Brattle St. & Concord Ave.), Cambridge, 617-497-5511; www.craigiestreetbistrot.com
◪ Fast embraced as a "promising" "new treasure" in the "02138 neighborhood", this "hidden" "reward" outside

get updates at zagat.com

Boston　　　　　　　　　　　　　F | D | S | C

Harvard Square is a "real find" for "creative, urbane and satisfying" French fare (chef-owner Tony Maws has "got it right"); it's an "authentic re-creation of a Parisian bistro" through and through, from the "memorable", daily changing menu to the "cozy" "European"-style quarters to the service with a "Continental flair", though some early reports say it needs to "work out a few kinks."

Cuchi Cuchi ⑤　　　　　　　20 | 24 | 21 | $33
795 Main St. (Windsor St.), Cambridge, 617-864-2929; www.cuchicuchi.cc

☑ "Doesn't the name say it all?" ask fans of this "festive", "happening scene" near Central Square, where the "funky" space sort of looks "like a favorite grandmother's attic"; "transforming" the concept of tapas, the Eclectic menu showcases an "eclectic" "variety of delicious" "small plates" designed to be shared, inspired by cuisines from around the world and presented by a "patient" staff that's happy to "explain" the dishes; rigid types, however, moan it can be "hard to make up a coherent meal."

Daedalus　　　　　　　　　17 | 18 | 16 | $27
45½ Mt. Auburn St. (bet. Bow & DeWolfe Sts.), Cambridge, 617-349-0071

☑ "MBA types", "graduate students" of all fields and academic "wanna-bes" "fill this popular venue" where the "upstairs greenhouse" room (replete with a glass ceiling) gives off an "airy, sophisticated feel" that lends Harvard Square "some real character"; the kitchen turns out fairly satisfactory New American fare at "reasonable prices", though given the "hit-or-miss" execution, most gourmands suggest that this scene may make for a "better bar than restaurant."

Daily Catch　　　　　　　　22 | 8 | 15 | $27
323 Hanover St. (bet. Prince & Richmond Sts.), 617-523-8567 ⌿
John Joseph Moakley Federal Courthse., 2 Northern Ave. (Sleeper St.), 617-338-3093
441A Harvard St. (bet. Beacon St. & Commonwealth Ave.), Brookline, 617-734-5696
Augustine's Plaza, 124 Broadway/Rte. 1 (Lynn Fells Pkwy.), Saugus, 781-231-3280
www.dailycatch.com

☑ "Finally, a place that understands the importance of garlic" praise worshipers of this "no-frills" "calamari heaven", now a quartet in the Boston area; the "large portions" of "delicious" Sicilian seafood dishes and "fresh pastas" are "served piping hot in the frying pan", so though you're practically eating "in the kitchen at these tiny steam baths", with food this "fresh" the "decor is not what you're here for"; N.B. the waterfront branch was set to open shortly after we went to press.

subscribe to zagat.com

Boston F D S C

Dakota's 18 | 18 | 18 | $32
101 Arch Street Bldg., 34 Summer St. (Arch St.), 617-737-1777

☑ Many "power brokers" recommend this "smart"-looking "business" "hot spot" for a "refined" Traditional American meal, even though it can be "extremely noisy" (with "all that marble" and tile and "nothing to deaden the sound", "don't plan on having any long conversations"); critics, however, declare that though it may be "one of the few choices in the Financial District", it probably "wouldn't make it anywhere else."

DALÍ 25 | 24 | 22 | $31
415 Washington St. (Beacon St.), Somerville, 617-661-3254; www.dalirestaurant.com

■ With its "sexy", "surrealistic" surroundings, this "tapas paradise" in Somerville manages to be "outrageous and romantic at the same time"; whether you come for a "memorable" "dinner for two" or a "boisterous" fiesta "for 12", you'll be treated to the "best" "authentic" Spanish cuisine in Boston, presented with "gracious, old-world" style; if you're on a budget, just watch what you order because the check "adds up fast."

Dalia's Bistro & Wine Bar – | – | – | M
1657 Beacon St. (Winthrop Rd.), Brookline, 617-730-8040

A "breath of fresh air blew into" Brookline when this contemporary "neighborhood bistro" and wine bar took over the site of Duckworth Lane; settle into a gray velvet banquette and have a "tasty" full-course New American–Mediterranean meal or opt for a lighter 'bistro plate'; though it's "still working out the kinks common to a new place", early admirers "expect great things from it" ("everything is better with practice").

Dalya's 21 | 19 | 21 | $37
20 North Rd. (Rte. 62), Bedford, 781-275-0700; www.dalyas.com

☑ "For those who want city dining without city driving", this "surprisingly elegant" farmhouse tucked away in an "out-of-the-way location" in Bedford is a "great choice" for an "evening out with friends"; appointed with antiques, wrought-iron chandeliers and wood floors, it's a "relaxing" backdrop for "quite good" Mediterranean (and some American) dishes, though cynics charge "it's what you expect out in the suburbs – boring and predictable."

Davide Ristorante ▽ 24 | 21 | 23 | $47
326 Commercial St. (bet. Clark & North Sts.), 617-227-5745

☑ "Why don't more people know" about this "quiet", "romantic" North End "find" ponder perplexed partisans who are plenty pleased by its "impressive" Northern Italian menu (especially the "fantastic homemade pastas"),

get updates at zagat.com

Boston

| F | D | S | C |

"outstanding wines" and "elegant yet comfortable" environs; regulars rave that there's "not a bad selection in the house" and add that the staff is "courteous and helpful", but penny-pinchers complain "not a good value" (the "food isn't on par with the prices").

Davio's
| – | – | – | E |

75 Arlington St. (Stuart St.), 617-357-4810
Royal Sonesta Hotel, 5 Cambridge Pkwy.
(opp. Cambridgeside Galleria), Cambridge, 617-661-4810
www.davios.com

Newly relocated to "fabulous-looking" steakhouse-style digs opposite the Park Plaza Hotel, the Back Bay flagship of this "upscale" duo offers a mix of "reliably good" Northern Italian classics and more "creative" fare, while the high-ceilinged offshoot at Cambridge's Royal Sonesta Hotel features a similar menu, paired with a "priceless" "view of the Charles River and the Boston skyline"; those "not impressed", however, deem it a "safe choice", but "nondistinctive" and "overpriced."

Delfino
| 24 | 19 | 22 | $29 |

754 South St. (bet. Belgrade Ave. & Washington St.), Roslindale, 617-327-8359; www.delfinorestaurant.com

☑ "Dee-lish" is the verdict on this "lovely" little "storefront" "smack in the middle" of "up-and-coming" Roslindale, which imports "North End quality to the suburbs"; it's a "good bet" for a dining experience that's "refined yet family-friendly", with "fantastic" "traditional" Italian cooking and "reasonable prices"; the "wait can be long" (no reservations are taken), though, and the tables are packed "so close you could eat off your neighbor's plate."

Delux Cafe ●✗⌿
| 19 | 18 | 16 | $18 |

100 Chandler St. (Clarendon St.), 617-338-5258

☑ The "cool kids' hangout in the otherwise overpriced South End", this colorful, "postage stamp"–sized spot ("well worth a little squish") with "unusually cheeky" decor and rotating exhibits by local artists is one of the "best little bars in Boston"; the monthly changing menu of Eclectic "comfort food" will "leave you very satisfied", which explains why it's "packed all the time" with "suits and bikers" alike, despite service that can be "painfully slow."

Deluxe Town Diner
| 18 | 16 | 17 | $15 |

627 Mt. Auburn St. (Bigelow Ave.), Watertown, 617-924-9789

☑ "Nothing could be finer" than this "terrific nouveau diner" chirp fans of this landmark building in Watertown that's been updated with a bit of "style"; you'll find "all the standard" American items on the menu (notably "fantastic breakfasts"), as well as an "interesting" choice of more "inventive" dishes, all made with "fresh ingredients" and

Boston | F | D | S | C |

"without the greasy spoon flavor"; sure, it's "slightly pricier" than the average hash house, but it's "more upscale" too.

Demos ⊄ | 19 | 4 | 13 | $12 |
146 Lexington St. (Pond St.), Waltham, 781-893-8359
60-64 Mt. Auburn St. (Main St.), Watertown, 617-924-9660
■ "Good Greek fare and plenty of it" attracts Athenian admirers to this pair of dives in Waltham and Watertown, where they can tuck into "heaping plates" of traditional "staples on the cheap" (the "kebabs are terrific"); you have to "wait on yourself" ("order at the counter") in the severely "spartan" setting, but "if ambiance isn't key", you can't beat the "budget prices."

Desmond O'Malley's | 14 | 17 | 18 | $22 |
30 Worcester Rd. (Rte. 9), Framingham, 508-875-9400
■ "Eat, drink and be merry" – or just "hang out and listen to a good band" – at this "bright spot on Route 9" in Framingham, a "fun", "relaxing" watering hole with a "great selection of beers on tap" and "decent" Irish pub grub; the wistful, though, wish that the dishes "were as good as their efforts" and warn too that it can get way "too loud to hear your companions."

Devlin's | 18 | 20 | 18 | $25 |
332 Washington St. (Market St.), Brighton, 617-779-8822;
www.edevlins.com
■ One of the "more upscale places" in Brighton, this "townie-tony" bistro is considered a "gourmet outpost" in the gastronomic wilderness and a good pick if you're looking for "something between high-end and pub" grub; though the mix of Traditional and New American fare is "not wildly sophisticated", you get "honest food at a fair price", delivered by a "super-friendly" staff; besides, it provides major "relief from all the college-kid hangouts."

Dish | 21 | 19 | 20 | $29 |
253 Shawmut Ave. (Milford St.), 617-426-7866;
www.southenddish.com
■ "Watch the neighborhood crowd meet and greet" while sampling a "creative" Eclectic menu at this "adorable little" South End bistro "known mostly to locals (who want to keep it that way)", who try to "snag a table outside" or "score" one of the "cozy" booths; "if parking weren't so bad", devotees would "eat here at least once a week" (it's "one of the best deals" in the neighborhood), but a melancholy minority maintains "they can dish it out, but they can't dish it up" all that well.

Diva Indian Bistro | 20 | 22 | 15 | $23 |
246 Elm St. (Chester St.), Somerville, 617-629-4963;
www.divabistro.com
■ "From the intriguing hanging lamps" to the windows that "open onto trendy Davis Square", this "stunning" Indian

Boston

F | D | S | C

bistro in Somerville is pure "eye candy", while the "gourmet" menu is almost good "enough to make you break into an aria"; critics, however, find it "more flash than substance", booing that the "mood can sometimes be destroyed" by the "frustratingly" "flaky" service.

Dodge Street Bar & Grill   ▽ 18 | 11 | 18 | $28
7 Dodge St. (bet. Lafayette & Washington Sts.), Salem, 978-745-0139; www.dodgestreet.com

☑ "Go for the live bands" (nightly) and "stay for the cheap drafts" at this "fun" "local" nightspot in Salem, where the "music and the vibe are great"; it's "kind of grungy, though that's part of its charm", but you better "be prepared to bump elbows with the college kids and former hippies-turned-yuppies with khakis and ponytails"; as for the American eats: the "bar is better than the restaurant", so "forget the food."

Dolphin Seafood   18 | 11 | 17 | $24
1105 Mass Ave. (Remington St.), Cambridge, 617-661-2937
12 Washington St. (Rte. 135), Natick, 508-655-0669 **S**
www.dolphinseafood.com

☑ For "plain old seafood" "without having to catch your own", fin fanatics make waves to this pair of "family" restaurants in Harvard Square and Natick that's known for its "consistently good" "fresh fish"; while the dishes are "nothing exotic", they're "well prepared" and served by a "competent" staff at "reasonable prices."

Dom's   ▽ 20 | 16 | 20 | $37
100 Salem St. (Bartlett St.), 617-367-8979

☑ "Forget about all those tourist spots in the North End" and "take a cab to this hideaway" ("forget trying to park" too) instead urge faithful followers who let owner Dom "take them under his wing"; he'll enthusiastically "cater to your meal desires" and compose a Northern Italian dinner just for you, a "personal" approach that boosters say ensures an "excellent dining experience"; do-it-yourselfers, though, who "don't need someone to help them order" "don't see the charm."

Donatello   23 | 19 | 21 | $41
44 Broadway/Rte. 1N (south of Rte. 95), Saugus, 781-233-9975; www.donatellorestaurant.com

☑ If you're north of Boston and you're craving an "old-fashioned" Italian meal, get your fix at this "pink"-hued Saugus standby, an "upscale" "suburban spot" that has long been feeding guests "fine" food; it's a "favorite" among loyal supporters, though skeptics who sniff "overrated" contend it's a "legend in its own mind."

Dong Khanh ⊅   ▽ 23 | 9 | 14 | $11
81-83 Harrison Ave. (Beach St.), 617-426-9410

■ "Come for a bowl of pho and a traditional iced coffee or tall fruit shake" recommend regulars who've discovered

Boston F | D | S | C

this "wonderful find in Chinatown", where you "can't go wrong with any item" on the "authentic" Vietnamese menu (the dishes are "done better than most" elsewhere); the "bare-bones" digs are definitely "no frills", and it "helps if you speak the language", but in any tongue this is "damn good", "quick" and "cheap" eating.

Doyle's Cafe ◐ — 14 | 19 | 15 | $19
3484 Washington St. (Williams St.), Jamaica Plain, 617-524-2345

☑ "Rub elbows with local politicians" at this "quintessential" Boston "institution" that has functioned as a "comfortable neighborhood Irish pub before such pubs were fashionable"; since 1882, this "venerable" "hangout" has been a "place to see and be seen in Jamaica Plain", and its "old tavern feel" still has "lots of character"; granted, the Traditional American grub is "ho-hum", but at least it's "affordable for most every budget."

Durgin Park — 16 | 12 | 13 | $27
Faneuil Hall Mktpl., 340 N. Market St. (Congress St.), 617-227-2038; www.durgin-park.com

☑ "Granddad loved it" and so do the busloads of "tourists" who line up at this Faneuil Hall "legend" that's been around since 1827; you still "expect Paul Revere to walk in at any moment" while you're chowing down on "hungry man's portions" of "simple" New England "home cooking" at "long" "communal" tables in cavernous quarters filled with "local color"; it's "as Boston as it gets", but critics charge "not as good as in the old days" (even its "notoriously" "sassy" service "isn't as rude as it used to be").

Dynasty ◐ — 15 | 11 | 10 | $21
33 Edinboro St. (bet. Beach & Essex Sts.), 617-350-7777

☑ As big as a "megaplex" and open till 4 AM, this "plain" Chinatown fallback will do for "good dim sum" and other "decent" Chinese "standards"; insiders suggest going with "someone who knows how to order here, because many staffers don't speak much English", but foes ask with so many options practically "next door, why bother?" – "if it ever ruled", this dynasty has "long been overthrown."

EAST COAST GRILL & RAW BAR — 25 | 17 | 20 | $35
1271 Cambridge St. (Prospect St.), Cambridge, 617-491-6568; www.eastcoastgrill.net

■ Even "after all these years", this "dressed-down" Inman Square grill remains one of the "biggest food thrills in the Boston area", because chef-owner Chris Schlesinger's "passion comes through in each dish" – from the "way cool raw bar" selections to the "amazing" "spiced-up seafood" to the "incredible" oak-smoked pit BBQ, all served by an "exceptionally friendly" staff that's "efficient" "even under pressure"; though it "gets so loud you can't

Boston   F | D | S | C

hear yourself think", this "exciting" "hot spot" is a "deeply entrenched favorite" for good reason.

Eastern Pier Seafood   ▽ 20 | 15 | 15 | $18
146 Northern Ave. (Seaport Blvd.), 617-423-7756
■ Though you "can't tell from the outside", this modest Chinese seafood house near the World Trade Center boasts a "fabulous view" of the harbor; it's an appropriately aquatic setting for "great food outside of Chinatown", featuring "far above-average" Cantonese fare such as salt-and-pepper shrimp.

East Ocean City ●   23 | 13 | 17 | $23
25 Beach St. (bet. Harrison Ave. & Washington St.), 617-542-2504
■ The "key word is ocean" at this "reliable" Chinatown venue where "you can watch the fresh fish" from the tanks ("every type imaginable") virtually "swim over to your table"; as you'd expect, the "authentic" Cantonese-style seafood specialties are "terrific" (the "ginger-scallion lobster is the best", though the spicy-salted squid also comes "highly recommended"); given too the "affordable prices" and late hours (till 4 AM), "no one cares about the decor" or lack thereof.

eat   22 | 18 | 23 | $30
253 Washington St. (Union Sq.), Somerville, 617-776-2889; www.eatrestaurant.com
■ "You feel like an insider when you eat at eat", a most "welcoming, unpretentious" "neighborhood" "charmer" in Somerville that's so "comfortable" it "feels like home"; enthusiasts are "very fond" of the "limited" but "ever-changing" menu of "gourmet" American "comfort food" – "carefully prepared" and "not at all boring" – and the "sweet" service, adding that the fact that "there are always chefs from other restaurants dining at the bar on their nights off must be a good sign."

Edwardian Tea Room ⊄   _ | _ | _ | M
1332 Mass Ave. (Park Ave.), Arlington, 781-648-6508
Housed in a former pharmacy, this spacious Arlington Heights site has been recently recast as an English-style tea salon with Edwardian-era decor and Oriental rugs; teetotalers can settle in for a quiet break while sipping and sampling from a select menu of scones, cakes and finger sandwiches; for homesick Londoners, an elaborate high tea is served on Sundays.

Elbow Room   18 | 21 | 17 | $22
1430 Commonwealth Ave. (Kelton St.), Brighton, 617-738-9990
◪ "Cozy enough for a conversation yet lively enough to start a conga line", this "cool" bistro is an "active scene for twentysomething" singles ("finally, a place for those of

Boston

F | D | S | C

us who have already graduated but still like a little fun"); perhaps as "classy as a place in Brighton can be", it appeals with "solid" New American "comfort food" at "plebian prices", not to mention "awesome martinis", but more mature types feel it's "better for the bar action than the food" and warn too of the "suicidal parking situation."

El Cafetal
▽ 20 | 9 | 17 | $17

479 Cambridge St. (Brighton Ave.), Brighton, 617-789-4009

■ Cooking "authentic *comida colombiana*" "like your South American grandmother might make", this modest "local treasure" in Brighton comforts with "tasty", "hearty" and "cheap" fare served "promptly" by "friendly" folks; "don't expect to find Americanized vittles" here, but do be aware that having a "little knowledge of Spanish wouldn't hurt" (or else "be prepared to do lots of pointing"); P.S. don't miss the "very good fruit nectars."

El Coqui
— | — | — | I

561 Cambridge St. (7th St.), Cambridge, 617-876-6500

Named for the Puerto Rican tree frog and its eponymous song, the latest addition to the East Cambridge melting pot is this bare-bones eatery that specializes in stick-to-your-ribs Caribbean fare; the satisfying dishes – along the lines of *tostones,* salt cod stew and *pernil* (roast pork shoulder) – are the kind of solid island cooking that a native grandmother might make; N.B. be sure to check out the collection of amphibians in the back room.

ELEPHANT WALK
23 | 21 | 20 | $32

2067 Mass Ave. (bet. Hadley & Russell Sts.), Cambridge, 617-492-6900; www.elephantwalk.com

☑ "Run, don't walk", to this "established favorite" in Porter Square distinguished by its "vibrant", "varied" menu that showcases both French and Cambodian cuisines; the "intoxicatingly aromatic" "flavor rush" is "like nothing else in Boston", and combined with "beautiful" "tropical" decor, makes for an "exotic" "treat"; the legions of loyalists who "dream about this place" have "never had a disappointing meal here", plus the prices won't "strain your pocketbook"; N.B. the Boston branch near Kenmore Square is temporarily closed due to fire.

El Oriental de Cuba
21 | 6 | 12 | $13

416 Centre St. (Paul Gore St.), Jamaica Plain, 617-524-6464

■ Once you've tried this "yummy" "taste of Cuba" in Jamaica Plain, amigos are sure that "you'll start getting weekly cravings" for its "filling" specialties that "smack of authenticity" (the Cuban sandwiches are "fantastic", but "on Fridays, go for the roast pork special"); though a "school cafeteria may have better decor" than this "hole-in-the-wall" and the "slow" staff is still on island time ("be prepared to wait"), these "cheap" eats are the "real thing."

get updates at zagat.com

Boston

F | D | S | C

El Pelón Taqueria — 22 | 10 | 15 | $11
92 Peterborough St. (bet. Jersey & Kilmarnock Sts.), 617-262-9090; www.elpelon.com

■ "Why eat hot dogs at Fenway Park?" wonder aficionados when you can feast on "authentic" Mexican food just a "five-minute stroll" away; at this "funky, kitschy" taqueria, the kitchen turns "super-fresh ingredients" into "simple" but "fabulous" things like fish tacos, burritos and chiles rellenos; not only are the "folks who work there cool", but the prices are "shockingly cheap."

El Sarape — 24 | 14 | 20 | $22
5 Commercial St. (Union St.), Braintree, 781-843-8005; www.elsarape.com

■ "This place is the real deal" attest advocates of this "unassuming" Braintree "jewel" that prepares the "best" "traditional" Mexican food in Boston; "don't be fooled by the informal" "south-of-the-border" atmosphere or the decor "straight out of a street market", because the kitchen sends forth "sublime", seriously "authentic" dishes that "bring you directly to Mexico."

Emma's Pizzeria ⌀ — 24 | 13 | 17 | $17
40 Hampshire St. (Portland St.), Cambridge, 617-864-8534

◪ Worshipers are convinced that the "pizza god lives" at this "laid-back" "yuppie haven" in Kendall Square, where the "perfect" "gourmet" pies (the "best in Boston") are an "epiphany on crust" and more than "ready for induction into the hall of fame"; though it's "perpetually crowded" with "biotech types", this "slice of nirvana is worth the hassle", even if a confounded contingent contends "sauce and cheese on a cracker doth not a pizza make."

Emperor's Garden — - | - | - | I
690 Washington St. (Kneeland St.), 617-482-8898

Busy and bustling, this one-time theater (with 1,000 seats) in Chinatown has "turned into a dim sum zoo", particularly on the weekends, with carts circulating through the "sweeping" space laden with "glorious" small plates; respondents who've tried it report a "real" Hong Kong–style "experience" and "good fun."

Enormous Room ⌀ — ▽ 22 | 26 | 19 | $23
567 Mass Ave., 2nd fl. (Pearl St.), Cambridge, 617-491-5550; www.enormous.tv

◪ "Feel like a pasha (while drinking like a fish)" at this "hottest new thing in town", a "sexy", "swanky" lounge upstairs from Central Square's Central Kitchen that always seems "like an orgy waiting to happen"; "recline on a divan while admiring the cool Cambridge crowd" and nibbling from platters "heaped" with "flavorful" Moroccan "finger foods"; it'd be an even more enjoyable "adventure", however, if the "staff noticed you were there."

Boston F | D | S | C

Epiphany ●   -|-|-| E
107 South St. (bet. East & Tufts Sts.), 617-338-7999;
www.epiphanyboston.com
Smartly outfitted in the emperor's red and black colors, this sleek new lounge in the Leather District brings an upscale Asian flavor to the neighborhood; the frequently changing menu mixes Eastern and Western elements, resulting in fusion cuisine like escargot spring rolls with seaweed salad and Maine lobster with butternut risotto and edamame.

Erawan of Siam   19|21|19|$21
469 Moody St. (High St.), Waltham, 781-899-3399
☑ "If you want to carry on a conversation" over "above-average" Thai fare ("definitely try the pad Thai"), this "quiet", "beautifully decorated" Waltham mainstay is a "tried-and-true" choice; the service is generally "fine" and a meal a "good value", but disappointed dissenters deem it "uneven", when not "dull."

Euno   21|21|21|$39
119 Salem St. (Cooper St.), 617-573-9406;
www.119euno.com
☑ Lots of "drippy candles", exposed-brick walls and a "great fireplace" make this "out-of-the-way place" feel like a "private", "romantic escape from the hubbub of the North End"; the "inventive" Italian fare is "served with charm" and the "open storefront" windows let in "soothing breezes" in "fine weather", so even if some "neighbors have the edge in the food category", a dinner here is "never disappointing" because they "try so hard."

Evoo ⑤   24|21|21|$42
118 Beacon St. (Washington St.), Somerville, 617-661-3866;
www.evoorestaurant.com
■ Chef-owner Peter McCarthy's "ambitious" Eclectic dishes are the "best thing that could happen to local produce" rave respondents about the "adventurous preparations" crafted at his "off-the-beaten-path" Somerville bistro; combining the "right mix of maximum flavor and minimalist decor", it turns out meals "so good" that it should definitely be a "destination for foodies from all over" – "despite the goofy name", an acronym for "extra virgin olive oil."

Excelsior   -|-|-| E
272 Boylston St. (bet. Arlington & S. Charles Sts.),
617-426-7878
Slated to open shortly after we go to press, this project is a joint venture between acclaimed chef Lydia Shire (Locke-Ober) and partners Tim Lynch and Ken Himmel (Grill 23 & Bar, Harvest); master designer Adam Tihany is revamping the Back Bay site overlooking the Public Garden that formerly housed Shire's Biba, which is expected to result in a backdrop as sophisticated as the New American menu

get updates at zagat.com

Boston | F | D | S | C |

(look for her signature eclectic elements) and 400-plus bottle wine list.

Fajitas & 'Ritas | 15 | 10 | 13 | $17 |
25 West St. (bet. Tremont & Washington Sts.), 617-426-1222
48 Boylston St. (bet. Harvard & Washington Sts.), Brookline, 617-566-1222
1237 Hancock St. (Washington St.), Quincy, 617-774-1200
www.fajitasandritas.com

◪ When you need a fix of "basic" Tex-Mex grub and "killer margaritas", this "festive" (or "cheesy") trio has "fun literally written all over it" – on the "graffiti-covered walls" (except at the Quincy branch), that is; the eats are "decent", but "if you're looking for fine dining, this is not the place for you", since it can be a "chaotic" "zoo" "reminiscent of high school lunchrooms", and "service – what service?"

Fava ∫ | 25 | 20 | 22 | $45 |
1027 Great Plain Ave. (bet. Chapel St. & Eaton Sq.), Needham, 781-455-8668; www.favarestaurant.com

◼ Carved into the granite walls of what once housed the Needham Center rail depot, this "gourmet" "sleeper in the suburbs" promises a "fabulous", "fresh culinary adventure with each visit"; Needham natives "love" that this "intimate neighborhood" "charmer" resides in their corner of the world, and "whether you find it tight and cramped or cozy and cute", Jeff Kaye's "inventive" New American dishes add up to a "brilliant meal from start to finish."

FEDERALIST | 25 | 25 | 25 | $65 |
XV Beacon Hotel, 15 Beacon St. (bet. Bowdoin & Somerset Sts.), 617-670-2515; www.xvbeacon.com

◼ "Wear your power suit" and bring your "gold card" to this "opulent" "dining experience" at the "luxurious" XV Beacon Hotel, where the "sophisticated" New American cuisine, "exquisite" wine list and "impeccable" service make it one of the city's "best special-occasion" spots; in these "regal" surroundings worthy of "Boston Brahmins", you could hardly "feel more elegant", but brace yourself for "sky-high prices" that could cause even the "bust of Ben Franklin to roll his eyes."

FIFTY SEVEN | 19 | 18 | 19 | $42 |
Radisson Hotel, 200 Stuart St. (bet. Arlington & S. Charles Sts.), 617-423-5700; www.fiftyseven.com

◪ "Convenient" "before a show", this "clubby" Theater District chophouse at the Radisson is "darn good for a hotel restaurant"; a "classic" lineup of "solid" steaks and seafood is "well presented" in a "comfortable", "uncrowded" space, but detractors lament that "while the potential is there, it just isn't up to the standard we've come to expect" from fine Boston establishments ("nothing distinguishes it").

Boston   F | D | S | C |

Figlia
20 | 16 | 20 | $34 |

22 Union St. (bet. Beacon St. & Langley Rd.), Newton, 617-244-8833

☑ Surveyors "swoon over the homemade pastas" and other "tasty" Italian fare offered on the "creative menu" at this "reliably good" "winner" in Newton Centre; regulars remark that the "cordial" servers seem to "really care whether you have a good time" but hint you may want to "bring earplugs and learn sign language", because the hardwood floors, granite-topped tables and faux-marble walls create a "noise level so bad some hesitate to return."

FIGS
21 | 16 | 17 | $26 |

42 Charles St. (bet. Chestnut & Mt. Vernon Sts.), 617-742-3447
67 Main St. (bet. Monument Ave. & Winthrop St.), Charlestown, 617-242-2229
1208 Boylston St. (bet. Hammond St. & Holly Ln.), Chestnut Hill, 617-738-9992
92 Central St. (Weston Rd.), Wellesley, 781-237-5788
www.toddenglish.com

☑ "For a night out that doesn't call for a change of clothes and a loan from the bank", this "yuppie" foursome of "upscale pizza parlors" pleases with just the "right amount of pizzazz"; the "nouvelle" pies headline a "simple" Italian menu with "enough choices to please the whole gang", but "be prepared to wait – and wait", since the "slow" staff seemingly "goes on a European tour during dinner"; still, it's the "most accessible" of celebrity chef Todd English's restaurants, and while it's "no Olives", it's "not the pits either."

Filippo Ristorante
∇ 17 | 16 | 18 | $29 |

283 Causeway St. (Endicott St.), 617-742-4143

☑ Handy to the Fleet Center, this "old-fashioned" North End Italian is a "good stop before an event", as the helpful staff "makes every effort to get you out on time without your feeling rushed"; sure, you "could do a lot better" than these "basic" eats and the decor is a "bit corny", but the faithful always enjoy a "fun" time.

Finale ◐
25 | 20 | 18 | $23 |

1 Columbus Ave. (Park Plaza), 617-423-3184
30 Dunster St. (bet. Mass Ave. & Mt. Auburn St.), Cambridge, 617-441-9797
www.finaledesserts.com

■ A "sweet tooth's best friend", this "upscale", late-night Theater District desserterie's "divine", "finely crafted" baked goods are "pure fantasy"; the menu of "light" bites is "good too", but "who needs to eat a meal" when they can "treat" themselves to such "over-the-top", "orgasmic pastries"?; the "only unpleasantness" is the "way-too-expensive" tab, but it's "worth a splurge now and then" for

get updates at zagat.com   **67**

Boston | F | D | S | C |

a "perfect finale to an evening"; N.B. there's another branch in Harvard Square.

Finz
| 18 | 20 | 17 | $31 |

Pickering Wharf, 76 Wharf St. (Derby St.), Salem, 978-744-8485; www.hipfinz.com

◪ On "historic Pickering Wharf", this "contemporary" seafood house affords a "lovely view of Salem Harbor", enhanced by an "open" room surrounded on three sides by walls of windows; the kitchen sends forth both "traditional and innovative" finny fare, though commentators carp it's a "pity the food doesn't live up" to the "great setting by the sea" and wish too that the "casual" "service were as sophisticated as the decor."

Fire & Ice
| 15 | 15 | 12 | $23 |

205 Berkeley St. (St. James Ave.), 617-482-3473
50 Church St. (bet. Brattle & Palmer Sts.), Cambridge, 617-547-9007 ◐
www.fire-ice.com

◪ Undeniably a "place to pig out" in the Back Bay and Harvard Square, this "chaotic", "all-you-can-eat" Eclectic twosome features a "unique concept" – assemble "your own dinner" from an "array of raw meats, fish and veggies", choose a sauce and "watch it all sizzle" as a chef cooks your meal on a "huge centerpiece" grill; it's "entertaining" for the "younger set" (as is the *Pee-Wee's Playhouse* decor), but gourmands gripe "everything ends up tasting the same."

Firefly
| 17 | 14 | 15 | $22 |

130 Dartmouth St. (bet. Columbus Ave. & Stuart Sts.), 617-262-4393

◪ Blown your cash "while shopping at Copley Place"? – then console yourself at this "bargain of the Back Bay", a "nice little cafe" that placates with all-American "home cooking"; while the food "isn't going to win any culinary acclaim", the service is "friendly" and the "relaxing" patio is "perfect for people-watching."

Fireplace
| 21 | 21 | 20 | $36 |

1634 Beacon St. (Washington St.), Brookline, 617-975-1900; www.fireplacerest.com

◪ "Like your mom would make if she were a good cook", the "flavorful" New England "comfort food" prepared at this "great neighborhood place" in Brookline "warms the stomach", while the "fireplace blazing in the background" "warms the rest"; the "cozy" space manages to feel both "homey" and "elegant", thanks in part to the "solicitous" servers, though a frustrated few sigh the "potential is there, but it doesn't always deliver."

Five North Square
| 21 | 17 | 19 | $30 |

5 North Sq. (Prince St.), 617-720-1050; www.5northsquare.com

◪ "Romantics" recommend that you "relax and enjoy" the traditional Italian food prepared at this "classic" North

Boston F | D | S | C

End standby, a "cozy", family-owned haven just three doors up from the Paul Revere House; the "great selection" of familiar favorites includes the "best eggplant parmesan in the city", but unsentimental sorts say the food is "not too interesting" and caution that the "tacky interior is not for the faint of heart."

Flash's ● 18 | 15 | 16 | $19
310 Stuart St. (Arlington St.), 617-574-8888

☑ Whether you're looking to down a "quick lunch", "catch up" "with friends" "after work" or "grab a bite after the theater", this "lively", late-night meeting place located where the Back Bay meets the South End is one of the "best buys in the neighborhood"; though it's "mainly a bar" (known for its "hipster cocktails"), the kitchen does turn out "hearty" Traditional American grub along with some "interesting" Spanish-style tapas.

Fleming's Prime Steakhouse 21 | 20 | 21 | $45
217 Stuart St. (bet. Arlington & S. Charles Sts.), 617-292-0808; www.flemingssteakhouse.com

☑ "Big, bold steaks", "side dishes that could be a meal in themselves" and a "great wine list" make plenty of hungry carnivores happy at this chain link in the Theater District; it's a "dark", "comfortable", roomy retreat where "they don't seat you on your neighbor's lap" and where "you can actually hear yourself think"; the service is "swift and efficient", key if you're heading to a show, but bellicose beefeaters bellow "there are much better in town."

flora 23 | 22 | 22 | $37
190 Mass Ave. (Lake St.), Arlington, 781-641-1664; www.florarestaurant.com

☑ "Fine dining" at a "reasonable price" has made this "pretty" Arlington New American a "suburban success story"; housed in a 1920s brick-and-granite bank building with barrel-vaulted ceilings and two-story-high windows, it features a "sophisticated" menu of "sumptuous" dishes brought to table by an "engaging" staff that exudes "lots of warmth", making dinner "always a pleasure"; even if a minority maintains it "lacks that little bit of flash to move it to the top tier", most embrace it as a "favorite local spot."

Florentina ⌀ ▽ 18 | 7 | 18 | $16
143 Main St. (bet. Broadway & 3rd St.), Cambridge, 617-577-8300

■ "Faster than you can get your money out of your wallet" you'll be served "hefty portions" (the "meat lasagna keeps you full for a week") of "typical" but "yummy" Italian food at this speedy spot that's popular with the "lunch crowd"; though there are no surprises at this "busy, no-nonsense" joint, it's one of the "best values in the Kendall Square" neighborhood; N.B. no dinner.

get updates at zagat.com

Boston | F | D | S | C |

Florentine Cafe — 20 | 21 | 18 | $33
333 Hanover St. (Prince St.), 617-227-1777

◪ "Get a window table and watch the street life" from this "fancy storefront", a North End "scene" that's a "blast to hang out" at "if you're looking for a lively (read: loud) spot" that's not your "typical red-sauce" cliché; the Italian menu is "surprisingly nouveau", and there's a "great bar" too, but the cognoscenti complain that the "food doesn't live up to the slick" surroundings.

flour bakery & café — 26 | 16 | 17 | $12
1595 Washington St. (Rutland St.), 617-267-4300;
www.flourbakery.com

■ "Every neighborhood's dream come true", this South End American "patisserie's" baked goods ("among the best in Boston") are "nirvana on a plate"; everything from its "fabulous pastries" (the "homemade Pop-Tarts are superb") to its "spectacular" cakes to its "designer sandwiches" is "incredibly tempting", so even if these "tasty treats" are a little "pricey" and the "limited seating" makes it a "tight squeeze", admirers can only applaud "flour power!"

Forest Cafe — 19 | 7 | 16 | $20
1682 Mass Ave. (bet. Hudson & Sacramento Sts.), Cambridge, 617-661-7810

◪ If you can "get past" the "dinginess" of this "real dive" near Porter Square, "you'll find better Mexican fare" than at many of its competitors; though it "feels like you're eating in a bar" (and you are), the "totally dependable" food is "*muy bien*" (the "seafood selections stand out", like the "great" shrimp enchiladas); besides, the "seedy" digs draw an "interesting townie crowd."

Franklin Cafe ◐ — 25 | 17 | 19 | $31
278 Shawmut Ave. (Hanson St.), 617-350-0010

■ "Dark, difficult and delicious" say the "city folk" who "love" this "hip" yet "unpretentious" South End "hangout" that's always packed with a "lively crowd" lined up for its "incredible" New American dishes; the "wait can be unbearable" (often "three or four deep at the bar"), though once you finally secure a table, "you're never rushed out" by the "friendly" servers; what's more the "prices are so reasonable", and the kitchen's open till 1:30 AM.

Franklin Cape Ann ◐ — 24 | 21 | 21 | $33
118 Main St. (bet. Hancock & Porter Sts.), Gloucester, 978-283-7888

■ Perhaps the "best bet for reducing Boston-bound traffic from northern New England", this late-night North Shore "sister of the South End original" gets kudos for its (nearly) "equally fine" New American menu; not only does its "amazing" cooking make it "one of the best places in Gloucester", its "cool", urbane ambiance is a "real treat", making the natives "thrilled to have this sophisticated yet accessible" "surprise" in their own backyard.

Frank's Steak House 15 10 16 $24

2310 Mass Ave. (Rice St.), Cambridge, 617-661-0666; www.frankssteakhouse.com

◪ "The '30s never died" at this "classic steakhouse" of "everyone's youth" north of Porter Square, where the "reliable meat 'n' potatoes" fare keeps it quite "busy"; neither the "old-school" menu nor the "time warp" decor has been "updated in years" (clearly), which nostalgists find "heartwarming", but critical carnivores contend that "this cow has lost its moo."

FUGAKYU 25 23 20 $33

1280 Beacon St. (Harvard St.), Brookline, 617-738-1268 ◐

621 Boston Post Rd./Rte. 20 (Horse Pond Rd.), Sudbury, 978-443-1668

■ "Welcome to sushi wonderland" – the "quality, variety and taste" of the raw fish prepared at this Japanese "circus" in Brookline (and its Sudbury sibling) are just "phenomenal", but the "crowds know it too (unfortunately)", so "beware the lines"; regulars recommend booking a "private" traditional "tatami room", since otherwise it can feel a bit like dining among a "mob" at "Disney World."

Full Moon 18 14 16 $23

138 Mass Ave. (Milton St.), Arlington, 781-646-1404

344 Huron Ave. (bet. Chilton & Fayerweather Sts.), Cambridge, 617-354-6699

◪ "Where Chardonnay and BRIO train sets are both readily available", these "kiddie-centric" "restaurants designed for families" in Arlington and Fresh Pond serve food "like you'd make at home – if you had the energy"; youngsters love the colorful play area, while grown-ups are grateful for the "decent" New American cooking, but even some parents suggest "skip it if you have no baby on board", because the "whining" and "chaos can be overwhelming."

Galleria Umberto $ ⊭ 24 6 14 $9

289 Hanover St. (bet. Prince & Richmond Sts.), 617-227-5709

■ Go early "before they run out of food" at this "favorite" Southern Italian "lunch spot" in the North End, where there's "always a line out the door"; it's the "genuine article", like a "corner luncheonette in Rome", and justly famous for making about the "best – and cheapest – pizza in Boston", as well as "great calzones" and rice balls that are "fried perfection"; who cares about the total "lack of decor" and "nonexistent" service?

Gallia $ 19 20 18 $42

1525 Washington St. (W. Brookline St.), 617-247-4455

◪ Nattily done up in shades of saffron and pomegranate, this "beautiful newcomer" to the South End welcomes

Boston   F | D | S | C

with a "warm" atmosphere that befits its sunny, "creative" Mediterranean fare; boosters, who'll "be sorry to see this place discovered", say the "well thought-out" menu brims with "tempting" choices, though the less impressed report some "rough patches."

Garden of Eden   19 | 15 | 14 | $18
571 Tremont St. (bet. Clarendon & Dartmouth Sts.), 617-247-8377; www.goeboston.com

At this "all-day delight" in the South End, the "consistently satisfying" Country French food "will make you want to sin again and again" declare devotees of its "delicious soups", "specialty sandwiches" and "indulgent pastries"; a "cool place to hang out", it's a "neighborhood-y" "yuppie heaven" with "top-notch people-watching" from the sidewalk cafe, but given the "lackadaisical" service, former congregants feel "this garden grows more and more overrun."

Gardner Museum Cafe   21 | 17 | 17 | $22
Isabella Stuart Gardner Museum, 280 Fenway (Palace Rd.), 617-566-1088

"Worth a visit just to walk by the fabulous Italianate courtyard", this "wonderful" little "nook" provides a "lovely rest stop" "after viewing some art" or before a "Sunday concert"; the "fresh", "light" French-influenced New American fare is "nicely prepared", and when the weather is clement the garden dining is particularly "delightful", making a "quiet lunch" in the Fenway feel almost like a "mini-vacation."

Gargoyles on the Square   24 | 21 | 23 | $38
219 Elm St. (Summer St.), Somerville, 617-776-5300

An "unsung hero", this "fantastic neighborhood" "gem" remains something of a Davis Square "surprise" for a "special" New American dinner in smart-looking environs; a "grown-up restaurant" with "awesome" fare, "stylish presentations", a "romantic" ambiance and "expert" service, it "makes staying out of Boston a pleasure"; some customers prefer to "eat at the bar" to "feel like one of the family" while enjoying a "very affordable meal", but everyone begs "don't let the secret out."

Geoffrey's Cafe Bar   18 | 16 | 15 | $25
160 Commonwealth Ave. (Dartmouth St.), 617-266-1122; www.geoffreyscafe.com

Near Newbury Street, this "funky" Back Bay hangout practices a "winning formula" of turning out American "homestyle cooking with flair"; given the "nice variety" of dishes on the menu (including "plenty of comfort foods"), "reliable" execution and "reasonable prices", habitués find it "easy to eat here weekly without having a bad meal", but note that the "colorful" staff can be "too busy with its own dramas" and "lose sight of why patrons are here."

Boston | F | D | S | C |

Giacomo's ⊘ | 23 | 15 | 18 | $28 |
431 Columbus Ave. (bet. Dartmouth & W. Newton Sts.), 617-536-5723
355 Hanover St. (bet. Fleet & Prince Sts.), 617-523-9026

☑ "Whether you're in the North End or the South End", the "excellent seafood", "perfect" pastas with "lick-your-plate-good" sauces and other "classic" Italian dishes prepared at this tiny, family-run twosome make it "worth the extra hour at the gym"; despite the "crazy lines", you'll be "in and out fast" because the staff "turns over tables" at a "frenetic" pace, but a mystified minority concludes "so overrated."

Ginza | 24 | 16 | 18 | $31 |
16 Hudson St. (bet. Beach & Kneeland Sts.), 617-338-2261 ◐
1002 Beacon St. (St. Mary's St.), Brookline, 617-566-9688

■ Continuing to rank among the "best in Boston", this "popular", "traditional" Japanese pair in Chinatown and Brookline is renowned for its "beautifully presented" "pieces of every type of fish you can imagine" ("like eating art"), "graciously" served by "modern-day geisha in kimonos"; connoisseurs are "never disappointed" by the "outstanding" sushi and "love the fact" that the Hudson Street original is "open damn late" (till 4 AM most nights).

Giuseppe's | – | – | – | M |
(fka Metro)
Porter Exchange Bldg., 1815 Mass Ave. (Roseland St.), Cambridge, 617-354-3727

The spacious Porter Square site that most recently housed the French brasserie Metro has morphed into this bustling North End–style trattoria, replete with red-and-white-checkered tablecloths and a menu of traditional red-sauce dishes; bring a crowd to share the hearty portions of old-fashioned Southern Italian cooking, offered at moderate prices that are sure to be crowd-pleasing as well.

Glenn's Restaurant & Cool Bar | ▽ 24 | 19 | 23 | $36 |
44 Merrimac St. (Newburyport Tpke.), Newburyport, 978-465-3811

■ "Adventurous meals prepared by someone obsessed with food" have made this "extremely comfortable" "hot spot" in Newburyport a "favorite" among the "locals" and "one of the better places north of Boston"; though the "interesting" Eclectic menu is "not huge", it changes daily, and "what is served is done well", "seasoned and spiced" just right; add on weekend jazz and blues, and the result is a "big-city performance in a small city."

Golden Temple ◐ | 18 | 20 | 18 | $27 |
1651 Beacon St. (bet. University & Winthrop Rds.), Brookline, 617-277-9722

☑ "No matter your religion", "this is one temple where you should worship" insist the faithful followers who "grew up

Boston   F | D | S | C

eating" at this Brookline "institution" and almost feel "like a member of the family"; with its "new take on old favorites" and "fancy" decor "right out of *Architectural Digest*", it may be the "hippest Chinese restaurant in the area", but purists who nix the setting as "garish" also deride the "Americanized" food as "culinary sacrilege."

Good Life ●   13 | 16 | 15 | $20
28 Kingston St. (bet. Bedford & Summer Sts.), 617-451-2622
720 Mass Ave. (bet. Inman & Prospect Sts.), Cambridge, 617-868-8800
www.the-goodlife-us.com

◪ "Sometimes you just need a burger and a strong martini", and that's the time to settle into a "big booth" at one of these "hip", "retro cocktail lounges" Downtown and in Central Square; groupies gather for the "Rat Pack" vibe, "cool jazz and hot drinks", but critical clubbers counsel "forget" the "boring" American "pub grub" at these "ersatz rec rooms."

Grafton Street Pub & Grill   15 | 19 | 16 | $23
1230 Mass Ave. (Bow St.), Cambridge, 617-497-0400

◪ Harvard Square habitués get their groove on at this "lively" "late-night scene" where "well-groomed young professionals and university seniors" like to get a bit "dressed up" before mingling; the New American fare may be "better than your average pub grub" (though still "boring"), but wags just wonder "how many upscale Irish bars does Cambridge need?"

Grand Canal   18 | 21 | 18 | $22
57 Canal St. (Causeway St.), 617-523-1112;
www.somerspubs.com

◪ It "feels like you've been transported across the pond" at this "authentic" Irish pub that brings a touch of Victorian elegance to the North Station neighborhood; given the "good selection of beers on tap" (22) and the "inviting" "vintage" setting, it's a "great" place to down a pint, while the "snappy" service will help get you to a "Fleet Center event" on time; overall, it's a "fun place to go anytime", but don't consider it a "food destination."

Grand Chau Chow ●   24 | 10 | 16 | $20
41-45 Beach St. (Harrison Ave.), 617-292-5166

◪ "One of the best Chinese restaurants in Chinatown", this "busy" "hole-in-the-wall's" "focus" is clearly on seafood; "watch your dinner swim around" in the fish tank, then "faster than Superman" it'll be on your plate, "fresh", "flavorful" and "most delicious"; "if you can stand the Formica" appointments and "brusque" service, you'll be "rewarded" with a "reliably" "authentic" meal, plus it's open till 3 or 4 AM every night.

Boston F | D | S | C |

Grapevine 26 | 21 | 23 | $39
26 Congress St. (Derby St.), Salem, 978-745-9335;
www.grapevinesalem.com

■ A "top pick for fine dining on the North Shore", this "gourmet" "treasure" across from Pickering Wharf in Salem "compares favorably with some of the best restaurants in Boston"; it's "hard to decide what to order among so many wonderful choices" on Kate Hammond's "adventurous", "seasonal" New American menu, but "it's all good" and it's delivered by a "welcoming" staff in a "romantic" dining room and out in the "lovely" garden.

Grasshopper 20 | 14 | 18 | $18
1 N. Beacon St. (Cambridge St.), Allston, 617-254-8883

☒ "You'll never know that you're not eating meat" at this Asian "hideaway" in Allston, a "paradise" for "die-hard vegetarians" and a "vital" resource for vegans; "it's amazing what they can do with tofu and seitan", creating "inventive" dishes that are "high-quality" and "satisfying" (there's even a "great non-dairy cheesecake for dessert"); unimpressed "omnivores", however, opine "no thanks."

Great Thai Chef ▽ 24 | 15 | 22 | $17
255 Washington St. (Union Sq.), Somerville, 617-625-9296

■ Though the name of this "unassuming" "neighborhood" "jewel" may be a tad "pretentious", it does in fact produce "great" Thai food; the Somerville surveyors who know about it praise its "consistently top-notch" cooking ("lighter" and "less greasy" than many in its category) and "friendly" service, finding it a "yummy" "place to be a regular"; what's more, the tabs are "inexpensive" and there's "often no wait."

Green Dragon Tavern ▽ 14 | 17 | 15 | $20
11 Marshall St. (Union St.), 617-367-0055;
www.somerspubs.com

☒ "If you're a history buff", this "atmospheric" Irish-American pub near Faneuil Hall that was "built in the 1650s" is a "must-visit along the Freedom Trail"; "unwind after a busy workday" at this "cozy" Revolution-era tavern and "sit at the same bar as John Hancock" and Paul Revere did before you, but though the grub may be "better than you'd expect", "go for the bands and the beers, not the food."

Green Papaya 18 | 12 | 17 | $19
475 Winter St. (Rte. 128, exit 27B), Waltham, 781-487-9988

■ "Shopping in suburbia" or working in the "Route 128 technology zone" and looking for a "dependable" place to "grab lunch" at a "good price"? – then try this "strip-mall" standby "just off the highway" in Waltham and sample its "well-executed", if "nothing unusual", Thai food ("if only the menu would branch out a little"); though it's always "packed" at midday, the "efficient" staff will get you "in and out in under an hour."

get updates at zagat.com 75

Boston

F | **D** | **S** | **C**

Green Street Grill
19 | 15 | 18 | $28

280 Green St. (bet. Magazine & Pearl Sts.), Cambridge, 617-876-1655; www.greenstreetgrill.com

▣ "Don't judge a book by its cover", as the "grungy exterior" of this "part bar, part restaurant" off Central Square belies the "creative" cooking and "happening" scene inside; chef Mark Romano (ex the Blue Room) has revamped the menu, mixing "toned-down" "Caribbean-inspired" flavors with New American fare to come up with an "inventive" roster of "delicious" dishes, though longtimers lament it "lacks the edge it used to have."

Greg's ⌀
▽ 15 | 7 | 17 | $17

821 Mt. Auburn St. (Belmont St.), Watertown, 617-491-0122

▣ "Talk about lasting power" – "Greg's has been around as long as mama" (longer, probably), and "you can count on both" for dishing up "stick-to-your-ribs" Southern Italian "home cooking"; the "plain", "old-fashioned" "standards" on the menu and the "red-checkered cloths" on the tables qualify this "no-frills" Watertown "bargain" as a veritable "time capsule", which is just fine with the "older folks who frequent this place", but those without blue hair suggest that it could use a "face-lift."

Grillfish
19 | 19 | 17 | $29

162 Columbus Ave. (bet. Arlington & Berkeley Sts.), 617-357-1620; www.grillfish.com

▣ As you'd expect from its name, this "festive" South End seafood house grills up "consistently good fish", prepared "simply" and served in a "hip" room with "great style" (if you're into "Gothic" lite); it's an easy option for "enjoying a night out with friends", but "be careful to seat your parents facing away" from the erotic mural ("not for the easily embarrassed") behind the stone bar, and beware too that the "noise" can be "deafening."

GRILL 23 & BAR
26 | 24 | 25 | $53

161 Berkeley St. (Stuart St.), 617-542-2255; www.grill23.com

■ "Hail to the chef", Jay Murray, who has made this Back Bay "class" act "more than just a steakhouse"; while continuing to thrill the cognoscenti with the "best" dry-aged prime cuts "in the city", the menu now also emphasizes "fabulous" seafood dishes as well as "more inventive" American fare, accompanied by a "magnificent wine list" and brought to table by "intelligent, professional" servers who "make you feel important"; enhanced by "clubby", "dignified" environs that are "perfect for business" wheels and deals, it exemplifies "power dining at its best."

Gusto ⌀
22 | 20 | 22 | $30

4174 Washington St. (Murray Hill Rd.), Roslindale, 617-363-9225

■ When you "don't feel like dealing with the North End" but crave an "excellent" Italian meal, head to Roslindale to

Boston | F | D | S | C |

this "surprisingly" "upscale" "haven" in the suburban "food desert" for "soul-satisfying" cooking "served without pretense"; the folks "couldn't be nicer" and the prices are "reasonable", leaving fans convinced that "every neighborhood should have a place like this."

G'Vanni's | 17 | 15 | 17 | $31 |
2 Prince St. (North Sq.), 617-523-0107

☑ "Be prepared to get real friendly with your neighbor" at this tiny Italian "staple", because the quarters are very "close"; expect "average food at better-than-average prices" (partisans advise "veal is the specialty – stick with that"), though detractors who feel that it's "resting on its reputation these days" lament that it's indicative of "what the North End has become infamous for."

Gyuhama ● | 21 | 13 | 18 | $28 |
827 Boylston St. (bet. Fairfield & Gloucester Sts.), 617-437-0188

☑ "Rock 'n' roll sushi is a great invention" cheer the fans who shake their booty to the beat of "turned-up music" till the wee hours at this "fun" Back Bay Japanese; the fare is "tasty" ("everything is fresh") and the service "swift", but aesthetes wish "they'd fix up" the "claustrophobic" basement digs, while gourmands ask "why settle for good in a city that has great?"

Halfway Cafe | 16 | 9 | 17 | $15 |
174 Washington St. (VFW Pkwy.), Dedham, 781-326-3336
820 Boston Post Rd./Rte. 20 (bet. Farm & Wayside Inn Rds.), Marlborough, 508-480-0688
394 Main St. (Lexington St.), Watertown, 617-926-3595
www.thehalfwaycafe.com

☑ If armchair athletes "could live on popcorn, beer" and "basic", "dirt-cheap" American "pub grub", they'd "never have to leave" this trio of suburban sports bars; though the "divey" digs "aren't much to look at", it's a "friendly" place to "watch the Sox", though un-sporting sorts warn "don't even bother" unless "your softball shirt and cleats are still on."

HAMERSLEY'S BISTRO | 27 | 24 | 24 | $54 |
553 Tremont St. (Clarendon St.), 617-423-2700; www.hamersleysbistro.com

■ "Much like the fabled Mary Poppins", this "perennial favorite" in the South End is "practically perfect in every way"; chef-owner Gordon Hamersley's "passion for great food" is obvious after one bite of his "stellar" yet "earthy" French–New American bistro fare (his "signature" roast chicken "pleases even fancy-food fanatics"), served by a "standout, welcoming" staff in an "intimate", "inviting" space; "haute prices" notwithstanding, this "neighborhood star turned world-class restaurant" "continues to shine."

get updates at zagat.com

Boston

| | F | D | S | C |

Harry's ●∉
16 | 10 | 17 | $19

149 Turnpike Rd./Rte. 9 (Lyman St.), Westborough, 508-366-8302

☐ "We've fried and gone to heaven" sigh devout disciples of this "old-fashioned diner" in Westborough, a "local institution" where "you'll feel like a regular on your first visit"; "mix with truckers and suburbanites, who all come for the perfect clams" (the "best" you'll find "west of Ipswich") or "anything" else from the fry-o-laters – but "forget the rest" of the "cheap" Traditional American items; N.B. Harry's Too next door offers Traditional American "comfort food" and "fine jazz on Thursdays."

Hartwell House ⑤
16 | 19 | 19 | $38

94 Hartwell Ave. (bet. Rtes. 4 & 225), Lexington, 781-862-5111; www.thehartwellhouse.com

☐ "Your grandmother will love" the "elegant" surroundings of this colonial manor in Lexington, which provides a "wonderful setting" for a "pleasant" meal; others, however, frown that the "formal" space "feels like a museum" and dismiss the "uninspired", "ordinary" Continental-American menu, concluding that this "domain of blue-haired ladies" is way "past its prime."

Harvard Gardens
15 | 15 | 14 | $25

316 Cambridge St. (Grove St.), 617-523-2727; www.harvardgardens.com

☐ "You never know who you'll meet" at this "happening singles scene" on Beacon Hill, a popular "after-work place" where a "post-college crowd" of "twentysomethings" "hangs out with friends" or "picks up" new ones; though it offers a menu of "decent" American "comfort fare", tipplers hint that the "cocktails trump the food", so "don't stray too far beyond" the drinks.

Harvest
25 | 23 | 23 | $45

44 Brattle St. (Church St.), Cambridge, 617-868-2255; www.the-harvest.com

■ "*Bon Appétit* meets *Metropolitan Home*" at this "smart" Harvard Square "classic" where the "confidently prepared" New American dishes make it a "favorite for all seasons"; the "inventive" menu (with some New England influences) is "unfussy" but "superb", and it's presented by a "sharp" staff in "sophisticated" surroundings, making it still "one of the best choices in Cambridge"; P.S. the garden terrace is "especially delightful" for a "romantic" rendezvous.

HELMAND
26 | 22 | 20 | $30

143 First St. (Bent St.), Cambridge, 617-492-4646; www.helmandrestaurant.sbweb.switchboard.com

■ Promising a most "enchanting" evening, this "unique dining experience" in East Cambridge entices with its "magical" Afghan specialties infused with "out-of-this-

Boston   F | D | S | C |

world flavors"; from the "outstanding flatbread" to the "divine" baby pumpkin appetizer to the "unbelievable" *qabelee* (rice baked with lamb shanks and raisins), the dishes accurately "reflect" the motherland's location "halfway between the Middle East and India"; after all, the "owner's brother is Afghanistan's president" – "how can it not be authentic?"

Henrietta's Table   21 | 19 | 19 | $35 |
Charles Hotel, 1 Bennett St. (University Rd.), Cambridge, 617-661-5005; www.charleshotel.com
■ It's possible to "take both a finicky child and a real foodie" to this "country" charmer set right in Harvard Square, whose "homey", "faux farmhouse" setting makes it feel just "like grandmother's kitchen"; whether for a "power breakfast" among the "tweedy bunch", an "excellent" weekend brunch ("we've never seen anything so elaborate") or "satisfying" New England "homestyle cooking" at lunch or dinner, a repast here is always "fresh and wholesome", with "local produce" as the "star."

Hilltop Steak House   15 | 10 | 14 | $25 |
210 Union St. (Rte. 3, exit 17), Braintree, 781-848-3363
855 Broadway/Rte. 1 (Lynn Fells Pkwy.), Saugus, 781-233-7700
www.hilltop-steak-house.com
☑ "When you're in the mood" for a "big steak" at an un-big price, this "lowbrow" pair of beefy outposts in Braintree and Saugus may fill the bill; "fancy it ain't, but tummy-filling it is", though know that "you'll feel like cattle yourself in the huge", "barn-like" space (know too that the "famous" plastic "cows out front are friendlier than the staff"), leading critical carnivores to "steer clear."

Hi-Rise Bread Co.   24 | 12 | 13 | $13 |
56 Brattle St. (Church St.), Cambridge, 617-492-3003
208 Concord Ave. (Huron Ave.), Cambridge, 617-876-8766
☑ "Filled with the welcoming smells" of "fresh-baked breads", "delicious pastries" and "addictive cookies", these "terminally hip bakeries" are a "totally Cantabrigian scene"; "mingle with academic types" and "locals with trust funds" at the "communal tables" while indulging in some sweet treats or a "huge, scrumptious" sandwich; it's "undeniably expensive" (wags call it the "Hi-Price") and the staff is "flighty", but the smitten swear it'd be hard to "get closer to heaven."

House of Blues   15 | 19 | 15 | $23 |
96 Winthrop St. (bet. Eliot & JFK Sts.), Cambridge, 617-491-2583; www.hob.com
☑ "Let's all say a big amen" for this "rocking" nightclub in Harvard Square, where the live nightly "music is enough to make a poor man smile"; though the Delta-inspired Southern "comfort food" is only "ok", at least it "won't give you the

get updates at zagat.com   79

Boston F | D | S | C |

blues" (fans suggest check out the "raucous" "Sunday gospel brunch", which nourishes both "body and soul"), but discerning types advise "skip the meal and head straight upstairs for the entertainment."

House of Siam   24 | 18 | 22 | $22 |
542 Columbus Ave. (Worcester St.), 617-267-1755; www.houseofsiam.com

■ South End denizens "can't say enough good things" about this "amazing" Siamese star where the "wonderful array of flavors" makes it one of the "best little Thai houses in the city"; given the "appetizing" dishes (with "just the right spice"), "relaxing" atmosphere and "wonderful" service, regulars have to ask "why cook when you can get a great, inexpensive meal" here?

House of Tibet Kitchen   21 | 14 | 20 | $16 |
235 Holland St. (Broadway), Somerville, 617-629-7567

■ "Buddha's gift to Somerville", this "little hole-in-the-wall" "soothes" with "fragrant", "flavorful" "comfort food, Tibetan-style" (the *momo* dumplings are "yum-yum"); the "exotic" menu offers "lots of new tastes to try", while the "calming" atmosphere and "happy" servers "make you feel at home", adding up to a "different, tasty bargain" ("vegetarians too will rejoice in the number of offerings").

House of Zen   _ | _ | _ | I |
16-18 Eliot St., 2nd fl. (JFK St.), Cambridge, 617-497-8288

The third establishment to occupy this Harvard Square site in the last couple of years, the "latest transformation sees the return of decent Chinese food"; tucked away in an upstairs room, it's a "simply" decorated place that features all the mainstream favorites, from moo shu pork to kung pao chicken to Mongolian beef; it's nothing extraordinary, but a meal is "enjoyable" enough and the prices are such that even students can afford it.

HUNGRY I   22 | 24 | 22 | $55 |
71½ Charles St. (bet. Mt. Vernon & Pinckney Sts.), 617-227-3524

■ "Step off of Beacon Hill and into a tiny village" in France when you descend the townhouse stairs to this "absolutely romantic" "jewel" that may be the "ultimate date place" ("don't let the name fool you"); the trio of fireplaces makes it "perfect on a cold winter night", while the "beautiful garden" is ideal for alfresco dining in the summer, but at any time an "attentive" staff brings forth "rich" Country French fare in a "softly lit" room; it's a *très* "transporting place" to take "your loved one" for any "special occasion."

ICARUS   26 | 24 | 24 | $51 |
3 Appleton St. (bet. Arlington & Berkeley Sts.), 617-426-1790; www.icarusrestaurant.com

■ While it may now draw "less attention than its trendier neighbors", "all restaurants should strive" to be as "classy"

Boston

F | **D** | **S** | **C**

---

as this "winged wonder", an "elegant" "institution" in the South End that "soars head and shoulders above most"; chef-owner Chris Douglass' "sophisticated" New American dishes are "deftly conceived and executed", and they're served by a "fabulous" staff that always "goes the extra bit to please" in a "refined" room "ideal for an evening of quiet conversation"; by all accounts, "this Icarus still flies high."

IL CAPRICCIO ⑤   27 | 22 | 25 | $50
888 Main St. (Prospect St.), Waltham, 781-894-2234

■ "Even the pickiest gourmets love" this Waltham "gem", esteemed as the "best – period" Italian ristorante in the Boston area; it "totally wows" with Richard Barron's "meticulously prepared" specialties from the Northern region of The Boot ("it's difficult not to want everything on the menu", but "do not miss the mushroom soufflé"), "spectacular wine list" and "accommodating" service; though the space is a "little cramped" and the prices are "fairly tough on the wallet", "oh, mama mia" is it "worth it."

Il Moro   ▽ 22 | 16 | 20 | $40
143 Pleasant St. (Washington St.), Marblehead, 781-639-8682

◪ "Reliable" for a "business dinner" yet "elegant" enough for a "romantic" meal, this North Shore trattoria satisfies with "simple, classic" Mediterranean-Italian cuisine; though penny-pinchers complain that it's a "little pricey" for a "small town", supporters swear it's "worth the drive" to Marblehead – "go, you won't regret it."

Imperial Seafood House ◐   ▽ 20 | 13 | 15 | $18
70 Beach St. (Edinboro St.), 617-426-8439

◪ "At this corner restaurant next to the Chinatown gate", the "solid" dim sum makes it a reasonable "alternative to waiting in line at more popular spots" in the neighborhood; a "steady" old standby, it "still turns out good, authentic" Chinese food, and it's even a "happening" spot "late at night" (the kitchen is open till 3 AM), but design divas declare the cavernous digs are "in dire need of a major renovation."

Independent   19 | 18 | 17 | $28
75 Union Sq. (Washington St.), Somerville, 617-440-6022; www.theindo.com

■ "Don't think that this is just another bar", because the chef at this "modern-looking" Somerville pub sure "can cook"; the "imaginative" kitchen just "keeps getting better", plating "gussied-up", "delicious" New American "comfort food" that's served by a "sweet, helpful" staff in a room that's "chic-er than you'd expect"; factor in live music on most nights and what you get is a "real surprise."

Indian Cafe   ▽ 23 | 15 | 21 | $21
1665 Beacon St. (Winthrop Rd.), Brookline, 617-277-1752

■ Looking for a "great place to be introduced to Indian food"? – Brookline boosters urge "put yourself in the

---

get updates at zagat.com

Boston F | D | S | C |

hands" of the "friendly" servers ("they'll come up with a wonderful sampling") at this "terrific local" mainstay that "consistently turns out quality" fare; what's more, the dishes come in "tremendous portions", and the quarters are "comfortable" and "quiet."

Indian Club ▽ 21 | 12 | 22 | $19 |
1755 Mass Ave. (Linnaean St.), Cambridge, 617-491-7750; www.indianclubrestaurant.com

◪ Though the decor "could use some help", the "excellent" Indian food offered at this "unpretentious" "neighborhood" joint "makes up for it"; advocates attest that "everything on the menu is worth trying", and it's easy to do so when the prices are so "reasonable"; it's within "walking distance of Harvard and Porter Squares", but skeptics snipe "keep walking – there are lots of better places."

India Pavilion ▽ 19 | 13 | 17 | $17 |
17 Central Sq. (Western Ave.), Cambridge, 617-547-7463

◪ Despite its "time-worn" setting, this small, "low-key" Indian veteran in Central Square continues to do brisk business thanks to its "solid", "well-spiced" "basics" and "inexpensive prices"; some surveyors, however, who have "revisited this old favorite", report that it has "lost part of its luster over the years" and advise "you can find much better in Cambridge."

India Quality 24 | 13 | 20 | $19 |
484 Commonwealth Ave. (Kenmore St.), 617-267-4499

■ Run by "such nice people", who "understand the meaning of the word 'spicy'", this long-standing "favorite" in Kenmore Square cooks the "best Indian food in Boston"; while there's "not much to be said for the atmosphere", it's definitely "hard to resist gorging on the savory", "authentic" dishes, and "you certainly get your money's worth."

Indigo ℐ ▽ 27 | 25 | 25 | $43 |
45 Chapel St. (Highland Ave.), Needham, 781-453-0002; www.indigo-needham.com

■ "Hidden in a strip mall", this "welcome addition to Needham's dining scene" is an "all-around fantastic restaurant"; from the "creative" New American cooking to the "beautiful", "modern" setting (done up in the namesake blue hue) to the staff that pays "attention to all the details", this "sophisticated" "suburban find" "has everything"; it's off to a very fine start, but better go soon – it'll be "mobbed once the word gets out."

Intrigue Cafe ▽ 21 | 26 | 22 | $30 |
Boston Harbor Hotel, 70 Rowes Wharf (Atlantic Ave.), 617-856-7744; www.bhh.com

◪ "What could be better than sitting outside" on the terrace "watching all the action" and taking in the "wonderful view of the harbor"? ask admirers of this casually "elegant"

Boston — F | D | S | C

cafe, a "little-known oasis in the heart of the waterfront district" (the "location can't be beat"); it's a "relaxing" place in which to partake of "good quality" New American fare, but epicures find the food "unremarkable for a hotel of its caliber."

Ironside Grill ▽ 14 | 13 | 15 | $29
25 Park St. (Warren St.), Charlestown, 617-242-1384; www.ironsidegrill.com

☒ "Pickings may be slim in Charlestown" if you're seeking an "affordable meal", but this Traditional American grill located near the U.S.S. Constitution is one option; the "varied menu" "sometimes succeeds", but the disgruntled moan "not very imaginative" and "usually disappointing", advising that a "more focused approach would probably garner better results."

Iruna ⚡ 16 | 11 | 16 | $23
56 JFK St. (Memorial Dr.), Cambridge, 617-868-5633

☒ "Down an alley off JFK Street", "tucked away from the bustle" of Harvard Square, this "tiny" Spanish "relic" seems "unchanged" after nearly 40 years; that's "reassuring" to loyalists looking only for a "simple", "traditional" meal with "great sangria", but for every amigo who embraces it as an "underappreciated" "survivor" "with character", there's a critic who yawns "nothing special."

Isabella 21 | 17 | 19 | $30
566 High St. (bet. Eastern Ave. & Washington St.), Dedham, 781-461-8485; www.isabellarestaurant.com

☒ A "rare suburban restaurant with an unusual menu and a desire to please", this "friendly" New American bistro is "innovative" "without being far out"; despite "weekend waits that can be uncomfortable" and "close quarters" that are always "too crowded", Dedham denizens declare "they try hard here", lauding it as a "great find outside Boston" (but "wishing it were bigger").

Island Hopper 18 | 17 | 18 | $21
91 Mass Ave. (bet. Commonwealth Ave. & Newbury St.), 617-266-1618; www.islandhopperrestaurant.com

☒ "After a busy day" of shopping in the Back Bay or for a "casual" dinner, take a trip to this "colorful", "exotic" "sleeper" that'll transport you to Southeast Asia with its "wide variety" of "interesting" dishes; the offerings are "beautifully presented" by a "welcoming" staff, and the "price is right", but purists feel the open kitchen exerts "too much effort in mixing various ethnic cuisines" and suggest it'd be "better off sticking to one type of food."

Istanbul Cafe 23 | 14 | 17 | $21
37 Bowdoin St. (Cambridge St.), 617-227-3434

■ "Worth ferreting out", this "little hideaway" "tucked away in a cellar" on Beacon Hill prepares Turkish food so

get updates at zagat.com

Boston

F | D | S | C

"consistently outstanding" that it's "just like being in Istanbul"; admirers adore the "fabulous" "home cooking" brought by an "accommodating" staff, but "you'd better love thy neighbor" because these quarters are "very close."

Ithaki Mediterranean Cuisine 23 | 21 | 22 | $36
25 Hammatt St. (Washington St.), Ipswich, 978-356-0099; www.ithakicuisine.com

■ "It's Greek to me and it's wonderful" rave insiders about this North Shore "secret", a "delightful surprise" where the "out-of-this-world" Hellenic and Mediterranean fare provides a "welcome change in this land of baked stuffed scrod"; not only is the "beautiful" room filled with "old-world charm", but the "tables are set far enough apart so that you can chat with your guests."

Jacob Wirth 16 | 17 | 17 | $26
31-37 Stuart St. (bet. Tremont & Washington Sts.), 617-338-8586; www.jacobwirthrestaurant.com

☑ "Step back in time to your grandfather's Boston", "have a big plate of wursts and kraut" and wait for infamous politician "James Michael Curley to walk in the door" of this piece of "history" in the Theater District; since 1868, it has been dishing up "hearty" German-American food, and it continues to be a "decent" pick for a "pre-show bite", but opponents vote "not Wirth it."

Jae's 20 | 18 | 18 | $28
520 Columbus Ave. (Concord Sq.), 617-421-9405
1223 Beacon St. (St. Paul St.), Brookline, 617-739-0000

☑ Such "artful", "imaginative" "sushi keeps our fins twitching" say afishionados of this still "creative" duo that was doing "Pan-Asian before it was trendy"; the "vast menu" of "fresh and healthful" dishes inspired by regions "from Bangkok to Sapporo" can "satisfy all the cravings" at your table, but brace yourself for the "loud" decibels ("fortunately", the "tropical fish" in the "immense" tanks "aren't adding to the noise").

Jake's Boss BBQ 18 | 5 | 11 | $14
3492 Washington St. (Williams St.), Jamaica Plain, 617-983-3701

☑ "Jake's is not only the boss, but the king" of "scrumptious BBQ" swear subjects who swoon for this "cheap rib joint" in Jamaica Plain; "order at the counter", "grab some napkins" and "plan on getting your hands dirty" when you chow down, but note that the staffers are on "Southern speed" and it may "take them longer to serve the food than for the kitchen to slow-cook it."

Jake's Dixie Roadhouse 18 | 14 | 16 | $25
220 Moody St. (bet. Main & Pine Sts.), Waltham, 781-894-4227; www.jakeandearls.com

☑ "End the day" with a "Southern treat" at this "lively" Waltham roadhouse where the "succulent" smoked brisket

Boston F | D | S | C |

and Memphis-style ribs are hot and "melt in your mouth" and the "excellent beers" are cold; while it has its staunch supporters, the barbecue cognoscenti are "disappointed" by the "so-so" vittles.

James's Gate   20 | 19 | 18 | $24 |
5-11 McBride St. (South St.), Jamaica Plain, 617-983-2000; www.jamessgate.com
■ "Everything you could ask for in a local pub" cheer regulars about this "uncontrived" Jamaica Plain watering hole that "gets our vote for casual sweater night"; whether you opt for a "surprisingly good" American meal in the "quiet" dining room or a "pint of Guinness and a tasty shepherd's pie" in the "lively" Irish bar, you'll be charmed by the "warm" "Celtic" atmosphere.

Jamjuli   20 | 16 | 18 | $23 |
1203 Walnut St. (Centre St.), Newton, 617-965-5655
◪ "If you actually want to talk to the people you're dining with", this "peaceful", "pleasant" Newton Highlands Thai is a "yummy" choice; the "fresh, delicately prepared" dishes are "nicely spiced" and always "dependable", and they're presented by a "well-intentioned" staff, but still, the negative nag "not up to par with others" in its category.

JASMINE BISTRO   24 | 18 | 26 | $30 |
412 Market St. (Washington St.), Brighton, 617-789-4676
■ "Customer satisfaction is number one on their minds" at this petite, "family-run" bistro that's "operated with pride" by "people who care"; the "thoughtful hosts" "give the star treatment" to all their guests while offering them "dazzling" dishes based on the "cuisines of several nations", mixing Hungarian and French fare with the flavors of the Near East, Middle East and the Mediterranean; enhanced by a "laid-back feel", it's a "gem in the wilds of Brighton."

Jasper White's Summer Shack   19 | 13 | 15 | $32 |
149 Alewife Brook Pkwy. (Cambridge Park Dr.), Cambridge, 617-520-9500; www.summershackrestaurant.com
◪ Reminiscent of a "Cape Cod beach shanty" (though quite a "cavernous" one), this "chaotic" "barn of a restaurant" in Fresh Pond is "full of families" who "love the party atmosphere" and the "long picnic table" seating; Jasper White's "pan-roasted lobster rules", while the rest of the New England seafood "classics" on the menu are "well prepared", but critics carp that this "tacky" "warehouse" has all the "ambiance of a roller-skating rink", not to mention that it's a "shack that charges mansion prices."

Jer-Ne   20 | 23 | 23 | $52 |
Ritz-Carlton Boston Common, 12 Avery St. (Tremont St.), 617-574-7176; www.ritzcarlton.com
◪ "Look fabulous and act rich if you go" to this "classy" dining room at the Ritz-Carlton Boston Common that's

get updates at zagat.com   85

Boston

F | D | S | C

appointed with "sophisticated", "modern Brahmin" decor (so unlike that of the dowager Ritz opposite the Public Garden); given the "serene" ambiance and generously spaced tables, it's an "excellent place for conversation" and the service is "impeccable", but those who feel that the New American menu "hasn't yet hit the mark" advise continue "on your jour-ney – don't bother stopping" here.

Jimmy's Harborside 18 | 17 | 18 | $39
242 Northern Ave. (Boston Fish Pier), 617-423-1000; www.jimmysharborside.com

▰ Longtime fans "keep expecting to see Frank Sinatra or Dean Martin walk" into this Boston "institution" on the waterfront, which since 1924 has been a "popular" place to "take visitors for some New England flavor"; "grandma may love" the "seafood dishes prepared the old-fashioned way", and for some, the "wonderful" harbor "view makes the evening worthwhile"; but schools of critics crab that this "tourist trap" is "long past its sell-by date."

Jimmy's Steer House 19 | 14 | 18 | $22
1111 Mass Ave. (Quincy St.), Arlington, 781-646-4450

▰ "Take your value-conscious relatives" for a "family meal" at this "moderately priced" steakhouse in Arlington that packs in the "early-bird-special crowd" and "singles" of the "over-60" persuasion, who appreciate the "big portions" of "competently prepared" fare and "very friendly" service; it's "not at all imaginative", but "you go here to not be surprised by anything", and the "formula must work" because "there's always a wait."

Joe's American Bar & Grill 16 | 15 | 16 | $25
100 Atlantic Ave. (Commercial Wharf), 617-367-8700
279 Dartmouth St. (Newbury St.), 617-536-4200
South Shore Plaza, 250 Granite St. (I-95, exit 6), Braintree, 781-848-0200
985 Providence Hwy. (Rtes. 1 & 128), Dedham, 781-329-0800
2087 Washington St./Rte. 53 (Rte. 123), Hanover, 781-878-1234
Northshore Mall, 210 Andover St./Rte. 114 (Rte. 128), Peabody, 978-532-9500
311 Mishawum Rd. (Washington St.), Woburn, 781-935-7200
www.joesamerican.com

▰ "Better than your average chain", at least "when you want the familiar", this "casual" all-American septet is a "pretty good" pick for a "hearty", "kid-friendly" meal; the "fairly generic" menu is "decent" and you "won't leave hungry", but wags recommend it only "if city life has you jonesing for the suburban-mall experience."

Joe Tecce's 16 | 16 | 16 | $30
61 N. Washington St. (Cooper St.), 617-742-6210

▰ Since 1948, this "touristy" North End "landmark" has been a "safe bet" for "big servings" of "old-school" "red-

Boston | F | D | S | C |

sauce" eats the "way your grandma made it"; the decor is "pure kitsch" ("almost a caricature of an Italian restaurant"), but those "who aren't too discriminating" swear it's "lots of fun and better than it gets credit for"; skeptics, however, yawn just "another joint relying on its past glories."

John Harvard's Brew House ● | 16 | 15 | 16 | $21 |
33 Dunster St. (bet. Mass Ave. & Mt. Auburn St.), Cambridge, 617-868-3585
1 Worcester Rd./Rte. 9 (bet. I-90 & Rte. 30), Framingham, 508-875-2337
www.johnharvards.com

◪ "Think twice if you're over 25" and considering stopping in one of these "faux quaint" brewhouse franchises, because the "noise is deafening" and the American pub grub "isn't much better than in the dorms"; that certainly doesn't deter the "college set" from "hanging out" – the Cambridge branch is "quintessential Harvard Square" (read: a "frat-boy scene") – and quaffing "craft beers."

Johnny D's Uptown | 17 | 14 | 16 | $20 |
17 Holland St. (College Ave.), Somerville, 617-776-2004;
www.johnnyds.com

◪ "Tops" for a "jazz brunch" "on the weekends" or to "catch a live act in the evening" throughout the week (blues, salsa, world beat, etc.), this Somerville club draws a "crowd of regulars" with its "fabulous" schedule; it's worth "booking a dinner seating just to get a better view" of the show, but note that the American pub grub, while "respectable", clearly "takes second stage to the music."

Johnny's Luncheonette | 18 | 15 | 15 | $17 |
1105 Mass Ave. (Remington St.), Cambridge, 617-495-0055
30 Langley Rd. (bet. Beacon & Centre Sts.), Newton, 617-527-3223

◪ Like a "flashback to the '50s", these "retro" luncheonettes in Harvard Square and Newton Centre attract both "families with screaming kids" and "area hipsters" wearing "thick black glasses, messenger bags and bed hair", who all crowd in for "enormous portions" of "all-American" "diner" food (including "breakfast at anytime"); even if naysayers nix it as "overpriced kitsch", better "get there early" or "you'll be salivating over someone else's omelet."

José's | 18 | 11 | 16 | $16 |
131 Sherman St. (Walden St.), Cambridge, 617-354-0335;
www.josesmexicanrestaurant.com

◪ "Everyone seems to have a great time", "particularly after a few of the huge margaritas", at this Tex-Mex "hole-in-the-wall" that's way "out of the way" between Fresh Pond and Porter Square; "all the food tastes the same here, but it's fresh" and "good enough" (at least it's "consistent) and comes in "large portions" at "bargain prices", so though

Boston | F | D | S | C |

the menu may be "unexciting", it's a "Cambridge place with parking – you can't beat that with a piñata stick!"

Joy Luck Café | 20 | 16 | 19 | $21 |
1037 Great Plain Ave. (Highland Ave.), Needham, 781-455-8908

☒ Offering "better food than many other Chinese restaurants in the area", this Needham "favorite" has found a niche for itself with its "light", "fresh take" on the genre (including some dishes that are "different" from what you find on "standard" menus); though the lukewarm conclude "good" but "nothing to write home about" (and advise "take your SUV and go Downtown" instead), most consider it a "find in the suburbs."

JP Seafood Cafe | 21 | 16 | 19 | $22 |
730 Centre St. (Harris Ave.), Jamaica Plain, 617-983-5177; www.jpseafoodcafe.com

■ "Bring on the sushi" cheer afishionados of the "delicious, inventive" finny fare prepared at this Japanese-Korean seafood house, a "true find" in "funky" Jamaica Plain; despite "the cramped tables", the "hippie-dippy" clientele embraces this "friendly, well-run enterprise", lauding the fish that's "as fresh as can be" and the "can't-be-beat lunch-box specials"; those from other towns just "wish it were in our neighborhood."

J's at Nashoba Valley Winery ▽ | 25 | 24 | 24 | $37 |
100 Wattaquadock Hill Rd. (Rte. 117), Bolton, 978-779-9816; www.nashobawinery.com

■ Nestled in the heart of Massachusetts' apple country, this rustic farmhouse at the Nashoba Valley Winery in Bolton boasts "picturesque views of the surrounding vineyards"; it's a most "lovely" backdrop for chef Steven Sprague's "unique, flavorful" New American cooking (you "can't find much better" "west of Route 495"), accompanied by "interesting" house wines and served by a "nice" staff, making it a "perfect spot for a special occasion or when you want to impress."

JULIEN ⑤ | 26 | 27 | 27 | $66 |
Le Méridien Hotel, 250 Franklin St. (bet. Oliver & Pearl Sts.), 617-451-1900; www.lemeridienboston.com

■ "What fine dining should be", this "plush" dining room at Le Méridien Hotel is one "amazing restaurant"; graced with "elaborately carved gold-leaf ceilings, glittery mirrors" and "tables nicely spaced for privacy", it's "elegant without being stuffy" and it makes each guest "feel like they have their own brigade of personal staffers who anticipate their every need" while proffering "luxurious", "absolutely exceptional" New French fare; yes, this "haute cuisine" comes at "haute prices", but the starry-eyed "only wish we had more special occasions" to celebrate here.

Boston　　　　　　　　　　　　　F | D | S | C |

Jumbo Seafood ◐　　　　24 | 10 | 18 | $22 |
7 Hudson St. (bet. Beach & Kneeland Sts.), 617-542-2823
■ "Seafood is the name of the game" at this "authentic" Chinatown "favorite", voted the "best Chinese restaurant in Boston; the "fish cannot be any fresher", as it "goes from swimming in the tank to your plate in minutes" (in particular, it's "justifiably famous for its lobster preparations" and "scrumptious" "salty, spicy squid"); "don't look too closely around" the bare-bones digs – just focus on all the "fabulous" "traditional" dishes with "jumbo taste" brought by "quick and efficient" servers at "very reasonable prices."

Karoun ✗　　　　20 | 18 | 18 | $27 |
839 Washington St. (Walnut St.), Newton, 617-964-3400
◪ "If you like shish kebab" and other "solid", "authentic" Middle Eastern and Armenian fare, this "enchanting surprise" in Newtonville is a "must"; it's always a "fun" night out here, especially on weekends, when a belly dancer entertains, and on Tuesdays, when salsa and tango lessons are offered, but dissenters feel it's "not about the food, it's about the atmosphere."

Kashmir　　　　24 | 20 | 19 | $28 |
279 Newbury St. (Gloucester St.), 617-536-1695;
www.kashmirindianrestaurant.com
◪ Cosseting with "gracious" service, this "crown jewel" in the Back Bay is a "classy" "destination" for "upscale" Indian dining (it's "worth the trip just for the breads" and "we could live off the chicken tikka masala"); the patio is a "wonderful" spot for "people-watching" (just the "place for lunch in the summer"), while the interior is "elegant" and "comfortable", but detractors caution "you're definitely paying for the beautiful decor" and the "golden location."

Kaya　　　　18 | 15 | 16 | $26 |
581 Boylston St. (bet. Clarendon & Dartmouth Sts.),
617-236-5858 ◐
1366 Beacon St. (Harvard St.), Brookline, 617-738-2244
1924 Mass Ave. (Porter Sq.), Cambridge, 617-497-5656 ◐
www.kayausa.com
◪ Take an "excursion to the Orient" recommend regulars at this "quiet" Asian trio, which may be "low on ambiance" but is "high on flavor"; the "diverse menu" of Japanese and Korean dishes includes "competent" sushi and "tasty" tableside BBQ, but the disappointed declare that given the "depressing" digs and "indifferent" service, "something is definitely missing" at this "unfulfilled promise."

Kebab Factory　　　　22 | 21 | 20 | $22 |
414 Washington St. (Beacon St.), Somerville, 617-354-4996;
www.kashmirspices.com
■ For a "twist on the traditional", "check out" this teensy Indian bistro in Somerville that "does a great job with the

Boston

F | D | S | C

classics" but "also offers a number of original dishes"; though its moniker may "scream suburban mall" experience, that couldn't be further from the truth considering the "clear flavors", "high-end" setting and "courteous" service – "now, if only they would change the name."

Kebab-N-Kurry 23 | 10 | 16 | $23
30 Mass Ave. (bet. Beacon & Marlborough Sts.), 617-536-9835; www.bombayclub.com

☑ "You'll feel like a student again" at this "Mass Avenue dive" that attracts lots of mouths with its "fabulous curries" ("so hot, so yummy", so almost-"cheap") and other "consistently" "excellent" Indian dishes; be warned, however, that the "very small" "subterranean digs" can seem "claustrophobic" ("you'll sit way too close to your neighbors, but the food is good enough that you may not care"), so you might want to "take it to go."

Khao Sarn Cuisine 23 | 19 | 21 | $23
250 Harvard St. (Beacon St.), Brookline, 617-566-7200

■ "Don't go bland" when you can venture far "beyond the usual" with the "mouth-popping flavors" produced at this "exotic", "restful" "find" in Coolidge Corner, which "offers many regional Thai dishes" from the North "that you don't see" at the average Siamese eatery; what's more, the staff is "eager to help you understand" the "authentic" specialties and they'll give you tips on the "proper way to eat them."

King & I 20 | 12 | 17 | $19
145 Charles St. (Cambridge St.), 617-227-3320

☑ "Given its location on Beacon Hill", "you'd expect prices to be much higher" than they are at this very "affordable" "neighborhood" Thai, which always pleases partisans with a "quick and tasty" meal; the menu is fairly "extensive", and the service "efficient", making it a "convenient" "low-maintenance" place to grab a bite, even if critics dismiss the "boring" food.

KingFish Hall 21 | 21 | 18 | $38
Faneuil Hall Mktpl., 188 S. Market St. (Chatham St.), 617-523-8862; www.toddenglish.com

☑ "Disneyland meets SeaWorld" at this "high-energy" seafood fantasy at Faneuil Hall that's a real "crowd-pleaser" among "tourists and Bostonians" due to its "whimsical" "Dali-esque" decor, "bright", "zippy" atmosphere and "imaginative menu" of "fish with or without a twist"; those, however, who gripe that the room is "way too noisy" and the service "snail-like" (the staff is "too glam to be prompt") warn you're "paying for all the Todd English hype."

King Fung Garden ∉ ▽ 24 | 3 | 19 | $14
74 Kneeland St. (bet. Hudson & Tyler Sts.), 617-357-5262

■ It doesn't get more "hole-in-the-wall" than this "tiny", "family-owned" "diamond in the rough" "tucked away in a

Boston F | D | S | C

hidden corner" of Chinatown, but "don't mind the decor", since the kitchen turns out such "amazing" Chinese food; "try the Peking duck" (the "best in the city"), "homemade noodles" and scallion pie (the "gold standard") for sure, but whatever you order, the "only thing smaller than the room is the check."

Kouzina ☒   24 | 16 | 21 | $29
1649 Beacon St. (Windsor Rd.), Newton, 617-558-7677
■ "Eager to please", this "warm", "wonderful" "treasure" has Waban all abuzz with its "spectacular", "innovative" (yet "not weird") Mediterranean menu that's "fun for all – kids, families and couples on date nights"; it's "always mobbed" in the highly "intimate" (only 20 seats) storefront space, but "if you can get in" (it's "worth the wait"), you'll be treated to a "delicious" meal served by "gracious" folks; this is "what a neighborhood place ought to be."

Kowloon ●   18 | 17 | 17 | $23
948 Broadway/Rte. 1 (Main St.), Saugus, 781-233-0077;
www.kowloonrestaurant.com
◪ A "throwback to the good old egg roll, spare rib and duck sauce days", this North Shore "temple of tackiness" may have "enough seating for the whole city of Saugus"; equally "huge" is the "retro menu" of Chinese, Polynesian and Thai dishes, which brings up "fond memories" among sentimental sorts of their "early" "Americanized" "dining experiences", but design divas deem the "over-the-top" "Boston meets the South Pacific" decor "in serious need of a visit from Martha Stewart."

La Campania ☒   26 | 23 | 23 | $47
504 Main St. (bet. Cross & Heard Sts.), Waltham, 781-894-4280
■ Widely esteemed as a "must for lovers of *la cucina Italiana*", this "charming" trattoria in Waltham feels "like a trip to Tuscany"; chef-owner John Maione's "phenomenal" cooking yields "flavors so memorable" "you'd lick the plate clean if you could get away with it", and it's served in a "cozy", "rustic" setting that makes for a "romantic spot for a special evening"; "tight quarters are the only drawback" at this "splurge in the suburbs."

La Casa de Pedro   23 | 16 | 19 | $25
51 Main St. (bet. Church & Pleasant Sts.), Watertown,
617-923-8025
■ Infused with the "warm greetings" of chef-owner Pedro Alarcon, "La Casa feels like your own casa" say sated surveyors who've sampled his "home-cooked Venezuelan delights" at this "little treasure" in Watertown; the "heaping portions" of "Latin-flavored" dishes are clearly "made with care", and you'll "leave stuffed to the gills", so despite "tables that are too close" together, this is "everything that a good local spot should be."

Boston

F | D | S | C

La Famiglia Giorgio   17 | 10 | 15 | $19
250 Newbury St. (bet. Fairfield & Gloucester Sts.), 617-247-1569
112 Salem St. (bet. Cooper & Parmenter Sts.), 617-367-6711

☑ While there's "nothing nouveau" about this pair of "no-frills" "spaghetti-and-meatballs type places" in the Back Bay and North End, its "obscenely" "gigantic portions" of "old-fashioned" Italian "home" cooking make it "popular with students on a budget" (and with "hungry football teams" too); you'd "better drive" here because "you'll need a car to bring home the monster-sized doggy bag", but the cognoscenti warn unless you favor "quantity, not quality", "fuhgeddaboudit."

La Groceria   17 | 13 | 16 | $25
853 Main St. (Mass Ave.), Cambridge, 617-497-4214; www.lagroceriarestaurant.com

☑ Since 1971, this "no-surprises" "standby" in Central Square has been a "popular MIT hangout", satisfying big appetites with "reliable" Italian "standards" "like your mama's pasta", "served fast" and at "affordable prices"; a cadre of critics, however, counsel "stick to the North End", since this "boring" place has definitely "gone downhill" over the years.

Lala Rokh   23 | 22 | 24 | $37
97 Mt. Vernon St. (Charles St.), 617-720-5511; www.lalarokh.com

■ As if "you've come to eat in" a private home, the staff "bends over backward to make patrons happy" at this "tranquil oasis" set in an "old townhouse on Beacon Hill", where the "adventurous are rewarded" with "lovingly prepared" Persian food; the "extremely attentive servers help customers navigate" the "exotic" menu, presented in an "inviting" setting (with "original artwork") that's highly "recommended for a romantic dinner."

Lam's   22 | 14 | 20 | $19
825 Washington St. (Walnut St.), Newton, 617-630-5222

■ Perhaps the "best little-known restaurant in Newtonville", this Vietnamese-Thai "surprise" is "welcoming and friendly to all", and a "wonderful" pick for a "delicious", "super-fresh" meal delivered "promptly"; though there may "not be much atmosphere", the "wide-ranging" menu ("just different enough") and "value for the money" more than compensate; "what a find in the suburbs."

Landing   18 | 20 | 20 | $37
81 Front St. (State St.), Marblehead, 781-631-1878; www.thelandingrestaurant.com

☑ "Get a window seat" to best take advantage of this Marblehead "beauty's" "can't-be-beat" "location right on

Boston F | D | S | C |

the harbor"; the pub offers lighter American bites, while the more "formal" dining room features a "varied menu" that "highlights the catch of the day", but "if only the food were more interesting" lament those who feel that its saving grace is its "prime piece of real estate."

La Paloma   22 | 14 | 19 | $20 |
195 Newport Ave. (Hobart St.), Quincy, 617-773-0512; www.lapalomarestaurant.com

■ "The whole family can eat their fill without emptying the wallet" at this "local" Mexican "favorite" that's "worth the drive to Quincy"; "don't let the strip-mall setting deceive you", because the kitchen does a "great job on all the favorites" and the "specials never disappoint either" (there's always a "line out the door to prove it"); well, at least the "awesome margaritas" make the "wait" more palatable.

La Summa   ∇ 23 | 17 | 22 | $28 |
30 Fleet St. (bet. Atlantic Ave. & Hanover St.), 617-523-9503

■ "To get the true feel of a great neighborhood", head to this "excellent alternative to the busy Hanover Street establishments"; an "old-time, family-style" Southern Italian fixture a bit "off the beaten path", it represents "what the North End used to be", feeding customers "outstanding", "authentic" dishes (notably the "best homemade pastas") in a "relaxing", "comfortable" environment at moderate prices; in sum, it's a "gem."

Laurel   20 | 19 | 19 | $28 |
142 Berkeley St. (Columbus Ave.), 617-424-6711; www.laurelgrillandbar.com

■ "Impress your date" "yet don't go home broke" by dining at this "mecca for the frugal gourmet", a "charming", "unheralded" "little place" that may be the "best bang for the buck" on the Back Bay–South End border; most of the "well-prepared" New American entrees are only $10 ("unheard of in pricey Boston!"), so not only do you get "fine dining" with "no attitude", it's a true "bargain."

LEGAL SEA FOODS   22 | 17 | 19 | $33 |
Copley Pl., 100 Huntington Ave. (bet. Dartmouth & Exeter Sts.), 617-266-7775
Long Wharf, 255 State St. (Atlantic Ave.), 617-227-3115
26 Park Plaza (Columbus Ave.), 617-426-4444
Prudential Ctr., 800 Boylston St. (bet. Fairfield & Gloucester Sts.), 617-266-6800
South Shore Plaza, 250 Granite St. (I-95, exit 6), Braintree, 781-356-3070
Burlington Mall, 1131 Middlesex Tpke. (Rte. 128), Burlington, 781-270-9700
5 Cambridge Ctr. (bet. Main & 6th Sts.), Cambridge, 617-864-3400

(continued)

get updates at zagat.com

Boston | F | D | S | C |

(continued)
LEGAL SEA FOODS
The Mall at Chestnut Hill, 43 Boylston St. (Hammond Pond Pkwy.), Chestnut Hill, 617-277-7300
50 Worcester Rd./Rte. 9 (Ring Rd.), Framingham, 508-766-0600
Northshore Mall, 210 Andover St./Rte. 114 (Rte. 128), Peabody, 978-532-4500
www.legalseafoods.com
Additional locations throughout the Boston area

◪ Voted the Most Popular restaurant in Boston, this "quintessential Boston seafood experience" "won't let you down" when you're looking for finny fare prepared "just the way you want it"; whether you're "taking out-of-town visitors" or "mom and dad", you can "depend" on this "solid performer"; sure, it's a "chain", but if you can "ignore all the tourists" and "wade through" the sea of "crowds" to "catch a table", you'll get "good, fresh fish – enough said."

Le Lyonnais ⌀ ▽ 23 | 19 | 23 | $44 |
416 Great Rd./Rte. 2A (Rte. 27), Acton, 978-263-9068

■ "*Bon appétit*" cheer Francophiles about the "excellent" "classic" French cuisine prepared at this "lovely" "old house" in Acton, which evokes the "feel" of a "country" home in France; the series of three "quiet", "intimate" rooms (plus a covered porch) makes it a "favorite for an anniversary dinner" or any other "special" "romantic" "event" if you're in the "far reaches of suburbia."

LE SOIR 26 | 23 | 24 | $52 |
51-53 Lincoln St. (bet. Chester & Columbus Sts.), Newton, 617-965-3100; www.lesoirbistro.com

■ "Escoffier would be proud" of chef-owner Mark Allen (ex Ritz-Carlton Dining Room), because "this guy can cook", and what comes out of his Newton Highlands kitchen is "out-of-this-world" French fare that "rivals almost any in Boston"; the Gallic "classics" are proffered in a "classy manner" in an "intimate", "elegant" bistro environment, leaving the smitten simply swooning "thank heaven" for this absolutely "memorable" taste of "Paris in the suburbs."

L'ESPALIER ⌀ 28 | 27 | 27 | $87 |
30 Gloucester St. (bet. Commonwealth Ave. & Newbury St.), 617-262-3023; www.lespalier.com

■ "To remind yourself that elegance still exists in the world", "indulge" in the "pure luxury" provided by this "exceptional" "class act" set in an "exquisite" townhouse in the Back Bay that's "perfect for a milestone celebration"; chef-owner Frank McClelland is a "genius", and he "layers textures and flavors in such brilliant ways" that "you're almost intoxicated" by his "sublime" "haute" New French

Boston

F | **D** | **S** | **C**

masterpieces; the "flawless" staff "treats everyone like a VIP", so despite prices that could nearly "include airfare to Paris", this is the "*crème de la crème*" of Boston.

Les Zygomates ⓢ

22 | 21 | 20 | $39

129 South St. (bet. Beach & Essex Sts.), 617-542-5108; www.winebar.com

■ "Bon vivants" won't want to miss this "truly French experience", a "chic" boîte in the Leather District that imports a slice of "Paris to Boston"; the "traditional" bistro menu gives you "plenty to smile about", but the "real star here is the wine list", with "fetching" selections available by the taste, glass, half-bottle or full bottle (there's even a $20 list of labels), plus a tasting event every Tuesday; throw in "live jazz almost every night" and all devotees want to know is "what more do you need in life?"

Limbo

– | – | – | E

49 Temple Pl. (bet. Tremont & Washington Sts.), 617-338-0280; www.limboboston.com

"There's no better place to be among friends" insist "dressed to impress" scenesters about this "absurdly hip" Downtown "scene"; the "very modern", multi-level space houses a first-floor dining room, a mezzanine and a "gorgeous" lounge worked by resident DJs ("great for after-work drinks"), while the "intimate basement" – the "best part" of a "fun night out on the town" here – hosts "live jazz" (a "treat") as well as funk, R&B and Latin music; the new Mediterranean menu "could be better", but the "groovy" ambiance "makes up for it."

Limoncello

22 | 19 | 22 | $33

190 North St. (Richmond St.), 617-523-4480; www.limoncelloboston.com

■ "Man wins lottery", fulfills "his lifetime dream", "opens North End restaurant" – that's the charmed story at this "convivial" trattoria "off the main drag"; "delightful" owner Maurizio Badolato's guests "strike gold" themselves too, considering the "marvelous" traditional Italian cooking, "Sunday dinner–type setting filled with lots of families" and "personable", accommodating service, not to mention that the signature "homemade limoncello will virtually knock your socks off."

Linwood Grill & BBQ

18 | 13 | 16 | $20

81 Kilmarnock St. (Queensberry St.), 617-247-8099

◪ "Solid" "renditions of barbecue" and other "filling Southern-style" vittles make fans "lick their lips" at this "funky" Fenway "dive" with a "comfortably" "laid-back" vibe; while it's "not the best BBQ in Boston", it's a convenient pit stop if you're heading to a Sox game, and the "cool yet unpretentious bar scene" in the adjacent club makes it a "great place to catch live music."

Boston | F | D | S | C |

Locke-Ober ⚥ | 21 | 24 | 22 | $60 |
3 Winter Pl. (bet. Tremont & Washington Sts.), 617-542-1340; www.locke-ober.com

☑ "It's not your father's Locke-Ober", but it still "tastes of old money" as "you're transported back in time" for a dining experience that's "Brahmin Boston at its best"; owner Lydia Shire (ex Biba) has "revitalized" this "elegant" Downtown "landmark" while still "maintaining some traditional favorites" on the Continental menu, but still, trendoids find it "way too stuffy" and gripe too about prices that'll "break the bank."

L'Osteria | 24 | 16 | 22 | $28 |
104 Salem St. (Cooper St.), 617-723-7847; www.losteria.com

■ "Satisfying to the max" for "all things red sauce", this "homey", "family-run" ristorante in the North End cooks up "old-fashioned, honest" "comfort food" "just like your Italian grandmother used to make (or you wish she did)"; while the fare may be "predictable" and "nothing fancy", that's "exactly why it's so beloved" (legions of loyalists say "we've been coming for many years and have never been disappointed") – *mangia, mangia!*

Lotus Blossom | 23 | 19 | 19 | $25 |
394 Boston Post Rd./Rte. 20 (Station Rd.), Sudbury, 978-443-0200; www.lotusblossomcuisine.com

■ "Always a crowd-pleaser", this "attractive", "upscale" neighborhood "jewel" in Sudbury is widely known for preparing some of the "best" Chinese food "in the western suburbs"; the menu features a "large variety" of dishes, all "consistently" "well prepared" and made with "high-quality" ingredients, "setting it apart from many others" and making it an especially "great choice if you can't make it to Chinatown."

Lucca ◐ | 23 | 21 | 22 | $38 |
226 Hanover St. (Cross St.), 617-742-9200; www.luccaboston.com

■ If you're in "search of something new", voters vouch for this "lively", late-night North End "hot spot", a "swanky place" that's "definitely a step above" the neighborhood's typical "red-sauce" establishments; the "well thought-out" Northern Italian menu (offering both "inventive" and "classic" dishes), "accommodating" service that elicits "bravos" and "fine bar" "ensure that you leave pleased" and return often.

Lucky's | ∇ 17 | 20 | 19 | $22 |
355 Congress St. (A St.), 617-357-5825; www.luckyslounge.com

■ "Bathed in red lights", this "cool" "basement" lounge in South Boston amid the Fort Point Channel office buildings

Boston

F | **D** | **S** | **C**

gives off the feel of a "speakeasy", or at least a "retro rumpus room" with Rat Pack flair; the "above-average" American pub grub is "more interesting than you'd expect", but this "hangout" is really about the "great bar scene", "live music" (bands Tuesday–Saturday, plus a tribute to Old Blue Eyes on 'Sinatra Sundays') and "good-looking crowd."

Lucy's – | – | – | M
242 Harvard St. (Beacon St.), Brookline, 617-232-5829; www.lucysbrookline.com
Flavorful, low-fat food is the focus at this smartly casual Brookline newcomer, a New American bistro brightened up with a Fiestaware color scheme and adorned with works by young, local artists; the Caribbean flavors that dot the menu recall chef Owen Tilley's (ex East Coast Grill) tenure on the West Indies island of Vieques, though the bill of fare also offers light bites (wood-oven pizzas, Mediterranean-influenced salads) and plenty of seafood choices.

LUMIÈRE 27 | 23 | 24 | $51
1293 Washington St. (Waltham St.), Newton, 617-244-9199; www.lumiererestaurant.com
■ "Everything sparkles" at this "suave", "sophisticated" West Newton star that "shines like a beacon in the suburbs"; chef-owner Michael Leviton's "stellar" New French preparations guarantee an "amazing culinary experience" that's only enhanced by the "gorgeous surroundings" and "gracious" service; granted, it's awfully "tough to get a reservation", but if you can snag a booking, you'll "thank heaven" for this "high-class" "enchantress."

Lyceum Bar & Grill 24 | 22 | 23 | $36
43 Church St. (Washington St.), Salem, 978-745-7665; www.lyceumsalem.com
■ "Classy", "clubby" and "comfortable", this "gem in the culinary wasteland of Salem" is "one of the better dining spots north of Boston"; the "superb", "creative" New American menu "includes a nice mix of choices for all tastes", attracting "busy lawyers by day (and their clients by night)", while the live piano music in the evening hits just the right note; "they never let us down", which is why it's "one of our favorites year in and year out."

Maddie's Sail Loft ⊄ ▽ 18 | 8 | 19 | $26
15 State St. (bet. Front & Washington Sts.), Marblehead, 781-631-9824
◪ Old salts say the "great fried" seafood is the thing to eat at this "boisterous" "local" "institution" in Marblehead that's "notorious for its over-the-top drinks"; the American menu may be totally "typical", but the eats are "better than average" and they're delivered with "no fluff" in "homey" digs; it's been a "favorite" "sailors' spot forever" – just beware that "their idea of dessert is another drink."

get updates at zagat.com

Boston

| F | D | S | C |

Maggiano's Little Italy | 18 | 18 | 19 | $29 |
4 Columbus Ave. (Arlington St.), 617-542-3456;
www.maggianos.com

◪ With "more food than at mama's on a Sunday night", you'll surely be "well fed" at this "red-sauce" franchise in the Theater District that dishes out "massive portions" of "honest" Italian fare with Frank Sinatra crooning in the background; "take the whole family or your pals from the office" – the staff is unfazed "even when you arrive with a table of 20" – but dissenters who deride the "quantity over quality" "formula" scoff "they might as well serve the food in a trough."

Magnolia's Southern Cuisine ⑤ | 23 | 18 | 22 | $28 |
1193 Cambridge St. (Tremont St.), Cambridge, 617-576-1971;
www.magnoliascuisine.com

■ "If you're hankering" for "classic" Southern "comfort" food "livened up" with "just the right amount of innovation" and a "touch" of Cajun spice, then this "funky" "bayou treasure" in Inman Square is your place; along with the "excellent" regular lineup of dishes, it features a 'festival menu', which changes monthly, while the "happy" servers always "make you feel at home"; "y'all stop by", y'hear?

Maison Robert ⑤ | 23 | 24 | 24 | $52 |
Old City Hall, 45 School St. (bet. Beacon & Tremont Sts.),
617-227-3370; www.maisonrobert.com

◪ "Civilized" and "sophisticated", this "oldie but goodie" remains a "lovely" destination for a "business lunch" or "romantic dinner" Downtown; quartered in the Old City Hall building, it's an oh-so-"elegant" retreat with a "Boston Brahmin" ambiance, "gracious" service and "predictably excellent" classic French cuisine; "perhaps it's a bit stuffy for the uninitiated, but it still provides memorable dining for the old guard"; P.S. for a "less formal" meal, the cafe's prix fixe bistro menus are a "real steal."

Mamma Maria | 26 | 23 | 23 | $45 |
3 North Sq. (Little Prince St.), 617-523-0077;
www.mammamaria.com

■ "Don't let the name fool you" – the "imaginative", regional Northern Italian fare served at this "romantic" townhouse is "not your mother's cooking"; the "skilled" servers "really know how to treat people well" (like mama does), but at home you probably wouldn't find such "gourmet" food or "fancy" appointments; it may be a "splurge", but it's one of the "best in the North End."

MANTRA ⑤ | 23 | 25 | 22 | $58 |
52 Temple Pl. (bet. Tremont & Washington Sts.), 617-542-8111;
www.mantrarestaurant.com

◪ "Dress in black" (or better yet, "wear Armani") and join the "glittery crowd" at this Downtown "scene" that's all

subscribe to zagat.com

Boston

F | **D** | **S** | **C**

"glitz and glamour"; set in a century-old former bank, its "mesmerizing" decor makes you "feel like you're on a movie set"; prepare for a "sophisticated" "gustatory adventure" orchestrated by chef Thomas John, whose "exotic" and "wildly inventive" style "melds New French and Indian flavors"; though foes harrumph that "'pretentious' doesn't even begin to describe" the "hipper-than-thou attitude", followers just sigh "nirvana."

Marché Boston ◐   15 | 16 | 11 | $20
Prudential Ctr., 800 Boylston St. (bet. Huntington & Mass Aves.), 617-578-9700; www.marcheusa.com

☑ Like the "United Nations of food courts", this "self-service" "international melting pot" at the Prudential Center allows customers to "eat sushi, pizza and Chinese stir-fry – in one meal"; it's a "cool" Eclectic marketplace "concept" that's best appreciated when you want a "quick bite" in the Back Bay but "can't decide on what kind of food", though critics warn that the "gimmick wears thin" and the "chaotic" setting feels like a "high school cafeteria."

Margo Bistro   ▁ | ▁ | ▁ | E
Harborside Inn, 185 State St. (Atlantic Ave.), 617-670-2033; www.margobistro.com

"Hidden by the Big Dig", this "beautiful" "undiscovered" "gem" in the Harborside Inn is a real "sleeper", a "calm", "delightful" oasis in the midst of the Financial District; though the verdict is still out on its just-introduced Traditional American–Italian menu, followers who lauded its previous incarnation as a New American bistro are willing to give it a chance.

Marino Ristorante   19 | 19 | 20 | $32
2465 Mass Ave. (bet. Porter Sq. & Rte. 16), Cambridge, 617-868-5454; www.marinoristorante.com

☑ "Every neighborhood should have a restaurant like this" say boosters of this "solid" standby north of Porter Square, which pleases with "consistently fine", "authentic" Italian dishes inspired by the region of Abruzzo; much of the "organic" produce is grown on the proprietor's "own farms", so you know it's "fresh", as are the "hearty" "homemade pastas", but critical Cantabrigians complain that the "faux-rustic" setting "feels like suburbia" and add that "they should serve earplugs" to drown out the "over-the-top" din.

Martha's Galley ✗   ▁ | ▁ | ▁ | M
179 Court St. (bet. Nelson St. & Rte. 44), Plymouth, 508-747-9200; www.marthasgalley.com

"Hard to find" but worth the hunt, this teensy, family-operated "find" set in a Plymouth strip mall surprises with its "amazing" New American menu; everything is homemade – the "owners even grow many of the vegetables" – and "really good", though the signature scallops in ginger sauce

get updates at zagat.com   99

Boston   F | D | S | C

is "our favorite"; still, some surveyors "can't get past the almost cafeteria"-like atmosphere or "strange format."

Mary Chung ⊄   21 | 7 | 16 | $17
464 Mass Ave. (Central Sq.), Cambridge, 617-864-1991
■ "Make way for the dumplings" cheer fans who "break a sweat" over the "hot and spicy" Chinese fare offered at this "longtime favorite of the MIT set" in Central Square; a "cheap" "hole-in-the-wall" it may be, but it's a "holy place among Cambridge's hackers and geeks", and "as the many repeat customers will testify", the "spartan surroundings" "don't matter", since "Mary's not afraid to turn up the heat on her dishes" (the *suan la chow show,* meaty Szechuan won tons in a spicy broth, is "phenomenal"); "long may she tingle our palates."

Masa   22 | 20 | 20 | $40
439 Tremont St. (Appleton St.), 617-338-8884
■ "Inventive combinations of ingredients" and "spicy", "intense tastes" earn kudos for this "cosmopolitan" Southwestern alternative, one of the more "underrated restaurants in the South End"; not only does it "fill the void between its overpriced and undersophisticated neighbors", but in a part of town "where attitude can reign supreme", the service is "exceedingly pleasant."

Ma Soba   19 | 18 | 17 | $29
156 Cambridge St. (Hancock St.), 617-973-6680
◪ "East meets West" at this "modern", "stylish" Pan-Asian establishment on Beacon Hill, where the "fusion-y" dishes "tingle your tongue" and the "sushi is very fresh"; while it's "probably not worth going out of your way" for (the "mélange" of flavors "sometimes doesn't quite work"), it's an "interesting" option for those who "live or work nearby", even if it is "relatively overpriced."

Massimino's Cucina Italia ⚡   23 | 15 | 21 | $29
207 Endicott St. (Commercial St.), 617-523-5959;
www.massiminosboston.com
■ "Like when you're visiting nonna", you'll be "treated like family" at this North End cucina by people who "aim to please"; though it's "squeezed for space" and a little "out of the way" (far "from the hustle and bustle of Hanover Street"), it's "convenient to the Fleet Center", and loyalists insist it's "worth it" for the "family-style" Italian "home cooking" offered at "moderate prices."

Matt Murphy's Pub ⊄   22 | 16 | 18 | $20
14 Harvard St. (bet. Kent St. & Webster Pl.), Brookline, 617-232-0188
■ "So authentic" you practically "need a passport to get through the door", this "comfy" "multi-generational gathering spot" in Brookline is "just like a neighborhood pub in Ireland" (though with "extraordinary food for a bar");

Boston | F | D | S | C |

"grab a pint", order some "top-notch" fish 'n' chips (served "in newspaper, as at the local chippy" in Dublin), "enjoy the live music" and you'll almost "forget which side of the pond you're on."

Maurizio's | 25 | 16 | 22 | $34 |
364 Hanover St. (Clark St.), 617-367-1123

■ "Don't tell" the "tourists" plead those in-the-know, but this "charming" Italian "storefront" is "consistently one of the top performers in the North End"; greeting you with a "big smile", the servers instantly "make you feel so welcome" and then they'll feed you "fantastic" "traditional" "favorites" that "bring comfort food to a whole new level" (don't miss the "wonderful handmade pastas"), making this a "real find", "tight" quarters notwithstanding.

McCormick & Schmick's | 20 | 19 | 20 | $37 |
Faneuil Hall Mktpl., N. Market Bldg. (North St.), 617-720-5522
Park Plaza Hotel, 34 Columbus Ave. (bet. Arlington & Charles Sts.), 617-482-3999
www.mccormickandschmicks.com

■ At this "fish house that looks like a steakhouse", expect a "varied, always changing" selection of "consistently" "fresh seafood from both coasts", served in an "environment like that of a men's club" ("all dark woods and high booths"); it "may be a chain", but it possesses a "winning formula", even if fin fanatics loyal to Legal carp "nothing to get excited about" here and counsel "fish elsewhere."

Merengue | – | – | – | I |
170 Blue Hill Ave. (Fairbury St.), Roxbury, 617-445-5403;
www.merengerestaurant.com

Bring the family or a gaggle of friends to this cheerful tropical table in Roxbury, where the "beautiful" colorful walls and "delightful" staff set the stage for an island experience; highlighting the Dominican menu are "wonderful" dishes such as fish with coconut sauce and *mofongo* (garlicky mashed plantains), best washed down with a refreshing *batido* (fruit shake).

Meritage | – | – | – | VE |
Boston Harbor Hotel, 70 Rowes Wharf (Atlantic Ave.), 617-439-3995; www.meritagetherestaurant.com

At this modern reincarnation of the waterfront Boston Harbor Hotel's jewel box of a dining room (formerly Rowes Wharf), chef Daniel Bruce indulges his passion for pairing food with wine; his creative, seasonally changing New American menu is organized by type of wine, under such categories as 'sparklers' (ideal with oyster ceviche), 'full-bodied whites' (with, say, lobster in saffron-tomato stew) or 'fruity reds' (pastrami-cured squab, perhaps?); what's more, each dish is available as a small or large plate, the better for oenophiles to sample more well-matched options.

Boston F | D | S | C

Metropolis Cafe 22 | 18 | 19 | $37
584 Tremont St. (bet. Clarendon & Dartmouth Sts.), 617-247-2931
■ While it may "look like a diner", it "feels like home" inside this "adorably" "funky" Eclectic bistro in the South End that seems about the size of a "minivan"; a "small restaurant with a big heart", it appeals with "creative comfort food with a twist" ("don't miss" the "warm chocolate pudding cake"), even if it's so "cramped" you could almost "eat off your neighbor's plate."

Middle East ● 18 | 12 | 14 | $17
472 Mass Ave. (Brookline St.), Cambridge, 617-492-9181; www.mideastclub.com
◪ A "college hangout" that draws a "hip crowd" with a "funkier-than-thou" "punk rock attitude", this "shabby-chic", "late-night" haunt in Central Square is a "mecca" for "local" "live music"; it "just happens" to also feature "wholesome" Middle Eastern food that's "easy on the wallet", though the "basic" grub is an afterthought; P.S. be forewarned that "you'll feel out of place if you're over 25."

Midwest Grill ● 21 | 14 | 20 | $26
1124 Cambridge St. (bet. Elm & Norfolk Sts.), Cambridge, 617-354-7536; www.midwestgrill.com
■ "Pay one price and eat all you can" ("go hungry") at this Brazilian churrascaria near Inman Square, a "carnivore's paradise" where "roving waiters" deliver "huge skewers of meat" "fresh from the grill" to your table in an "unending stream"; it's an "amazing bargain" and a "fun" time – the live samba and bossa nova tunes nightly only add to the "party" atmosphere.

Mike's City Diner 21 | 12 | 18 | $13
1714 Washington St. (Springfield St.), 617-267-9393
■ Offering a "slice of city life" "where hard hats and white coats mingle", this "old-fashioned" "greasy spoon" in the South End harks back to a "different era, before healthy diets and gentrification" became household words; the waitresses who "call you 'hon'" are "always there to refill that coffee" while slinging "all-American breakfasts" and lunches (no dinner); "honest eats at a great price" – no wonder the "lines are out the door on weekends."

Milk Street Cafe ⌀ 18 | 12 | 14 | $13
50 Milk St. (Devonshire St.), 617-542-3663
Post Office Sq. (Congress St.), 617-350-7275
www.milkstreetcafe.com
◪ "When you need to eat a healthy meal but don't feel like depriving" yourself, reviewers recommend this "cafeteria-style" deli for its "fresh vegetarian options", "wholesome kosher" dishes and some of "the best soups in the Financial District"; "there's no real decor or service", and it can get

Boston

F | D | S | C

awfully "crowded between 12 and 2", but it earns two "thumbs up" for purveying a "fast", "cheap" lunch; N.B. the Post Office Square outpost, set in a glass gazebo in the park, is takeout only, and neither branch offers dinner.

Miracle of Science Bar + Grill 17 | 16 | 15 | $16
321 Mass Ave. (State St.), Cambridge, 617-868-2866

◪ Quite the "hot spot for yuppies, graduate students" and "nerds" from nearby MIT, this Central Square watering hole is a "fabulous place to meet a Ph.D."; the "simple menu" of American pub grub "done well" includes "delicious burgers", and the bartenders will "gladly synthesize whatever liquid libation you desire", but note that the digs look eerily like "your eighth-grade chemistry lab" and that it can be "too noisy for anyone with normal hearing – or anyone over 35."

MISTRAL 26 | 25 | 23 | $58
223 Columbus Ave. (bet. Berkeley & Clarendon Sts.), 617-867-9300; www.mistralbistro.com

◪ "Where the elite meet to greet and eat" and where "food and glamour go hand in hand", this "stylish" "see-and-be-seen" "scene" pulls in "sexy" "hipsters" ("plenty of eye candy for both sexes to enjoy") to the South End–Back Bay border, because "you just can't help feeling fabulous" here; Jamie Mammano "continues to produce outstanding", "innovative" Provençal dishes, though some servers seem to "think they're the star attraction."

Monica's 24 | 18 | 21 | $32
143 Richmond St. (bet. Hanover & North Sts.), 617-227-0311

■ "Forget the pile-it-on tourist factories in the North End" and visit instead this "lovely" "local treasure" where the Italian dishes spun with an "imaginative twist" are "made with exquisite care"; the menu is "seasonal", but the "homemade pastas are always a treat", and it's presented in "relaxing" surroundings with original artwork, stained-glass windows and pastel walls; "we almost don't want to let anyone know how wonderful" it is.

Montien 21 | 17 | 20 | $27
63 Stuart St. (Tremont St.), 617-338-5600

■ "For a quick bite before curtain" time, consider this "pleasant", "peaceful" Thai "island" located in the heart of the Theater District; "ask for the menu they reserve for Thai customers for a vicarious visit to Bangkok" and you'll be treated to the "real" deal", and if you tell the "efficient", "accommodating" servers that "you're trying to make a show" they'll be sure to "get you out in time."

Morse Fish ∇ 19 | 3 | 18 | $15
1401 Washington St. (Union Park), 617-262-9375

■ "To satisfy your wish for fish", make waves to this "no-frills" but "mmm good" South End seafood shop where the

get updates at zagat.com 103

Boston   F | D | S | C

"friendly" folks will "perfectly" fry "to order" your choice of specimens; it's "great for what it is", there's "no pretense" at all and it's been catering to the community for more than a century – "how can you not be loyal to this place?"

Morton's of Chicago   25 | 19 | 23 | $56
1 Exeter Plaza (bet. Boylston & Exeter Sts.), 617-266-5858; www.mortons.com

☑ "The steak speaks for itself" at this beef "paradise", the Back Bay link in a "powerhouse" "chain that knows how to do it right"; "you're sure to spot a professional athlete, politician or CEO here" while forking into an "impressive" "cut of meat" delivered by a "solicitous" staff, but skeptics snipe that dining in a "stuffy", "noisy" "basement is less than desirable" – particularly at these "expense-account" prices.

Mother Anna's   22 | 14 | 21 | $27
211 Hanover St. (Cross St.), 617-523-8496; www.motherannas.com

■ "When you get that Sunday night craving for real Italian food like your grandmother used to make", this "friendly" North End "classic" will "hit the spot" with its "big portions" of "old-fashioned" "homestyle" cooking ("try any of the pastas", but "if you haven't had" the signature lobster ravioli "you haven't lived"); given too the "reasonable" prices (the "bill could be twice as much and you'd still leave with a huge smile on your face"), who cares if "Mother needs a face-lift"?

Mount Blue   18 | 19 | 17 | $26
707 Main St. (Central St.), Norwell, 781-659-0050; www.mountblue.com

☑ "Be cool by association" at this "festive", "funky" hangout in Norwell that's "owned in part by Aerosmith" rockers Steven Tyler and Joe Perry (as you'd expect the "great" "live music", Wednesday–Saturday, is a major draw); as for the "Eclectic" menu, groupies "give it points for trying to bring a touch of the city to the suburbs", and though they "want to like it" even they concede it's "lacking."

Mr. & Mrs. Bartley's   23 | 14 | 15 | $13
Burger Cottage ⓈⒻ
1246 Mass Ave. (Plympton St.), Cambridge, 617-354-6559; www.mrbartleys.com

■ "When your inner carnivore is raging", feed it an "amazing hamburger" prepared "any way you want" at this "cheesy", "retro" "college dive" that's "still the undisputed champ" of a patty on a bun (don't miss the "out-of-this-world onion rings" or "great lime rickeys" either); decorated "like a freshman dorm room" and worked by a "plucky" staff, it can be a total "madhouse", but since 1961 this "kitschy" "institution" has been "where Harvard Square 'meats'" – "long may it grill."

Boston   F | D | S | C

Mr. Crepe ⊘   21 | 10 | 14 | $10
83 Holland St. (Thorndike St.), Somerville, 617-628-1500
■ "Watching the crepe maker work his magic" at this Davis Square cafe is "like watching a masterpiece being created", "only in this case" you get to "eat the artwork" – "delightful combinations" of "sweet or savory" tastes wrapped in a delicate pancake; it's "much more interesting than the average sandwich", but beware that these "handcrafted" Eclectic "treats" "take forever" to make, and the "seating area is so small" it should be called "Mr. Cramped."

Mr. Sushi   19 | 13 | 18 | $23
693 Mass Ave. (bet. Central & Water Sts.), Arlington, 781-643-4175
329 Harvard St. (Babcock St.), Brookline, 617-731-1122
■ Ignore the "corny name" and concentrate instead on the "super-fresh sushi" sliced and diced at this "tasty" twosome in Arlington and Brookline, a local "favorite for a quiet night out" thanks to its "relaxing" atmosphere and "affordable" tabs; even if it "can't keep up" with the prime-time Japanese contenders around town, it's just "fine for a beginner" or "when you need a fix."

MuQueCa   – | – | – | I
1093 Cambridge St. (Elm St.), Cambridge, 617-354-3296
Though it's easy to walk right past this modest, wee Inman Square storefront, don't pass it by if you're looking for "authentic" Brazilian food; the "conscientious and attentive owners" take pride in the cuisine of their homeland, and they'll happily explain the specialties to novices, suggesting perhaps their *moqueca,* a Bahian-style seafood stew cooked in a clay pot, washed down with a glass from the natural juice bar.

NAKED FISH   18 | 18 | 17 | $29
Faneuil Hall Mktpl., 16-18 North St. (bet. Congress & Union Sts.), 617-742-3333
15 Middlesex Tpke. (Bedford St.), Billerica, 978-663-6500
725 Cochituate Rd. (Speen St.), Framingham, 508-820-9494
215 Broadway/Rte. 1 N. (bet. Carpenter & Daly Rds.), Lynnfield, 781-586-8300
455 Totten Pond Rd. (3rd Ave.), Waltham, 781-684-0500
95A Turnpike Rd./Rte. 9 (Rte. 30), Westborough, 508-366-5959
www.nakedfish.com
■ "You almost expect" to see "Desi Arnaz" at this "spirited" local chain that gives "fresh" fish a "Cuban flair"; amigos praise the "wide selection" of "well-prepared" dishes, "zany" decor and "rocking" tropical cocktails, but critics crab that though the "tepid flavors" may "appeal to the timid" in Boston, this "bland" "gimmick" "would be laughed out of Miami."

get updates at zagat.com

Boston | F | D | S | C |

Nara ⓢ ▽ 18 | 11 | 11 | $21
85 Wendell St. (Broad St.), 617-338-5935

☑ Some Japanese food junkies are willing to head "off the beaten path" and down a "hard-to-find" Financial District "back alley" to this "hidden" "hole-in-the-wall" to tuck into its "fresh sushi" and other "authentic", "delicately prepared" "standards"; connoisseurs, however, deem the fare "decent but outshined by superior competitors nearby" and deride the decor too ("far from appealing").

Neighborhood Restaurant & Bakery ∌ 21 | 10 | 13 | $14
25 Bow St. (bet. Somerville Ave. & Summer St.), Somerville, 617-623-9710

■ "Bring your appetite" to this "popular" family-owned "hole-in-the-wall" in Somerville for a "behemoth breakfast" or "filling" Portuguese lunch, and "sit outside under the grape arbor" when the weather is fine; the tabs are so "impossibly low" that it draws everyone from "students" to "guys who move furniture for a living", despite the "close quarters" with no frills; P.S. "wish they would open for dinner too."

New Bridge Cafe ∌ 22 | 4 | 13 | $19
650 Washington Ave. (Woodlawn Ave.), Chelsea, 617-884-0134; www.newbridgecafe.com

☑ "How do they offer" such "amazingly" "tempting steak tips" (the "best in the world") or "great BBQ" for "so little money?" marvel meat lovers about this pubby American dump in Chelsea that's long been a "cheap eats" "favorite" in the "neighborhood"; it's "nothing fancy" (in fact, it could use a seriously "major refurbishment"), but nobody can deny that it's "excellent food for the money."

New Ginza 23 | 18 | 21 | $28
63-65 Galen St. (Aldrich Rd.), Watertown, 617-923-2100; www.newginza.net

■ "Part of a new wave of more innovative" Japanese restaurants in the Boston area, this upscale-casual Watertown addition is making a name for itself with its "creative combinations" of "exquisite sushi and sashimi" as well as its "good variety of specialty rolls" ("this is not your typical *tekka maki* kind of place"); if you don't have a yen for raw fish, the menu also offers traditional cooked dishes, all served in an "aesthetically pleasing" room by a "quick" staff that's almost "overly solicitous."

New Jang Su BBQ ▽ 26 | 8 | 17 | $26
260 Cambridge St. (bet. Bedford & Winn Sts.), Burlington, 781-272-3787

■ "All the native Koreans know about" this "authentic BBQ" house in Burlington, and they come to satisfy their "craving" for the "real" deal; bring a gang of "friends to help" cook

Boston

| F | D | S | C |

"heavenly" kalbi and other "tasty" treats right "at your own table"; in short: "lovely food in an unlovely setting."

New Mother India | 20 | 17 | 19 | $21 |
336 Moody St. (Gordon St.), Waltham, 781-893-3311; www.newmotherindia.com

■ "Among the many choices in the area", this "casual, relaxing" Waltham mainstay is a "reliable" pick for Indian "standards" done well, "plus several dishes not seen elsewhere" in the neighborhood; the "extensive" menu and "great beer selection" are delivered by a "pleasant" staff at prices that are always "reasonable", while the "better-than-average" "lunch buffet" is an especially "good deal."

News ❶ | – | – | – | M |
150 Kneeland St. (South St.), 617-426-6397; www.newsboston.com

No Boston diner has ever looked as good as this stylish late-night addition to the Leather District, whose dark woods make the rooms feel more 'banker' than 'breakfast'; while the sprawling menu highlights American comfort foods like eggs and burgers, it also features upscale bar bites, pastas and sushi; and as befits its name, there's even a newsstand up front.

New Shanghai | 23 | 14 | 17 | $21 |
21 Hudson St. (bet. Beach & Kneeland Sts.), 617-338-6688

◪ Turning out "some of the most authentic Shanghainese food" in town, this "consistent" kitchen in the "competitive Chinatown market" remains a "perennial favorite" thanks to "delicious" cooking that "puts many other restaurants to shame"; "with this decor, the food must be great to draw in these crowds", even if the unconvinced shrug "unexciting."

Nightingale | 21 | 21 | 20 | $34 |
578 Tremont St. (bet. Clarendon & Dartmouth Sts.), 617-236-5658

◪ A "terrific new addition to the South End", this rising "star" with an "upscale feel" woos diners with a "wonderful" New American bistro menu of "refreshing" "comfort food" at the "right price"; the "snappy", "contemporary" decor startles some with its "bright" "lime-green walls" and red wood chairs, but the smitten swear "we'd go every night if we lived in the neighborhood"; even those who suggest that it "needs a little refining" "hope" this "energetic" "up-and-comer" "sticks around."

9 Tastes | – | – | – | M |
50 JFK St. (Winthrop St.), Cambridge, 617-547-6666

The owners of Spice Thai Cuisine have opened a spin-off in a revamped basement space in Harvard Square, nicely appointed with traditional Asian fixtures and lots of fresh flowers; the broad menu includes all the expected Bangkok standards, at prices that won't bankrupt a student who's short on baht.

get updates at zagat.com

Boston | F | D | S | C |

No Name ⊘ | 15 | 8 | 14 | $21 |
15 Fish Pier (Northern Ave.), 617-338-7539

☑ "You haven't been to Boston if you haven't been" to this "fun" waterfront "institution" that's "been around as long as the Fish Pier"; if you "overlook the tired surroundings", it's an "unpretentious" pick for "simple seafood", particularly "if you want it fried", but know that it's a "no-frills", "touristy" "tradition that you either love or hate", with those in the latter category sniping "no name, no flavor, no service."

NO. 9 PARK ⌁ | 26 | 23 | 25 | $58 |
9 Park St. (bet. Beacon & Tremont Sts.), 617-742-9991;
www.no9park.com

■ At her "tony" Beacon Hill "class act", "first-rate" chef-owner Barbara Lynch's "impeccable" cooking "sparkles" like the golden dome of the "nearby State House"; she "works magic" with her Country French and Italian dishes, constantly creating "new wonders to experience", while the "talented sommelier" has assembled "one of Boston's most adventurous wine lists"; enhancing the "memorable" experience is the "stylish" setting and "exquisite" service, making a meal "feel like a celebration."

No. 1 Noodle House | – | – | – | I |
51 Langley Rd. (bet. Beacon & Union Sts.), Newton, 617-527-8810

Imagine a Singaporean hawker stall transported to Newton Centre and you'll get a picture of this no-frills Asian noodle house; scan the color photos of dishes posted on the wall, then order at the counter from a menu of Malay classics (such as *mee goreng,* Indian-style fried noodles), along with Chinese and Thai options; the digs may be lacking in atmosphere, but the prices are street-food cheap.

Not Your Average Joe's | 16 | 16 | 16 | $22 |
645 Mass Ave. (Water St.), Arlington, 781-643-1666
105 Chapel St. (bet. Great Plain Ave. & May St.), Needham, 781-453-9300
15 Mazzeo Dr. (West St.), Randolph, 781-961-7200
55 Main St. (Galen St.), Watertown, 617-926-9229
www.notyouraveragejoes.com

☑ "Families love" this "comfortable" quartet where the rooms are done up in a "vibrant" "colorful" style and the "midpriced" American menu (including brick-oven pizzas) offers a "slightly eclectic" "twist on comfort food"; critics, though, who conclude "less than average, Joe", cite food that "doesn't always hit the mark" (nor does it "go out on a creative limb") and service that equally "runs hot or cold."

OAK ROOM | 25 | 27 | 26 | $59 |
Fairmont Copley Plaza, 138 St. James Ave. (bet. Dartmouth & Trinity Sts.), 617-267-5300

■ "If you're looking to romance a carnivore", take "your significant other" to this "upper-crust" dining room at the

Boston   F | D | S | C

Fairmont Copley Plaza, one of "the most elegant spots in Boston"; the Traditional American menu showcases some of the "best steaks in town", proffered in "opulent" environs by a "top-notch" staff that treats you "like royalty"; it's "worth the splurge" for "discerning" patrons "who want to spoil themselves" – who cares if Back Bay "hipsters" find it a "bit stuffy"?

O Cantinho   ▽ 19 | 16 | 20 | $14
1128 Cambridge St. (bet. Columbia & Prospect Sts.), Cambridge, 617-354-3443; www.atasca.com

■ Even "picky foodniks from NY" are "pleasantly surprised" to discover this tiny, "delightful nook in Inman Square", a "perfect neighborhood" cafe that's "still kind of a secret"; the "tasty" Portuguese fare is "wonderful" and "really cheap", and the servers "so sweet" that those in-the-know are "reluctant to tell people about it."

Oceana   ▽ 20 | 21 | 20 | $42
Boston Marriott Long Wharf, 296 State St. (Atlantic Ave.), 617-227-0800

◪ Red, white and blue, with an "excellent" harbor view too sums up the crisp, nautical style featured at this spacious Marriott Long Wharf dining room (designed like a cruise ship); the seafood-slanted American menu is "nothing special", though supporters say the Sunday brunch buffet offers "lots of variety and good quality"; still, the consensus is that "given its location, it should be a destination – it's not", so "with all the other choices in town, you're better off going somewhere else."

Ocean Wealth   21 | 9 | 14 | $21
8 Tyler St. (Beach St.), 617-423-1338

■ "Go with a group for maximum sampling" of the "wealth of fresh seafood" offered at this "authentic", late-night (till 4 AM) Chinese "haven" in Chinatown, where "regulars just ignore" the lack of atmosphere, since "their faces are in the food, enjoying every bite"; though it helps to bring "someone fluent in Cantonese cuisine", otherwise just "point to other tables and order what they're having."

O'Fado   ▽ 21 | 14 | 21 | $25
72 Walnut St. (Harris St.), Peabody, 978-531-7369

◪ "Flavorful from start to finish", this "authentic" fixture is a "treasure for Portuguese cuisine in Peabody"; "don't miss the pork or shellfish dishes" – "just like those served in Lisbon" – best washed down with "wine poured from stoneware pitchers"; it's a "real find in a city proud of its diversity", though doubters deem it "not great."

Oga   25 | 21 | 22 | $35
915 Worcester Rd./Rte. 9 (Rte. 27), Natick, 508-653-4338

■ A "welcome addition to MetroWest", this Natick "gem" serves some of the most "creative and delicious" Japanese

get updates at zagat.com

Boston | F | D | S | C |

cuisine "in the area"; "if you love sushi, you'll love" chef-owner Toru Oga's "awesome", "spectacularly presented" specimens, which highlight "innovative offerings" that are "hard to come by" elsewhere; furthermore, the "lovely, modern" room has "great feng shui" (and sure "beats the view of the traffic on Route 9").

OISHII | 29 | 13 | 19 | $34 |

612 Hammond St. (Boylston St.), Chestnut Hill, 617-277-7888
Mill Village, 365 Boston Post Rd./Rte. 20 (Concord Rd.), Sudbury, 978-440-8300

■ Even "sushi snobs" agree that the "heaven on rice" at this "tiny" twosome in Chestnut Hill and Sudbury is the "best" in the state – in fact, with the "freshest fish in town", it was voted No. 1 for Food in the Boston area; the "creative maki and hand rolls are exceptional", "taking a favorite item to a whole new level", while the omakase extravaganza elicits a chorus of "oh my Gods"; the "seating is sardine-like" to the extreme, but it's "worth the wait to watch the chef create works of art" that rival even "Nobu's."

OLEANA | 26 | 21 | 22 | $41 |

134 Hampshire St. (bet. Columbia & Prospect Sts.), Cambridge, 617-661-0505

■ "Carried away on a magic carpet ride" of "exotic" Mediterranean flavors, enchanted enthusiasts of this "delightful" spot near Inman Square exclaim it's "as though our taste buds won the lottery"; indeed, chef-partner Ana Sortun is clearly "not afraid to challenge your palate", and she "succeeds with" "well-conceived" dishes that evoke the "warmth of sun-soaked" climes; the atmosphere indoors is "sophisticated, yet warm and comfortable", though the hot tables are out on the patio that feels like an urban "oasis."

Olé, Mexican Grill | 22 | 18 | 19 | $23 |

203A Broadway (bet. Adams & Foster Sts.), Arlington, 781-643-2299 *S*
11 Springfield St. (bet. Beacon & Cambridge Sts.), Cambridge, 617-492-4495
www.olearlington.com

■ Colorful and "festive", this pair of "absolute charmers" in Inman Square and Arlington is well known for its "real", "gourmet" Mexican food, from the "*muy bien*" "guacamole made fresh at tableside" to the "mouthwatering" entrees napped with "rich, complex sauces"; add "friendly, fast service" and "superb value" for the peso and you have the recipe for a "great night out."

OLIO *S* | 27 | 16 | 23 | $44 |

655 Washington St. (Rte. 128, exit 2A), Canton, 781-821-2396; www.oliorestaurant.com

■ "Lucky Canton" – though chef-owner Paul Turano is now in charge, this "exquisite" "gem" "hasn't skipped a

Boston

beat"; the New American fare is still "on par with the best Downtown restaurants", making grateful guests glad to have "such a quality" "find" south of Boston, while the service is "casual yet professional"; the olive-green surroundings are "relaxing", though with only 30 seats, it's not much bigger than a "sardine can."

OLIVES   25 | 21 | 21 | $50

10 City Sq. (Main St.), Charlestown, 617-242-1999; www.toddenglish.com

☑ Celebrity chef Todd English's "empire started here" in "charming" Charlestown years ago, but groupies of his Mediterranean "flagship" gush that this "bustling scene" "still wows"; "like the circus", his "complicated" dishes have so "many things going on" that it can get a "little overwhelming", though fans insist that his "layers and layers" of flavors are "always an awesome experience"; brace yourself too for the "unbearable noise" produced in the "too-tight quarters", despite the opinion of some scenesters who snipe that it "lacks the old buzz."

On the Park   23 | 16 | 20 | $33

1 Union Park (Shawmut Ave.), 617-426-0862

☑ Admirers "love the simplicity" of this "unpretentious" "little" "neighborhood bistro" that may be one of the "biggest bangs for your dining dollar in the South End"; it "doesn't look like much from the outside", so it may be "easy to miss", but inside is a warm, "cozy" room where a "personable" staff brings to table "wonderful" New American dishes; "adding to the pleasure of the meal is a tame noise level that allows you to converse", so even if a few grouse that it "isn't keeping up" with the "great places" nearby, most feel it's "underrated."

Orleans ●   19 | 19 | 16 | $30

65 Holland St. (Wallace St.), Somerville, 617-591-2100

■ "Sip a martini and lounge on a plush sofa" at this Somerville bistro that manages to be both "chic" and "comfortable"; it's a "great place to hang out", particularly "in the summer, when the windows are open", though at any time the "well-executed" New American fare is "better than you may expect"; a "nice addition" to the area, it obviously has "potential."

Osushi   – | – | – | M

Westin Copley Place, 10 Huntington Ave. (Dartmouth St.), 617-266-2788; www.osushirestaurant.com

It's all sushi all the time at this small but smart Back Bay Japanese newcomer housed on the second level of the Westin Copley Place; snag a seat at the teeny counter or at one of the handful of tables (the best look out over Dartmouth Street) scattered in the stylish red-and-black room and order up raw fish in all its glory.

Boston

| | F | D | S | C |

Other Side Cosmic Cafe ◐ ⊄   20 | 14 | 14 | $13
407 Newbury St. (Mass Ave.), 617-536-9477

■ Like a "transplant from the West Coast", this "cosmically cool" American cafe "hidden away" at the far end of Newbury Street in the Back Bay is an "arty", "vegetarian-friendly" retreat that's ideal when you're in the mood to "people-watch" while "drinking a smoothie" and "grabbing some munchies" amid "hippies and other funky types"; and, get this, the "juice bar" offers both "wheat-grass shots" and 50 kinds of beer.

Out of the Blue ⊄   23 | 11 | 20 | $22
382 Highland Ave. (Cutter Ave.), Somerville, 617-776-5020; www.outofthebluerestaurant.com

■ While it "may not look fabulous", this "casual" "little" Italian seafood house in Davis Square "does it right", turning out "large portions" of "surprisingly" "delicious", "fresh" fish dishes and "terrific" pastas in an aquatic-themed room decorated with "entertaining murals"; the service is "extremely friendly" and the prices "very fair", leading denizens to conclude "understated but overachieving."

Pagliuca's   20 | 11 | 18 | $26
14 Parmenter St. (Hanover St.), 617-367-1504

◪ "You won't leave hungry or poor" when you dine at this "old-school" North End standby where the "portions are enormous" but the "prices are not"; expect "simple" Italian cooking "typical" of traditional neighborhood ristorantes ("before the yuppies hit town"), served in an "informal", "homey" atmosphere that makes it a "great place to bring the family"; if a few feel it "isn't memorable", lots of mouths happily "keep coming back for more."

Palm   19 | 17 | 19 | $48
Westin Copley Place, 200 Dartmouth St. (bet. St. James Ave. & Stuart St.), 617-867-9292; www.thepalm.com

◪ A "shrine to expense-account dining", this clubby temple of meat at the Westin Copley Place rustles up "huge steaks" for "gents" on a "business lunch or dinner"; the "quality is consistent" and the "caricatures on the walls" lend some character, but critical carnivores complain that this "soulless" "chain" feels like a "stuffy old boys' club."

Paolo's Trattoria ⌀   22 | 20 | 21 | $28
251 Main St. (Lawnwood Ave.), Charlestown, 617-242-7229

■ "Homemade everything" served in a "warm", "casual environment" by a staff that "aims to please" makes this "cute", "unpretentious" trattoria with a "family feel" "one of Charlestown's better deals"; the "wonderfully rustic" Italian menu (including "fantastic wood-oven pizzas") is accented with the Mediterranean flavors of the chef's Greek heritage, resulting in "excellent" dishes like lamb al Greco, though a few hard-to-please types find it "lacking."

Boston   F | D | S | C

Papa Razzi   17 | 16 | 16 | $27
*271 Dartmouth St. (bet. Boylston & Newbury Sts.),
617-536-9200
2 Wall St. (Rte. 3A), Burlington, 781-229-0100
Cambridgeside Galleria, 100 Cambridgeside Pl. (bet. 1st St. &
Land Blvd.), Cambridge, 617-577-0009
The Mall at Chestnut Hill, 199 Boylston St.
(Hammond Pond Pkwy.), Chestnut Hill, 617-527-6600
768 Elm St. (Concord Tpke./Rte. 2), Concord, 978-371-0030
Merchants Row, 2087 Washington St. (Rte. 123), Hanover,
781-982-2800
16 Washington St. (Rte. 128, exit 21), Wellesley,
781-235-4747
www.backbayrestaurantgroup.com*

"After a hard day of shopping" or for a "dependable" supper out any time "you don't feel like cooking", "satisfy" your appetite at these "kid"-friendly Italian trattorias that may be "as good as it gets for a chain"; though it's "nothing to write home about", the food is "surprisingly" "well done, if predictable" (hard to go wrong with the "tasty" wood-fired thin-crust pizzas), the setting is "comfy", the service is "usually good" and the tabs "won't break the bank."

Parish Cafe ●   21 | 13 | 15 | $20
361 Boylston St. (Arlington St.), 617-247-4777

Banking on a "clever idea", this "cool" American cafe in the Back Bay has found a niche for itself by offering "delicious sandwiches" made from recipes "created by the best chefs in the city"; it's a "fun place" "for a nosh with friends", you can get a "civilized meal even at 1 AM" and the patio is "kicking in the summer" – "too bad the service isn't better."

Parker's   ▽ 17 | 20 | 17 | $37
*Omni Parker House, 60 School St. (Tremont St.), 617-227-8600;
www.omniparkerhouse.com*

"History" buffs hail this "old Boston" landmark at the 1856 Omni Parker House, home of the "famous" Parker House rolls, baked scrod and Boston cream pie (which adherents insist is still "out of this world"); beyond these enduring favorites, though, the classic New England menu is quite "average", while the service is "as quick as a turtle", leading critics to lament what a "waste of a beautiful room."

Passage to India   ▽ 21 | 11 | 19 | $17
*1900 Mass Ave. (Somerville Ave.), Cambridge, 617-497-6113;
www.passageindia.com*

■ Despite its "utilitarian" setting in an "unprepossessing storefront" in Porter Square, this "consistently good" – and "good value" – "sentimental favorite" "makes some of the more flavorful Indian dishes around"; the staff is particularly "accommodating and gracious", always "treating you royally", and the all-you-can-eat lunch buffet is a bargain.

Boston F | D | S | C

Peach Farm ◐   22 | 8 | 16 | $20
4 Tyler St. (Beach St.), 617-482-1116

■ Ignore the "cramped quarters" at this "basement" dive in Chinatown and zero in on "genuine" "Hong Kong–style" dishes, especially "amazing seafood" "entrees you won't see everywhere else" (think frogs with garlic); "some of the best items are written on the wall", so ask the "waiter to translate" or bring friends who speak the language; as a bonus, it's open till 3 AM.

Peking Cuisine   20 | 12 | 21 | $19
10 Tyler St. (bet. Beach & Kneeland Sts.), 617-542-5857
870 Walnut St. (Beacon St.), Newton, 617-969-0888

☑ At this Chinatown Chinese, the staff is like a "well-oiled machine and it'll get you out before the office even notices that you've gone on a lunch break", while the Newton Centre offshoot is "frequented by families", particularly on "too-tired-to-cook evenings"; despite "some misses" on the menu, both branches are "friendly", "unassuming" spots that "deliver" generally "tasty" Chinese food.

Pellino's   25 | 16 | 20 | $40
261 Washington St. (bet. Atlantic Ave. & Pleasant St.), Marblehead, 781-631-3344; www.pellinos.com

☑ "One of the better dining establishments north of Boston", this "romantic" "find" "brings a touch of the North End" to seaside Marblehead; "you feel that each dish" on the "superb", ever-changing Northern Italian menu is "made especially for you", and there's a "terrific" wine list to boot – if only the digs weren't so "cramped."

Penang ◐   22 | 18 | 17 | $22
685 Washington St. (Kneeland St.), 617-451-6373
57 JFK St. (bet. Eliot & Winthrop Sts.), Cambridge, 617-234-3988

☑ With its "consistently excellent renditions of a complex cuisine", this "crowd-pleasing" duo helped "put Malaysian fare on the Boston map"; whether you opt for the "tiki hut" setting of the Chinatown locale or the "trendy industrial" environs of the Harvard Square branch, "be adventurous" and sample the menu's "exotic combinations of flavors" (regulars recommend "go with a big group" to "try more dishes"), but beware that "popularity" has its price (read: prepare for a "mob" scene).

P.F. Chang's China Bistro   20 | 19 | 18 | $26
8 Park Plaza (bet. Boylston & Stuart Sts.), 617-573-0821; www.pfchangs.com

☑ "Embarrassing" to admit, "but we love" the "new spin" on Chinese food taken by this "Disney-esque" franchise in the Theater District say sheepish supporters; "don't expect authentic", though the "jazzed-up", "Americanized" chow (the famous "lettuce wraps are a must") has plenty of fans,

Boston　　　　　　　　　　　　　　　　F | D | S | C |

so expect "long waits, especially before show time"; purists who avoid this "homogenized chain", however, choose to "walk a couple of blocks to Chinatown" for the real thing.

Phoenicia　　　　　　　　　　　　　15 | 9 | 14 | $19 |
240 Cambridge St. (Garden St.), 617-523-4606
☑ In the mood for "something different"? – loyalists say it's "worth the trip" to this "out-of-the-way" dive on the back side of Beacon Hill for "solid", "reliable" Lebanese cooking at "very reasonable" prices; dissenters, however, who feel it "could be better", find the "uninspired" food "not overly flavorful or interesting."

Pho Hoa　　　　　　　　　　　∇ 17 | 8 | 11 | $14 |
17 Beach St. (Washington St.), 617-423-3934
1356 Dorchester Ave. (Kimball St.), Dorchester, 617-287-9746
www.phohoa.com
☑ Though "not for vegetarians", "if you're hungry and adventurous", this pair of "neighborhood" Vietnamese "joints" will fortify you with "movie theater–sized bowls" of "good and cheap" pho; part of an international chain of noodle soup shops, the Dorchester link is set in Boston's "largest Vietnamese community", while the Chinatown branch brings the same "authentic" menu (which "helpfully explains it all") to the city center, but detractors find it merely "serviceable."

Pho Lemon Grass　　　　　　　　22 | 18 | 20 | $20 |
239 Harvard St. (Webster St.), Brookline, 617-731-8600
☑ "Only in Brookline would they have an expensive pho joint" perhaps, but this Coolidge Corner Vietnamese does "maintain consistently high standards", offering "fresh", "delicious" dishes (the namesake beef noodle soup is especially "great on a cold winter day") and "nice" ambiance; hotheads dismiss the fare as too "bland", but clearly the "muted flavors play well to this suburban crowd."

PHO PASTEUR　　　　　　　　　23 | 13 | 17 | $18 |
119 Newbury St. (bet. Clarendon & Dartmouth Sts.), 617-262-8200
123 Stuart St. (Tremont St.), 617-742-2436
682 Washington St. (Beach St.), 617-482-7467
137 Brighton Ave. (Harvard Ave.), Allston, 617-783-2340
35 Dunster St. (Mt. Auburn St.), Cambridge, 617-864-4100
Atrium Mall, 300 Boylston St. (Florence St.), Chestnut Hill, 617-928-0900
☑ "Pure aromatherapy", the "huge bowls of" "fragrant", "steaming soup" prepared at this "local" sextet "inspire regular cravings" ("fortunately, addicts can choose from among multiple locations"); it "deserves kudos" for giving Boston a "sensational" taste of Vietnam's "delectable delights", served by a "zippy" staff that delivers "food in a flash" in digs that "aren't intimidating" for first-timers; the

Boston | F | D | S | C |

Pho République ◐   21 | 22 | 19 | $28 |
1415 Washington St. (Union Park), 617-262-0005
☑ "Add a few scorpion bowls and you never know what will happen" at this "trendy" South End "see-and-be-seen" scene that "sizzles with energy"; the opium-den couches, neon lanterns and "naughty red lighting" give it a "Sin City aura" (sort of like a "funky" "stage set of *Miss Saigon*"), forming an "exotic" backdrop for "unique" Vietnamese-inspired bites that "rock", but if you're looking for authentic cooking, go "elsewhere."

Piattini   21 | 18 | 19 | $29 |
226 Newbury St. (bet. Exeter & Fairfield Sts.), 617-536-2020
☑ The kind of place that could easily become a "regular after-work destination", this "tiny" "jewel" on Newbury Street specializes in the eponymous piattini, "tapas-style" small plates that are a "fun way to do Italian"; accompany the dishes with an "interesting" "wine flight (the perfect takeoff)", and get "comfortable" in the "cozy" quarters with "no attitude"; it's a "great concept" for the Back Bay, even if the food is a bit "uneven."

Picante Mexican Grill   18 | 11 | 13 | $11 |
735 Mass Ave. (bet. Inman & Prospect Sts.), Cambridge, 617-576-6394
217 Elm St. (bet. Cutter & Grove Sts.), Somerville, 617-628-6394
www.picantemex.com
☑ "Fresh, flavorful" and "filling" Cal-Mex fare makes this "inexpensive" twosome in Central and Davis Squares a "reliable bet"; the "yummy" burritos "always hit the mark" and the "cool salsa bar" includes some of the "best *pico de gallo* in Boston" ("be sure to try the exceptional limeade" too), but the "spare" decor and "fast-foodish" atmosphere lead some reviewers to "recommend takeout."

Piccola Venezia   18 | 18 | 19 | $24 |
263 Hanover St. (bet. Cross & Richmond Sts.), 617-523-3888
☑ "Bring visiting relatives" "looking for the traditional" to this "family"-friendly Italian throwback in the North End for "huge portions" of "basic" "red-sauce" fare at "affordable prices"; "homey touches abound", from the "warm, advice-giving" servers to the "old-world" setting, but detractors deride the "predictable" dishes as for "tourists" only and ask "with phenomenal spots within 50 yards away, why even bother?"

Piccolo Nido ⑤   ∇ 22 | 18 | 22 | $31 |
257 North St. (Lewis St.), 617-742-4272; www.piccolonido.com
☑ "Hear Italian spoken all the time" at this "cozy little" trattoria tucked a bit "out of the way" in the North End,

Boston | F | D | S | C |

"one of the warmest places around"; amid rustic quarters with a "family feel", tuck into "excellent", homestyle dishes (the risotto is "fantastic") that are "definitely a cut above many others" in the neighborhood, but those who find it "inconsistent" lament "not as good as we had hoped."

Pigalle | 26 | 21 | 24 | $54 |

75 S. Charles St. (bet. Stuart St. & Warrenton Pl.), 617-423-4944

■ "Ooh-la-la", "this is a winner" coo devotees of this "top-notch" "performer" in the Theater District, a "sophisticated" bistro that's a "testament to doing it right"; Marc Orfaly "really cares" about pleasing his guests, which he does "beautifully" well by "seductively" putting a "contemporary twist" on the French classics; his "outstanding" creations are turned out by a "smart, well-informed" staff in an "intimate" room, a "romantic hideaway" that's best enjoyed with "someone you love"; "bravo!"

Pinang | – | – | – | M |

Faneuil Hall Mktpl. (bet. Chatham & Clinton Sts.), 617-227-6866; www.pinangfavor.com

Not to be confused with the similarly named Penang, this Faneuil Hall newcomer scored some prime real estate at one corner of Quincy Market, the better to showcase still-novel-in-Boston Malaysian fare; expect a big, open room with quarry tile floors, floor-to-ceiling windows and a spacious patio on which to scope out the passing pedestrian parade; early enthusiasts only wonder is the food or the people-watching more spicy?

Pit Stop Bar-B-Q ∉ | ∇ 21 | 4 | 16 | $14 |

888 Morton St. (Evans St.), Mattapan, 617-436-0485

■ "Friendly" folks run this "literal hole-in-the-wall" (it's such a "little shed" that "if you blink you might miss it") in Mattapan that "never disappoints" with its "fabulous" Southern BBQ; the "ribs are amazing", slathered with the "best – no contest" "tangy sauce" (the "coleslaw deserves accolades" too), but note that with only four seats it's largely a "take-out" operation; P.S. "open Thursday–Saturday."

Pizzeria Regina ∉ | 24 | 9 | 13 | $14 |

226 Faneuil Hall Mktpl. (Thatcher St.), 617-227-8180
11½ Thatcher St. (N. Margin St.), 617-227-0765
Auburn Mall, 385 Southbridge St. (Auburn St.), Auburn, 508-721-0090
South Shore Plaza, 250 Granite St. (I-95, exit 6), Braintree, 781-848-8700
Burlington Mall, 1131 Middlesex Tpke. (Rte. 128), Burlington, 781-270-4212
101 Independence Mall Way (Raboth Rd.), Kingston, 781-585-6444

(continued)

Boston | F | D | S | C |

(continued)
Pizzeria Regina
Solomon Pond Mall, 580 Donald Lynch Blvd. (River Rd. W.), Marlborough, 508-303-6999
■ "You can't beat this little slice of heaven on a plate" avow worshipers of this Boston "landmark" that makes just about the "best" "old-fashioned" pizzas "in town"; "go to the North End location for the real experience" (the other branches "aren't as good" as the "original"), though if you "hesitate a nanosecond while ordering" expect some "abuse" from the "sassy" staff (the "brusque" treatment is "part of the charm"); the decor "hasn't changed since our parents were dating", but "if pizza is a religion, Regina is God."

Plaza Garibaldi   ▽ | 18 | 18 | 23 | $26 |
1141 Revere Beach Pkwy. (bet. Broadway & Rte. 1), Revere, 781-284-6005
☑ "For a fun night out", "bring a large party" to this "lively" Latin nightclub in the "highly unlikely location" of Revere, which features an extensive tequila selection and a strolling "mariachi band" on weekends; the Mexican food may be just "ok", but the "music is a treat."

Plaza III - | 21 | 18 | 19 | $48 |
The Kansas City Steakhouse
Faneuil Hall Mktpl., 101 S. Market St. (Merchants Row), 617-720-5570; www.plazaiii.com
☑ "If it's a good steak you want" "close to Downtown", this bi-level Midwestern import is "one of the better choices at Faneuil Hall" for a "dependable" all-American meal; it's "not the Capital Grille, but it is a "less expensive" "place to go for big red meat" "with all the fixings", though critics charge that other than its "prime location", there's "nothing noteworthy about it" ("adequate" but "typical").

Polcari's | 16 | 15 | 16 | $23 |
92 Broadway/Rte. 1N (Walnut St.), Saugus, 781-233-3765
309 Montvale Ave. (bet. Central & Washington Sts.), Woburn, 781-938-1900
☑ "Bring a hearty appetite" to tackle "generous portions" of Italian food that's "better than your average chain"; it's "festive" and "family friendly", though to some it feels like a "theme park" ("Little Italy Land"), while foes urge avoid the "disappointing" food (except for the pies brought in from Pizzeria Regina) and "go to the North End instead."

Pomodoro ⊄ | 24 | 11 | 18 | $30 |
319 Hanover St. (bet. Prince & Richmond Sts.), 617-367-4348
☑ "You can barely move" inside this "closet-like" "hole-in-the-wall" in the North End that's the ultimate in "no frills" – no reservations, no credit cards, "no bathroom" even (!); the "wine list consists of 'we got red, we got white'", and there are only 24 seats (expect a "wait"), but the "incredible"

118   subscribe to zagat.com

Boston F D S C

Italian cooking "packs such a punch" that it makes it all "completely worth it"; ignore everything else – "come for the food, period."

Ponte Vecchio ▽ 24 | 16 | 22 | $37
435 Newbury St. (Topsfield Fairgrounds), Danvers, 978-777-9188
■ "Good for a special occasion", this Danvers ristorante has long been a North Shore favorite for "fine" "old-fashioned" Italian dining; "don't confuse the staff's formality with stuffiness" – "it's just the European style" – though if the "authentic" fare is "what you come for" but you're looking for a more "casual" meal, the "pleasant" wine bar and cafe next door (under the same ownership) is "just as good" – without the "white tablecloths."

Porcini's 20 | 15 | 19 | $29
68 School St. (Arsenal St.), Watertown, 617-924-2221; www.porcinis.com
■ "Oh my, these guys can cook" exclaim enthusiasts of the "excellent" Italian kitchen at this "underrated", "out-of-the-way place" in Watertown that's ideal "for suburbanites who want a nice evening out without going Downtown"; those in-the-know who appreciate that they "can always get a table", even out on the "cute patio on a summer night", are understandably "reluctant to recommend" this "most pleasant find."

Pravda 116 ⑤ 15 | 21 | 15 | $35
116 Boylston St. (bet. Charles & Tremont Sts.), 617-482-7799; www.pravda116.com
☑ "If you consider vodka a main course", you'll feel right at home hanging around the "impressive ice bar" at this "swanky" Theater District nightclub (better "wear black and be cool", though); the "international crowd" "comes for the scene" (and to "take itself a bit too seriously"), but certainly not for the New American menu, which just "doesn't cut it."

Prezza ⑤ 26 | 22 | 23 | $48
24 Fleet St. (Hanover St.), 617-227-1577; www.prezza.com
■ "Not your typical red-sauce joint", this "surprisingly urbane" ristorante "feels more like Manhattan" than the North End, and it turns out "modern" Italian fare (don't pass up the "handmade pastas") so "fabulous" that it's "too good" to waste on a "first date" ("save it for the second"); backed by a "superior wine list", "appealing" decor and "polished, cordial" service, it adds up to a "place you want to visit again and again"; any wonder that fans "would swim across the Charles" for a dinner here?

Prose 22 | 11 | 15 | $33
352A Mass Ave. (Wyman Terrace), Arlington, 781-648-2800
☑ As the chef "changes" the "experimental" New American menu "daily" to best take advantage of "local, seasonal

Boston

F | D | S | C

ingredients", a meal at this "tiny", "personal" ("eccentric", even), "neighborhood-y" "alternative" in Arlington is "always" a "refreshing" "surprise"; don't come "if you're in a hurry, because like Heinz ketchup it's s-l-o-w good", and even if some find that "it sometimes works and sometimes doesn't", at least the experience is "interesting."

Punjab
24 | 17 | 19 | $20

473 Mass Ave. (bet. Medford St. & Swan Pl.), Arlington, 781-643-0943; www.punjabfoods.net

■ Regulars "hope it stays a well-kept local secret", but the "Saturday night lines indicate otherwise" at this Arlington "storefront" "gem"; clearly, the "word is out" about the "absolutely delectable" Indian food "prepared to order" here – "aromatic", "spicy" and "addicting" (the "superb" "naan bread takes the cake", though the chicken tikka masala is "out of this world" too) – and served by a "helpful" staff, which "makes up for" the "cramped quarters."

Punjabi Dhaba ●⊄
23 | 5 | 13 | $10

225 Hampshire St. (Cambridge St.), Cambridge, 617-547-8272

■ At this "roadside cafe", expect a "bustling", "cafeteria-style" setting replete with "Hindi music pumping" and a "constant loop of Indian movies" on the "overhead TV"; despite the "very basic" digs, the Indian "fast food" is "excellent", "authentic" and "generously portioned"; for "cheap eats" in Inman Square, "this is the place to go."

Purple Cactus Burrito & Wrap Bar
16 | 11 | 15 | $9

674 Centre St. (Seaverns Ave.), Jamaica Plain, 617-522-7422

◪ When you're jonesing for a "big burrito on the cheap" or just want to "grab a bite" on a night "when you don't feel like cooking", this Jamaica Plain standby can hit the spot with its "fresh", "reasonably healthy" Californian-Mexican burritos and wraps; boosters cheer that lots of "tasty noshing options abound" on the menu, but opponents find it "hit-or-miss."

RADIUS ⌀
26 | 25 | 25 | $62

8 High St. (bet. Federal & Summer Sts.), 617-426-1234; www.radiusrestaurant.com

■ "Feel like a master of the universe" at this "sumptuous experience" in the Financial District that "everyone should indulge in"; Michael Schlow "deserves to wear the tall hat", because his "cutting-edge" New French interpretations are "exquisite"; "top-notch" "across the board", it pulls in a "stylish crowd" and power "suits" with its "high-energy", "minimalist" design and "professional" service; "be prepared to drop some dough", but dinner here is "not just a meal – it's an event", and it's "one of the best in the city."

Boston F D S C

Raffael's ▽ 19 | 21 | 21 | $29
State Street Complex, 7th fl., 1 Enterprise Dr. (Newport Ave.), North Quincy, 617-328-1600; www.raffaels.com
☒ Affording a "great" "view of the Boston skyline" through "lots of windows", this "elegant" establishment "tucked away" in an office building in North Quincy satisfies some South Shore surveyors who "want a night out" without "driving into the city"; naysayers, however, who feel it's "ripe for a change", nix the "pedestrian" Italian-Continental dishes ("expensive for the quality").

Rangoli 24 | 15 | 19 | $21
129 Brighton Ave. (Harvard Ave.), Allston, 617-562-0200; www.rangoliboston.com
■ A "must for those willing to adventure" into "unusual" Southern Indian cooking, this Allston "gem" is the place to go "when you need a dosa fix"; the extensive menu offers "lots" of "unique" dishes "you don't encounter" at its competitors, all "unfailingly delicious" and delivered by an "efficient" staff at "reasonable prices" – just don't mind the "far from inspiring" setting.

Real Pizza ⊄ 22 | 7 | 13 | $15
359 Huron Ave. (Fayerweather St.), Cambridge, 617-497-4497
■ "Like Perrier to a man in the desert", the "gourmet pizzas" baked at this yuppie pie parlor (owned by Hi-Rise Bread Co.'s Rene Becker) near Fresh Pond are "totally satisfying"; addicts "can't resist" the "yummy crusts" topped with "innovative" "combinations" of "fresh ingredients", but note that since the joint has only a few seats, "most of the business is takeout"; be warned too of the "hefty price tags."

Redbones BBQ ⊄ 23 | 14 | 18 | $20
55 Chester St. (Elm St.), Somerville, 617-628-2200; www.redbones.com
■ "If you like pig or cow, you can't go wrong" at this "hopping" "institution" in Somerville, known for serving up "finger-licking good" BBQ in the "funkiest of digs"; "wash down" the "monstrous portions" of "divine" Memphis-style ribs with "one of the many beers on tap" or a "jar of lemonade"; "sadly, it's no secret", so "be prepared to camp out for a table", but this "heaven for homesick Southerners" will make you "want to yell yee-haw!"

Red Fez ☽ 17 | 19 | 17 | $30
1222 Washington St. (bet. E. Berkeley & Waltham Sts.), 617-338-6060; www.theredfez.com
☒ Recently reborn in the South End, this "trendy den" that first opened in 1940 is "giving off groovy vibes" to a whole new generation of "hipsters"; it's the latest "'in' place" for mingling with the "beautiful people" in "dark, private"-feeling surroundings (the "back deck is a must on warm

get updates at zagat.com

Boston | F | D | S | C |

summer nights") while nibbling off "yummy" "meze plates" from the Middle Eastern–Mediterranean menu that was built for "sharing"; it's "full of exotic flavor", but still, hard-to-please sorts "were hoping for more."

Redline | 15 | 17 | 16 | $22 |
59 JFK St. (bet. Eliot & Winthrop Sts.), Cambridge, 617-491-9851; www.redlinecambridge.com
Attracting "students" and "twentysomethings", this "happening" "joint" in Harvard Square is a "friendly enough" gathering place to "hang out with friends and have some drinks"; the New American menu "aspires to something" "higher" than the standard pub grub, even if it "inevitably falls flat", but be warned that the "bar scene" is way "louder than any Red Line train."

Red Raven ∇ | 26 | 23 | 23 | $31 |
75 Congress St. (Derby St.), Salem, 978-745-8558; www.redravensalem.com
■ "What fun!" – "like eating a gourmet dinner in a Salvador Dalí painting" cheer fans of this "unique place" in Salem that's always "full of surprises"; "you'll never meet friendlier people" than those who populate this "funky", "sexy", over-the-top space, enjoying "eclectic", "first-rate" New American dishes and sipping specialty 'noodletini' cocktails (a "must-have, but only if you've appointed a designated driver"); "long live the Raven."

Red Rock Bistro | 20 | 22 | 19 | $39 |
141 Humphrey St./Rte. 129 (Redington St.), Swampscott, 781-595-1414
The "smashing view of the Boston skyline" from every table is the obvious reason to visit this contemporary "bistro by the sea" that some North Shore neighbors assert is a "treasure on the water in Swampscott", though the New American fare is generally "well prepared" (particularly the "great fish" dishes); the "live jazz" on weekends is a swell touch, but the unimpressed are "taken aback by such prices" for "too hit-or-miss" food.

Red Sauce ∇ | 18 | 16 | 18 | $22 |
48 Whiting St./Rte. 53 (Rte. 228), Hingham, 781-740-0880
1114 Beacon St. (Walnut St.), Newton, 617-965-0110
516 Adams St. (Barry St.), Quincy, 617-745-9700
343 Arsenal St. (Arlington St.), Watertown, 617-924-6400
www.nakedrestaurants.com
Joey Crugnale, the entrepreneur "who started Bertucci's and the Naked Fish", has come up with yet another "new chain of restaurants", with the concept of serving "real" Italian food in a "relaxing" family-friendly setting at "very affordable prices"; some early reports call it a "good try" (at least "you know what you're going to get"), but skeptics shrug "nothing special" (feels too "formulaic").

Boston   F | D | S | C

Restaurante Cesaria   – | – | – | I
266 Bowdoin St. (bet. Hamilton & Quincy Sts.), Dorchester, 617-282-1998; www.restaurantecesaria.com
Unusually classy for the otherwise modest neighborhood, this attractive Dorchester newcomer is appointed with yellow sponge-painted walls, ceiling fans and murals of the waterfront; it's a sunny backdrop for the kitchen's down-home Cape Verdean cooking, comforting, highly seasoned Portuguese-like dishes influenced by the cuisines of Africa.

Rhythm & Spice   18 | 15 | 16 | $23
315 Mass Ave. (State St.), Cambridge, 617-497-0977; www.rspice.com
■ "Like a trip to Jamaica", mon, this "casual" Central Square grill delivers the "total Caribbean experience" – a "colorful" setting, "live island bands", a "great selection of rum drinks" (that "should come with warning labels"); "if you need goat, this is the place to go", though the menu also offers "flavorful" items like conch fritters, jerk chicken and stewed oxtail.

RIALTO   26 | 25 | 25 | $57
Charles Hotel, 1 Bennett St. (University Rd.), Cambridge, 617-661-5050; www.rialto-restaurant.com
■ "Be still my beating heart" swoon the smitten who've just savored a "knock-your-socks-off" dinner at the Charles Hotel's flagship dining room, an "ethereal" experience that's "lost none of its sparkle" over the years; the "elegantly understated" surroundings pull in an "upper-crust-meets-Cambridge-academic" crowd that appreciates "sublime" Mediterranean fare that "sings with every bite"; you may need to "bring an extra credit card", but it's "worth every penny" to "worship" at "Jody Adams' shrine."

Ristorante Fiore   19 | 19 | 18 | $33
250 Hanover St. (bet. Parmenter & Richmond Sts.), 617-371-1176; www.ristorantefiore.com
◪ "Romantics" whisper that on a balmy "summer evening", the "nice rooftop deck" at this "attractive" ristorante on the North End's "main drag" is the place to be; it's "comfortable" too in the "spacious" interior below, but though the kitchen's Italian "standards" are "above average", they "don't match up to the fancy decor" say the "disappointed", who "wouldn't rush to go back."

Ristorante Lucia   17 | 15 | 17 | $35
415 Hanover St. (Hanover Ave.), 617-367-2353 ☻
5-13 Mt. Vernon St. (bet. Main & Washington Sts.), Winchester, 781-729-0515 ⓢ
www.luciaristorante.com
◪ Replete with elaborate "faux Sistine Chapel frescoes" "covering the ceiling", the decor at this Italian twosome in the North End and Winchester is pure "old-style" "kitsch";

Boston

F | D | S | C

supporters say the "huge portions" of Abruzzo-inspired cooking are "tasty" (and caution "be careful how much you order" or most of your food will "go home in a doggy bag"), but a minority moans "tired in every way."

Ristorante Marcellino — | — | — | E
11 Cooper St. (Pine St.), Waltham, 781-647-5458
For years, this Waltham site was home to Marcellino, then it became a steakhouse and now it's Marcellino again, an upscale ristorante that goes back to its Southern Italian roots; this is a big place with an equally big menu, ranging from brick-oven pizzas to pastas to more contemporary Italo-inspired creations; you could bring the kids, but you could dress up for a romantic date too.

Ristorante Toscano 21 | 17 | 18 | $42
41-47 Charles St. (bet. Chestnut & Mt. Vernon Sts.), 617-723-4090; www.ristorantetoscanoboston.com
◪ "Beacon Hill's answer to the North End" may be this "underrated" Charles Street contender that pleases locals with "authentic", "wonderful" Northern Italian cooking; the dishes are served by a "warm" staff in a rustic Tuscan setting with exposed-brick walls hung with antique objects and hand-painted plates, making for an "enjoyable evening" for most, but critics shrug "nothing to write home about."

Ritz-Carlton Dining Room — | — | — | VE
Ritz-Carlton Boston, 15 Arlington St. (Newbury St.), 617-536-5700; www.ritz-carlton.com
Fresh from a multimillion-dollar face-lift, the Back Bay's venerable grande dame has reopened with a brighter, more youthful look (though, rest assured, its famous cobalt-blue crystal chandeliers remain, more sparkly than ever); new top toque Tony Esnault confidently executes a French menu that intersperses beloved classics (such as the legendary Grand Marnier soufflé) with contemporary creations, while early reports indicate that the polished Ritz service remains ever so white-gloved; N.B. jacket required, *naturellement*.

Riva — | — | — | M
116 Front St. (Otis Pl.), Scituate, 781-545-5881
"We're so fortunate to have this restaurant in our little town" say Scituate surveyors who've sampled this "tiny" "charmer" "near the harbor", owned by Jimmy Burke (Tuscan Grill); "great for both breakfast and dinner" (no lunch), the Italian dishes "prepared with the freshest local ingredients" will "fill you up and then some", while the "outdoor bar in the back jumps in the summer."

Rod Dee ●⌀ 23 | 4 | 13 | $12
94 Peterborough St. (Kilmarnock St.), 617-859-0969
1430 Beacon St. (Summit Ave.), Brookline, 617-738-4977
■ "Don't be afraid" of the extremely "divey" "storefront" digs at this Fenway and Brookline twosome, because inside

Boston   F | D | S | C

await "exquisite" Thai "delights" that "blow away" the fare offered at "many fancy restaurants"; the "outstanding" dishes are among the "most authentic in Boston" (and "as spicy as you want them"), and the "prices surely can't be beat", but best to "call ahead for pickup or prepare to wrestle for one of the few tables" on the premises.

Roka   20 | 15 | 19 | $24
1001 Mass Ave. (bet. Dana & Ellery Sts.), Cambridge, 617-661-0344

☑ While it's "not fancy or trendy", this "neighborhood sushi joint" between Harvard and Central Squares is a "feel-good spot" that's been satisfying Cantabrigians' yens for more than two decades with its "solid" Japanese fare, "artful plating" and "interesting sake selection", but dissenters who deride the "ordinary" offerings opine "not the best choice in the area."

Rosebud Diner   15 | 18 | 17 | $15
381 Summer St. (bet. Cutter & Elm Sts.), Somerville, 617-666-6015

☑ "Nothing beats the smiles and 'hello, honey'" greetings showered upon the patrons of this "genuine" "retro" diner in Davis Square, at least when you're looking for a "good, plain" "all-American" meal (or the "perfect hangover breakfast"); "sometimes you need a place like this" for "home cooking, away from home", but nostalgists who nix the "bland" grub sigh "she ain't what she used to be."

Rouge   – | – | – | E
480 Columbus Ave. (bet. W. Newton St. & Rutland Sq.), 617-867-0600; www.rougeboston.com

At this latest South End venture from Andy Husbands (Sister Sorel, Tremont 647), the menu takes its culinary cues from New Orleans and the Southern states surrounding it; the deep red walls in the bordello-inspired bar set a voodooistic Crescent City mood, while the more sedately attired dining room seems less 'madam' and more 'yes, ma'am.'

Royal East   19 | 13 | 17 | $20
782 Main St. (Windsor St.), Cambridge, 617-661-1660

☑ Just a "stone's throw from MIT", this Central Square "favorite" can fill the bill when you're "craving" "solid" Chinese food; granted, the dishes aren't "Chinatown quality", but at least it's "convenient" if "you're stuck in Cambridge", and if you're planning on bringing a large "group", the "accommodating" staff will be "happy" to arrange a multicourse "banquet" for your party.

Rubin's   18 | 9 | 14 | $18
500 Harvard St. (Kenwood St.), Brookline, 617-731-8787; www.rubinskosher.com

☑ Still the "best of its kind in the area", this "throwback" in Brookline is an "old-fashioned" "kosher deli" ("like those

Boston   F | D | S | C

in the Bronx 45 years ago") that makes everything from scratch (don't miss the "excellent Romanian pastrami"); not only does it serve the same satisfying fare that "your Jewish mother cooked for you", but it also offers some newfangled items like kosher sushi; if it doesn't "live up to New York" standards, at least it "tries."

Rustic Kitchen   – | – | – | E
(fka Todd English Rustic Kitchen)
Faneuil Hall Mktpl., 200 Quincy Mkt. (Clinton St.), 617-523-6334
Though "it's not Todd English's kitchen anymore" (the celebrity chef's former partner is now the proprietor) and the "touristy" locale at Faneuil Hall is "not so rustic either", both "those who like basic fare and those who want a little gourmet" remain generally pleased with the Mediterranean fare; skeptics, however, are reserving judgment "since it changed ownership"; N.B. executive chef Bill Bradley (ex Carmen) came onboard post-*Survey*, and word is that he'll introduce a more contemporary Italian menu.

Sabur   ▽ 23 | 22 | 24 | $29
212 Holland St. (Broadway), Somerville, 617-776-7890;
www.saburrestaurant.com
■ More than "living up to its tag line – 'exotic Mediterranean cuisine'" – this Somerville alternative earns praise for its "unusual, special" menu that reflects the flavors and aromas of cultures from the owners' native Yugoslavia to Italy, Greece, Southern France, North Africa and beyond; the "warmth" of the "lovely" room appointed with "beautiful copper tables" and a hearth is "matched only by the warmth of the staff"; besides, "where else around here can you get Bosnian cooking?"

Saffron   20 | 20 | 17 | $31
279A Newbury St. (Gloucester St.), 617-536-9766;
www.saffronboston.com
◪ "Smart and sophisticated", this "chic" Back Bay "beauty" pleases partisans with its "delightful take" on Indian food; the "eclectic" menu features not "just the same old tandoori chicken", but also "interesting" dishes such as cottage cheese ravioli and crab curry, though purists pan the "weird combos" that don't always gel into a "cohesive whole" and warn about "disorganized" service; in any case, the "divine" patio is a "great spot for people-watching."

Sage ⌀   26 | 19 | 23 | $43
69 Prince St. (Salem St.), 617-248-8814;
www.sageboston.com
■ "Good things come in small packages" is a proverb proved true at this "teeny" "treasure" "tucked away" in the North End; a "chef's chef", Anthony Susi never fails to tantalize taste buds with his monthly-"changing menu" of "fabulous", "gourmet" Northern Italian and New American fare, and

Boston F | D | S | C |

he'll make you feel "like you've come to his home and he's cooking just for you"; the "downside: the cramped seating."

Saigon ⌀ ▽ 23 | 13 | 20 | $15 |
431 Cambridge St. (Harvard Ave.), Allston, 617-254-3373
■ "Regulars" of this "cozy" Allston "hideaway" are almost "scared to tell you how good it is", but they can't keep mum about its "flat-out delicious" "homestyle" Vietnamese cooking; the "delicate", "subtly flavored" fare (the "old standbys plus some inventive" dishes) are served at "dirt-cheap" prices by "accommodating", "smiling" servers; factor in the fact that the "sincere" owners" "couldn't be sweeter" and the result is a "quiet little star."

Saint – | – | – | E |
90 Exeter St. (bet. Boylston St. & Huntington Ave.), 617-236-1134; www.saintnitery.com
Calling itself a 'nitery', this oh-so-chic lounge has taken over the cavernous Back Bay digs once occupied by Cafe Budapest; though one room, with its bordello-style decor and velvety red wallpaper, recalls the site's Middle Europa origins, the main space is pure Manhattan (blue neon pillars, buttery leather couches); local star chef Rene Michelena has put together an Eclectic menu of Asian-influenced small plates, but the scene seems to be the point here.

Sakurabana ℳ 23 | 10 | 16 | $28 |
57 Broad St. (Milk St.), 617-542-4311; www.sakuraboston.com
■ "One of the benefits of working" in the Financial District is that you can dine at this "homey" "gem of a sushi bar", which "caters to the lunch crowd" with "excellent" meals (some prefer to visit "for dinner, when it's not packed" and the pace is "pleasantly slow"); "they spend their money on quality fish, not furnishings" here, so if you're looking for a "reliable" Japanese "value" "without all the hype", this "unpretentious" "hole"-in-the-wall will "not disappoint."

SALTS ℳ 27 | 22 | 25 | $45 |
798 Main St. (Windsor St.), Cambridge, 617-876-8444
■ Producing an "exhilarating" "infusion of flavor with every single bite", the "superb" New American fare "influenced by Eastern Europe" (an homage to his Romanian and Russian heritage) executed by "skillful" chef Steve Rosen at his "intimate" bistro near Central Square is "inventive enough to delight without being overwrought"; together with his wife Lisa, they've created a "tasteful, understated" cocoon, "cramped" space notwithstanding.

Sandrine's 22 | 22 | 21 | $43 |
8 Holyoke St. (Mass Ave.), Cambridge, 617-497-5300; www.sandrines.com
◪ "As close as you can come to Alsace without a plane ticket", this Harvard Square "jewel" "feels like Strasbourg"

get updates at zagat.com 127

Boston　　　　　　　　　　　　　　F | D | S | C

the minute "you walk through the door"; the "solid" French bistro dishes, "full of bacon and other good things", and "refined", "civilized" ambiance make it a "welcome stalwart against too much innovation", though faultfinders nitpick "good but doesn't blow you away."

S&S　　　　　　　　　　　　　　　17 | 11 | 14 | $17
1334 Cambridge St. (bet. Hampshire & Prospect Sts.), Cambridge, 617-354-0777
Still "packing them in" for a "good old comfort-food brunch" on weekends – just as it has since 1919 – this Inman Square "staple" is upholding its reputation as an indispensable "local institution"; the deli menu, as ever, is "dependable" and "formidable", and the servers remain "endearingly rude", but kvetching kritics are convinced that serious "Jewish delis in Boston have gone the way of the hula hoop."

Santarpio's Pizza ●⊄　　　　　　23 | 6 | 13 | $16
111 Chelsea St. (Porter St.), East Boston, 617-567-9871
"What a dive, but what a pizza!" exclaim enthusiasts who'll "stop on the way from Logan just for a top-quality pie" dished up with "little frills or fanfare" at this "old-fashioned" East Boston landmark; despite the "gruff service", "thin-crust fans are in heaven" (we "love the BBQ lamb" too), but perplexed participants propose that the reason "people rave" about the food here is "because they've only eaten airplane peanuts all day."

Saporito's　　　　　　　　　　　26 | 16 | 23 | $40
11 Rockland Circle (George Washington Blvd.), Hull, 781-925-3023
It may be "kind of a shock when you pull up" at this "unassuming", "laid-back" cottage near Nantasket Beach, but "inside is dining bliss"; "still shining after more than 15 years", it remains a "favorite" South Shore destination for "intriguing" Northern Italian cuisine that would stand up to that of any "fine Boston restaurant", leading patrons to plead "please keep" "Hull's only treasure" a "secret."

Sapporo　　　　　　　　　　　∇ 22 | 15 | 21 | $24
81 Union St. (Beacon St.), Newton, 617-964-8044
"What it lacks in atmosphere", this "serene" Asian retreat housed in a Newton Centre "basement" "more than makes up" for with "freshly prepared sushi", "high-quality" cooked Japanese dishes and "lovely" Korean offerings; it's all served by a "gracious" staff that welcomes "regulars" with a "wide smile", and it's a "good value", which explains why "neighbors return again and again."

Saraceno　　　　　　　　　　　21 | 18 | 21 | $35
286 Hanover St. (bet. Parmenter & Prince Sts.), 617-227-5353
"When you're in the mood for" "well-prepared traditional" Italian food, this "old-world" ristorante in the North End

Boston

| F | D | S | C |

will satisfy with "sound" cooking that "ends up exceeding your expectations", turned out by a "friendly" staff in a "charming" "maze of rooms" (each with a different design motif); trendoids, however, "turn up their noses at the unimaginative menu and stodgy decor."

Savannah Grill ▽ 18 | 12 | 19 | $21

233A Elm St. (Grove St.), Somerville, 617-666-4200

🔲 Despite the fact that its "name creates a serious identity crisis" – is it Southern, or named for the African plains? – this "low-key" addition to Davis Square is filling a niche with its "well-prepared" Mediterranean fare; the "tasty" dishes are "appealing", and they're delivered by a "down-to-earth" staff in a simple "storefront" setting.

Scoozi 18 | 10 | 14 | $16

237 Newbury St. (Fairfield St.), 617-247-8847

🔲 "Take your cell phone to fit in with the crowd" of "young" "Euro" "poseurs" at this "cool" cafe on Newbury Street, where "if you can get a seat on the sidewalk patio", you'll take in prime "people-watching"; the Italian-accented New American menu runs the likes of "upscale" "pressed sandwiches", "crisp, light" designer pizzas and other "quick bites", though dissenters deride this wanna-be as the "Armani Cafe for those who can't afford" the original.

Scutra – | – | – | E

92 Summer St. (Mill St.), Arlington, 781-316-1816

Out of the limelight in Arlington, this warm and inviting (if tiny) new neighborhood "hideaway" shines in a "cute space" appointed with "romantic" golden hues; chef-owner Didier Baugniet's bistro menu looks to the sunnier climes of the Mediterranean, with influences from Italy, France and other countries in the region, yielding beautifully plated dishes made with "tender loving care."

Seasons 25 | 22 | 23 | $47

Millennium Bostonian Hotel, 24 North St. (Faneuil Hall Mktpl.), 617-523-4119; www.millennium-hotels.com

🔲 Deserving of a "prominent spot" among the city's "fine-dining" choices, this "sophisticated" destination in the Millennium Bostonian Hotel opposite Faneuil Hall has long been known for its "artistic" New American cuisine and "elegant" decor; though it's "not what it used to be" – as a "cutting-edge" leader in the field "in the '80s", it functioned as a launching pad for a number of notable local chefs – it continues to be a "wonderful place to celebrate", even if it's "often forgotten."

Second Street Cafe 𝒮 ⌀ ▽ 21 | 11 | 21 | $12

89 Second St. (bet. Hurley & Spring Sts.), Cambridge, 617-661-1311

■ Local techies, corporate types and courthouse workers are pleased to report that this New American addition in

get updates at zagat.com 129

Boston

| F | D | S | C |

East Cambridge is a "big improvement over the food court"; it's "worth a hike from Kendall Square" to tuck into "delicious salads", "outstanding sandwiches", "gourmet specials" and "very good cookies" at prices that are "cheap" for the quality; "what a great cafe", but "let's hear it for later hours."

Sel de la Terre 24 | 22 | 22 | $43
255 State St. (Atlantic Ave.), 617-720-1300; www.seldelaterre.com

☑ "One can live on bread and olive oil alone", at least if it's the "to-die-for" renditions offered at this "lovely" Provençal "oasis" in the "middle" of the waterfront "tourist zone"; the "simple, delicious" bistro dishes "transport you right to the French countryside", while the "personable" servers contribute to "that certain *je ne sais quoi*"; if a minority moans "not memorable", most maintain it's simply "Sel de la Terre-ific."

Seoul Food 21 | 8 | 20 | $17
1759 Mass Ave. (bet. Forest & Roseland Sts.), Cambridge, 617-864-6299

■ "Three cheers for this mom-and-pop place" near Porter Square, where the "kind", "hardworking owners" cook up "hearty", "delectable" dishes "just like your mother would have made – if she were Korean"; though the teensy, "unpretentious" storefront digs are "not particularly inviting", the "endearing husband-and-wife team" will "make you feel so at home."

Sepal 21 | 11 | 16 | $16
17 Nichols Ave. (Arlington St.), Watertown, 617-924-5753

☑ The "basics of Middle Eastern cuisine get the high-class treatment" at this "warm", homey Watertown "bargain" run by an enthusiastic chef-owner who "cares"; "wonderfully healthy", "flavorful" "vegetarian selections abound" on the "authentic" menu, notably the "best falafel in the Boston area, hands down", and combined with "incredibly nice", if "snail-like", service "make up for the forgettable interior."

Serafina Ristorante ∇ 19 | 18 | 20 | $40
195 Sudbury Rd. (Thoreau St.), Concord, 978-371-9050

☑ "What a find in surburban Concord" cheer boosters of this Italian ristorante that brings a touch of "city style" to MetroWest; the "yum" "Tuscan-style" fare, lively bar scene and "thoughtful" service "lure" back neighbors "time and again", but detractors yawn "just the same old shtick."

711 Grill ∇ 19 | 15 | 18 | $22
711 Centre St. (bet. Burroughs Pl. & Harris Ave.), Jamaica Plain, 617-522-1221

☑ "Super-duper" Southeast Asian cooking marked by "wonderful flavors" and "delicate sauces" pleases patrons at this informal eatery in Jamaica Plain; the "delicious" Vietnamese and Thai fare ("excellent options for vegetarians and omnivores alike"), especially the "interesting specials",

Boston

F | D | S | C

draws praise, as does the "friendly" service, but the "bare-bones" digs make aesthetes "want to just get takeout."

75 Chestnut 21 | 24 | 22 | $44
75 Chestnut St. (bet. Brimmer & River Sts.), 617-227-2175; www.75chestnut.com

☑ "Don't let the blue bloods scare you away" from this "hidden gem" "off-the-beaten-path" in the flats of Beacon Hill, which provides a "taste of old Boston" that's "perfect" for "when your parents are in town"; it "feels like a private club", with a "well-mannered" staff ("efficient yet not intrusive") bringing to table "solid" New American dishes; the "gentry" recommends it for an "unaffected, unrushed", "classically New England experience", even if detractors dub it an "overpriced *Cheers* with better upholstery."

Shabu-Zen 24 | 18 | 19 | $22
16 Tyler St. (bet. Beach & Kneeland Sts.), 617-292-8828; www.shabuzen.com

■ Billed as the "first shabu-shabu specialist in Boston", this Japanese "haven" in Chinatown is loads of "fun", particularly if you come with a "large group of friends"; starting with "very fresh ingredients", you cook at the table your choice of meat or seafood, along with vegetables and noodles, "family-style" in a "hot pot" filled with simmering broth, then dunk each morsel in a dipping sauce; the result is a "tasty" "communal" eating experience.

Shalimar of India ▽ 22 | 13 | 18 | $19
546 Mass Ave. (Central Sq.), Cambridge, 617-547-9280

☑ "Lots of regulars frequent" this "old standby" in Central Square because the "solid" Indian kitchen "does it right"; though the "standard" menu is "nothing fancy", the dishes are "consistent in taste and quality", and the lunch buffet is a particularly "good" "value"; the bottom line: "never great but never disappointing."

Shangri-La – | – | – | I
149 Belmont St. (bet. Exeter St. & Oxford Ave.), Belmont, 617-489-1488

"In a totally unexpected storefront location in Belmont", a Taiwanese family runs this little surprise that brings "real" "Chinatown" quality to the "suburbs"; the "remarkably large menu" features plenty of "authentic", "well-prepared" dishes, including some "unusual" items that you don't often see around town, served by an "efficient" – despite the occasional language barrier – staff.

Shanti: Taste of India – | – | – | M
277B Huntington Ave. (Mass Ave.), 617-867-9700
1111 Dorchester Ave. (Savin Hill Ave.), Dorchester, 617-929-3900
www.shantiboston.com

Ticket-holders are "delighted to find this addition to the Symphony district", a "cut above many other choices" in

Boston

F | D | S | C

this neighborhood; along with "good-quality" Indian fare (both classic and modern), the interesting, extensive South Asian menu also offers Pakistani and Bangladeshi specialties ("you can get goat" in a variety of ways!), presented in a smartly outfitted space; P.S. if you're south of the city, "try the Dorchester branch."

Sherborn Inn 17 | 18 | 17 | $32
Sherborn Inn, 33 N. Main St./Rte. 16 (Rte. 27), Sherborn, 508-655-9521; www.sherborninn.com

◪ Appealing to the "horsey set", this "historic" "country inn" in Sherborn can "suit almost any mood", as it allows guests the "choice" of having a "casual" New England meal in the cozy 1827 tavern or supping on New American fare in the "more formal dining rooms"; though everyone agrees that the environs are "comfortably" "quaint", gourmets grumble about the "mediocre" food and "inconsistent" service; at least there's live jazz on Tuesday nights.

Shilla 18 | 12 | 16 | $28
57 JFK St. (Winthrop St.), Cambridge, 617-547-7971

◪ Providing a "convenient stop" in Harvard Square for "decent" sushi and "reliable" Korean fare, this "no-frills" neighborhood "mainstay" attracts lots of Cambridge "students and faculty" members; despite the "spartan" setting, it's a "peaceful" place worked by a staff that "aims to please", but malcontents caution "don't get your hopes up", since "something must've happened to the food on the way from Asia."

Shogun 20 | 13 | 18 | $23
1385 Washington St. (Elm St.), Newton, 617-965-6699

◪ "The owners and servers are very friendly" and "treat customers well" at this "unpretentious" "neighborhood" Japanese "standby" in West Newton that's a handy pit stop "on the way to the movies" or for a "family night out"; it's "always busy" because the sushi is "always fresh", but connoisseurs suggest "there are lots of better alternatives."

Sichuan Garden 22 | 13 | 18 | $20
295 Washington St. (Harvard St.), Brookline, 617-734-1870

■ "Ask about the Chinese-language menu if you're feeling adventurous" when you visit this Szechuan "must-try" in Brookline that's "fantastic for the hot and spicy crowd"; insiders advise that it's important to "order the right things", so "convince the waiter to explain" to you the "non-English" bill of fare, and you'll be rewarded with the "most authentic" dishes you can "get in this part of the world."

Sidney's Grille 20 | 20 | 18 | $33
University Park Hotel @ MIT, 20 Sidney St. (bet. Franklin & Green Sts.), Cambridge, 617-494-0011; www.sidneysgrille.com

◪ Surveyors are split about this spacious New American dining room at the University Park Hotel @ MIT near Central

Boston   F | D | S | C

Square: proponents say the "surprisingly good" fare and contemporary setting make it "great" for both "business" dealings and for "casual meetings with friends", but foes dismiss it as thoroughly "unremarkable" and caution about "spotty" service.

SILKS   25 | 25 | 26 | $60
Stonehedge Inn, 160 Pawtucket Blvd. (Rte. 113), Tyngsboro, 978-649-4400; www.stonehedgeinn.com/silks

■ "Valentine's Day will never be the same" if you take your sweetheart to Tyngsboro's luxurious Stonehedge Inn for a most "special meal"; nestled amid acres of horse country, this "gorgeous" "jewel" is "one of the most romantic restaurants in all Massachusetts", providing an "elegant" backdrop for Eric Brujan's "exquisite" French masterpieces and a "world-class" wine list, proffered by a "pampering" staff well versed in "formal" European-style service; "we only wish we could afford it more often."

Silvertone Bar & Grill ⌀   20 | 17 | 18 | $20
69 Bromfield St. (Tremont St.), 617-338-7887

■ "Boston could use more places" like this "local joint" Downtown that's simultaneously a "hip and civilized" place for a "drink and a bite to eat"; the "cool clientele" craves its Traditional American "comfort food" – "old-fashioned home-cooked meals" including "meatloaf like your mom made" and "mac 'n' cheese" that's even "better" – paired with a select wine list known for its low markup and offered at "affordable" prices; regulars only "wish they had more room" in the "subterranean" digs.

Siros   21 | 21 | 18 | $33
Granite Plaza, 703 Granite St. (Rte. 37), Braintree, 781-848-4500
1217 Main St. (Rte. 53), Hingham, 781-749-4500
Clarion Hotel, 45 Hull Shore Dr. (Nantasket Ave.), Hull, 781-925-3604
Marina Bay, 307 Victory Rd. (Boardwalk), North Quincy, 617-472-4500
www.sirosrestaurants.com

◪ Whether you "sit outside" at this Italian quartet's Marina Bay branch to best take in the "beautiful" "view of the Boston skyline", bask in the Hull site's "perfect location on Nantasket Beach" or visit the other South Shore venues, you can expect "reliable" cooking served in "lovely" settings; the "disappointed", however, are "not in a hurry to go back" given the "unsophisticated" dishes that come with "gourmet prices."

Sister Sorel   23 | 18 | 20 | $27
645 Tremont St. (W. Brookline St.), 617-266-4600

◪ "Everything always seems to go right" at this "more casual" "next-door companion" to Tremont 647, a "cool",

get updates at zagat.com

Boston F | D | S | C |

loungey place to hang out "with friends" and maybe "meet a couple of new ones"; it "shares the same kitchen" with its older "sister" but features "lighter, less expensive" New American bites, though as with many South End spots, brace yourself for "crowded" conditions.

Skellig - | - | - | I |
240 Moody St. (Pine St), Waltham, 781-647-0679; www.theskellig.com

The proprietors of the Burren in Somerville have opened a similar outpost in Waltham, hoping to attract suburbanites with their signature mix of Guinness on tap, Irish-American pub grub and live music; the high-ceilinged space manages to feel both airy and cozy, with walls lined with photographs of bands – quite appropriate decorations, since the owners are musicians themselves.

Skewers 19 | 5 | 14 | $12 |
92 Mt. Auburn St. (JFK St.), Cambridge, 617-491-3079

☑ "If you blink, you may miss" this "student favorite", a "basement hole-in-the-wall" that's long been a Harvard Square mainstay for "economical" kebabs and other "consistently tasty" Middle Eastern fare; you get a "large meal for a small price", but you might want to consider "takeout", since obviously "no one goes here" for the "dungeon"-like atmosphere.

Skipjack's 18 | 16 | 18 | $31 |
199 Clarendon St. (bet. Boylston St. & St. James Ave.), 617-536-3500
1400 Worcester St. (Rte. 9), Natick, 508-628-9900
55 Needham St. (Boylston St.), Newton, 617-964-4244
www.skipjacks.com

☑ "You can depend" on this "aquatic-themed" local trio for "tasty", "fresh" seafood, simply prepared; though "it may not be the most exciting place in the world", to the "mainstream" majority, "predictability can be good", but critics who "yawn" over this "bland corporate" concept counsel "skip it."

Sol Azteca 20 | 19 | 18 | $26 |
914A Beacon St. (bet. Park Dr. & St. Mary's St.), Brookline, 617-262-0909
75 Union St. (Beacon St.), Newton, 617-964-0920
www.solaztecarestaurants.com

☑ Bringing a "bit of old Mexico" to New England, this "beautifully decorated" pair of "sure bets" in Brookline and Newton Centre has been satisfying amigos with "consistently good" "traditional" Mexican fare and "mighty refreshing sangria" since 1974 (not to mention "excellent patio dining"); even regulars, though, suggest it's "time for a few changes in the menu" and warn that the service is "forgettable – if they don't forget about you first."

Boston F | D | S | C

Solea Restaurant & Tapas Bar 22 | 21 | 20 | $30
388 Moody St. (Cushing St.), Waltham, 781-894-1805;
www.solearestaurant.com

■ "Taste the tapas, sip the sangria and you're transported to Spain" say aficionados of this "warm and cozy" Waltham room where both the suburban set and the high-tech crowd "go to un-stress"; "try as many things as you can" from the "selection of wonderful small plates" ("every bite is a treat"), served by people who "give the place a nice feel without being too friendly."

Sonsie ☾ 19 | 20 | 18 | $34
327 Newbury St. (bet. Hereford St. & Mass Ave.),
617-351-2500

☑ Sit "at the open-air tables" near the streetside French doors to "see and be seen" or retreat to the rear for a "romantic candlelit dinner" at this "swank", late-night Back Bay restaurant/lounge where the "innovative" Eclectic menu is a mere "appetizer to the people-watching" ("wear black" and "go looking your very best" to fit in among the "hip" "Euro crowd"); "it's been around for a while", but it's "still a chic place", though down-to-earth types charge "its 15 minutes should be up."

Sorella's ⌀ 20 | 8 | 14 | $12
386-388 Centre St. (Perkins St.), Jamaica Plain,
617-524-2016

☑ "On a quest for the perfect" American breakfast? – then "come early" to this "homey" Jamaica Plain cafe where a "crowd" always gathers for "pancake/waffle combos", "from pumpkin to peanut butter to gingerbread", that are "heaven-sent", as well as "creative" omelets bursting with "too many ingredients" ("is there anything they won't put in one?"); the "disappointed", however, claim that its "reputation is unwarranted."

Sorento's 20 | 14 | 15 | $24
86 Peterborough St. (bet. Jersey & Kilmarnock Sts.), 617-424-7070;
www.sorentos.com

☑ "Locals favor" this "unassuming" Fenway "faithful" for its "simple", "reasonably priced" Italian cooking when they're "headed for a baseball game" or just looking for a "pleasant place to get together with friends"; the "solid pastas" and "better-than-average pizzas" are "guaranteed crowd-pleasers", but "don't come if you're in a hurry."

Sound Bites ⌀ 24 | 9 | 13 | $11
708 Broadway (Boston Ave.), Somerville, 617-623-8338

☑ "Put up with it, you'll love it" maintain morning mavens who brave the weekend "lines out the door" at "the" place for "absolutely amazing" American breakfasts in Somerville; the "portions are as gargantuan as the restaurant is tiny", so "don't go if you want to relax and chat" (the waiters will

get updates at zagat.com

Boston

F | D | S | C

practically "throw you out if you linger too long", making for a "surreal adventure in comic abuse"); N.B. no dinner, but at lunch the menu is Middle Eastern.

South Street Diner ● ▽ 20 | 15 | 18 | $12
178 Kneeland St. (South St.), 617-350-0028

■ For pancakes all day long, this "cheap" Leather District "dive" is hard to beat; it's a Traditional American "greasy spoon" near South Station where the "jukebox is always on", the staff is "funky and sweet" and the "late-night characters make it even better"; however, "if you're the type of person who blots pizza with a napkin, stay at home" "and leave the perfect fried eggs to the rest of us."

Soya's 20 | 18 | 22 | $23
108 Oak St. (Needham St.), Newton, 617-527-8580

☑ At this "new kid on the block" in Newton Upper Falls, the menu offers an "interesting mix of Asian cuisines", from Malaysian and Indonesian to Thai and Chinese; early enthusiasts give kudos to the "wonderful spices" and "combinations that you can't find elsewhere in the suburbs" but caution that it's "still ironing out the kinks."

Spice Thai Cuisine 20 | 14 | 17 | $17
24 Holyoke St. (Mt. Auburn St.), Cambridge, 617-868-9560; www.spicethaicuisine.com

☑ "When you have a hankering" for Thai food in Harvard Square, this "friendly" spot can provide a fix with its "colorful, tasty" dishes packed with "so much flavor"; the "owner makes sure you're taken care of" by the "quick" servers, even though it's "always busy", but for those not on the wagon, the "lack of a liquor license is a problem."

Spinnaker ▽ 13 | 23 | 15 | $36
Hyatt Regency Cambridge, 575 Memorial Dr. (Amesbury St.), Cambridge, 617-492-1234; www.hyatt.com

☑ It's "all about the view" at Boston's only "revolving" rooftop restaurant, perched high atop the Hyatt Regency Cambridge, though "on a beautiful night" it's "worth it" just for the "splendid" vista of the city skyline and the Charles River; the Traditional American fare is "adequate" – if you're entertaining "out-of-town guests" – but if it weren't for the "spinning", there'd really be no reason to dine on the "bland" "hotel food" at this "tired" spot; N.B. open only for dinner Friday–Sunday and Sunday brunch.

Spire 20 | 22 | 19 | $54
Nine Zero Hotel, 90 Tremont St. (Park St.), 617-772-0202; www.spirerestaurant.com

☑ "Andy Warhol meets James Beard" at this "chic" new addition to the Downtown "scene", the "minimalist" dining room on the second floor of the boutique Nine Zero Hotel, where the "artistic" decor is generating a "lot of buzz"; the kitchen is "trying hard", but "at these prices, everything

Boston F | D | S | C

should be first-rate", and so far, epicures conclude, the New French fare — while "well crafted" — isn't "living up to the hype"; perhaps with time, "things will smooth out."

Square Café ▽ 20 | 23 | 20 | $35
150 North St. (bet. Central & Main Sts.), Hingham, 781-740-4060

☒ "Nothing square about this square" say surveyors who've sought out this "winner" in Hingham, a "great place to meet an old friend or significant other" or "have dinner with your mom"; the Peter Niemitz–designed interior with its plaid banquettes is "beautiful", but even reviewers who "really want to love it" lament that the New French fare is "uneven."

Stars on Hingham Harbor 17 | 14 | 17 | $21
2-4 Otis St. (North St./Rte. 3A), Hingham, 781-749-3200; www.eatwellinc.com

☒ Set in a '50s-style diner, this retro "meeting spot" on picturesque Hingham Harbor gets points from "local" South Shore families (expect "lots of kids" around) for its "fun" "hometown feel"; it's the "type of place where you'll run into old high school friends" while tucking into "great breakfasts" and other "filling" American eats ("stick to the basics"); it's "nothing special, but it's priced accordingly."

Stars on Huntington – | – | – | I
393 Huntington Ave. (Forsythe), 617-536-3232; www.starsboston.com

"In a neighborhood of few choices", this "casually hip" American place near the Northeastern campus is handy to the MFA or for a "pre-Symphony" meal; design divas give it a "thumbs up" for its "stylish", "modern" decor, but the verdict is still out on the revamped, less expensive menu, which highlights a student-friendly selection of comfort foods ranging from chicken wings to burgers to meatloaf.

Stellina 22 | 17 | 19 | $32
47 Main St./Rte. 20 (Rte. 16), Watertown, 617-924-9475

☒ A "long-running hit that shows no sign of letting up", this "cute little trattoria" "transports you far from Watertown" to The Boot; the "chef uses the freshest seasonal ingredients" to create "wonderfully imaginative" Italian dishes (addicts "crave the warm tomato salad" with goat cheese) turned out by a "gracious" staff; it's "crowded and loud", yet it can be "romantic" enough for a "tête-à-tête", at least if you dine alfresco out on the expanded garden patio replete with a bubbling fountain.

Stephanie's on Newbury 18 | 19 | 17 | $31
190 Newbury St. (Exeter St.), 617-236-0990

☒ "Outdoors is where it's happening" at this "quintessential" Back Bay cafe where the "location, location, location" makes it a "trendy" "people-watching scene"; the "ladies who lunch" laud the "surefire" New American menu,

get updates at zagat.com

Boston F | D | S | C

particularly the "big, yummy salads", though everything comes "spiced with a dose of Newbury Street attitude" according to pragmatists who "wish the food were better."

Stockyard 17 | 13 | 16 | $25
135 Market St. (N. Beacon St.), Brighton, 617-782-4700; www.stockyardrestaurant.com
■ "When you want a beer with your meat, instead of a cigar and a martini", rustle on over to this "old-fashioned family steakhouse" in Brighton that's like a "blast from the past"; "senior citizens, politicians and college students" alike appreciate the "consistently" prepared, "affordable" meals, though "underwhelmed" carnivores moo that this "throwback" "should be put out to pasture."

Stone Soup ▽ 27 | 15 | 23 | $40
0 Central St. (Market St.), Ipswich, 978-356-4222
■ If you can squeeze into this teensy cafe in quaint Ipswich, you'll be treated to some of the most "excellent" Eclectic cooking on the North Shore; chef-partner Mark Macklin is a "wizard with whatever fresh local ingredients catch his eye", though you may have to "wait till almost next year" if you want to come for dinner (Thursday–Saturday only), as the coveted tables are routinely booked six months in advance, but a "wonderful" breakfast or lunch is the next best thing.

Suishaya ● ▽ 21 | 11 | 19 | $25
2 Tyler St. (Beach St.), 617-423-3848
■ "For cheap sushi", a "bento box" lunch or a "late-night snack", this modest Asian option in Chinatown can fill the bill till 2 AM; fin fans favor the "fresh" raw fish, while others opt for the "good" Korean barbecue – either way, the "service and prices are less pretentious" than at many other maki outlets, but if the "cramped dining area" "doesn't take away from the experience" "it doesn't add to it either."

Sultan's Kitchen 24 | 9 | 16 | $14
72 Broad St. (bet. Franklin & Milk Sts.), 617-338-7819
■ Just "follow the long lines" to this Financial District "favorite", a "bustling" chef-owned "Turkish delight" that'll "knock your socks off" with "outstanding" Middle Eastern "specialties that never disappoint"; order at the counter, get served by a "lightning-fast" staff, then sit upstairs or get it to go – sample these "exotic", "economical" selections and you'll be "swearing off the old deli sandwich routine."

Sunset Cafe ▽ 21 | 17 | 20 | $23
851 Cambridge St. (bet. Hunting & Willow Sts.), Cambridge, 617-547-2938; www.thesunsetcafe.net
■ "When the musicians are on the menu" (on weekends), this "family-friendly" Portuguese cafe outside of Inman Square can sure get "crowded", but the traditional guitar music "adds so much to the ambiance" (you'll feel "as if

Boston

| F | D | S | C |

you're in Lisbon"); loyalists "enjoy" the "tasty" Iberian dishes from a menu that has "something for everyone, even the unadventurous."

Sunset Grill & Tap ◐ | 18 | 16 | 16 | $18 |
130 Brighton Ave. (Harvard Ave.), Allston, 617-254-1331; www.allstonsfinest.com

▨ A "beer lover's dream come true", this late-night "college hangout" in Allston claims to offer the "best selection in Boston", with "more than 100" brews "on tap" and even more by the bottle; the bar stocks "every kind you ever wanted to try and some you never knew existed" (the choices can "blow your mind"), the better to wash down the "typical" Traditional American "pub food" (at least the "burgers won't let you down").

Sweet Basil ⊄ | 26 | 11 | 19 | $27 |
942 Great Plain Ave. (Highland Ave.), Needham, 781-444-9600

■ "Some of the best Italian food outside the North End" can be savored at this Needham "jewel", a wee (ok, "claustrophobic") BYO trattoria that makes you feel "like you're eating in a friend's kitchen"; though "you'll hear every word your fellow diners say", the "squished-together tables don't deter foodies" who are only too happy to eat the "zesty", "garlicky" dishes brought by a "friendly" staff that's "quick to offer suggestions"; just "bring cash" (no plastic) and a bottle of wine, or consider "getting takeout" to avoid the "long lines."

Taberna de Haro ✄ | 22 | 17 | 19 | $29 |
999 Beacon St. (St. Mary's St.), Brookline, 617-277-8272

▨ "Forget the imposters" – "if you love garlic, olives and olive oil", this "warm and friendly" Spanish taberna in Brookline is the "real thing"; the "owners are excellent hosts", and their "open kitchen" turns out plate after plate of "tasty" tapas, smartly teamed with an exclusively Iberian wine list; "watch out", though, because "all those little dishes add up fast", and note too that the "cozy" digs "could use a bit more elbow room."

Tacos El Charro | 19 | 11 | 15 | $16 |
349 Centre St. (Jackson Sq.), Jamaica Plain, 617-983-9275

▨ Go for the "live music" and the "neighborhood feeling" on "weekend evenings", when a "mariachi band pleases young and old alike" at this "solid" Mexican joint in Jamaica Plain; the "authentic", "hearty" dishes are "popular for a reason", but be forewarned that this "fun" fiesta can get "so loud you can't hear your dinner companions."

Tacos Lupita ⊄ | ▽ 23 | 4 | 16 | $9 |
13 Elm St. (Porter St.), Somerville, 617-666-0677

▨ Aficionados "can't say enough good things" about this Somerville dive that's a "mile ahead of other taquerias in

get updates at zagat.com

Boston   F | D | S | C

the area"; from the "really good", crowd-pleasing burritos to the more unusual-in-Boston *huaraches* and *pupusas,* all the "authentic" Mexican and El Salvadoran eats are "made to order", so while it can be "a challenge to place your order if you don't speak Spanish", it's "worth" the effort.

Taiwan Cafe ●⇗   24 | 11 | 17 | $16
34 Oxford St. (Beach St.), 617-426-8181
■ Curious palates "recommend" the "real" Taiwanese cuisine offered at this "no-frills" "upstairs nook" that highlights "lots" of "unique" (or, depending on your perspective, "strange") specialties that "other restaurants might hide away on their Chinese-language menus" (such as "stinky fermented tofu", pork intestines, five-spice duck tongue, salt-and-pepper frog); "if you know what to order", it makes for a "delicious" "change of pace from the usual Chinatown fare", and it's "amazingly" "cheap" too.

Takeshima   23 | 13 | 21 | $25
308 Harvard St. (Beacon St.), Brookline, 617-566-0200
■ "Reliably high-quality sushi" and a "wide choice" of other "well-prepared" dishes "delight all eaters" at this "modest" Coolidge Corner "alternative" to Brookline's more "hyped" Japanese restaurants; while it may not be a "mind-blowing *Iron Chef*" experience, the "service with a smile" from the "hospitable" staff makes this "old standby" a "friendly" "neighborhood" choice.

TANGIERINO   21 | 26 | 18 | $39
83 Main St. (Pleasant St.), Charlestown, 617-242-6009; www.tangierino.com
◪ "Lit by candlelight" and festooned with plump cushions, this "beautifully decorated" Charlestown choice features an "intimate, lounge-y" setting that's "perfect" for a "first date" or even to woo "potential in-laws"; "unique flavors abound" in the "exotic", "mouthwatering" Moroccan dishes, especially in the North African–inspired tapas, but the consensus is the service "needs work."

Tango ⌀   – | – | – | M
464 Mass Ave. (Medford St.), Arlington, 781-443-9000
With the feel of a bustling bistro, this cheery Argentinean storefront done up in bright yellow and exposed brick brings the tastes of the pampas to Arlington; that means plenty of grilled meats and roast chicken bolstered by garlicky chimichurri sauce and delivered by a helpful staff at moderate prices; add on an enthusiastic owner and no wonder amigos applaud "*muy bien!*"

Tanjore   23 | 16 | 19 | $21
18 Eliot St. (Bennett St.), Cambridge, 617-868-1900; www.tanjorerestaurant.com
■ "Standing out from the crowd", this "modern" Harvard Square "find" is renowned for preparing the "best Indian

Boston | F | D | S | C |

food in Cambridge"; the "specialty" of the house is its selection of "excellent" "smaller dishes" to "mix and match" ("think Indian tapas" such as "fabulous dosas"), though the "regional" menu offers many other options (that "actually taste different from one another"), including plenty of "vegetarian" plates, presented by a "helpful, efficient" staff in a "conversation-friendly" atmosphere.

Tantawan ▽ 20 | 10 | 20 | $18
356 Arsenal St. (School St.), Watertown, 617-926-8371

■ Thai food lovers are excited about this "terrific find" set in an "ex-diner" in Watertown, where the cooking is "as delicious as the building's exterior is unassuming"; it's run by a "lovely family" who'll "help you with the menu", though regulars recommend that if you "stick with the more traditional" choices ("rather than the Americanized ones) you'll have a "great meal" at a "reasonable price."

Tapeo 23 | 21 | 19 | $30
266 Newbury St. (bet. Fairfield & Gloucester Sts.), 617-267-4799; www.tapeo.com

■ "Fantastic tapas and sinfully good sangria are the main attractions" at this "lively" Spanish "fiesta" in the Back Bay that's "perfect for snobby gourmands and stingy grad students alike"; the "starter-size portions add up to a mouthwatering meal" (like a "symphony in garlic"), and even if it's "not quite as romantic as its sister restaurant Dalí", it does boast the "added benefit of outdoor dining" right on Newbury Street.

Taqueria la Mexicana 23 | 8 | 17 | $9
247 Washington St. (Union Sq.), Somerville, 617-776-5232; www.lataqueria.com

■ "Tamales are the stars" at this Somerville taqueria that's "way better than the overhyped burrito shacks" around town; with only a "few tables and hardly any staff", it "barely qualifies as a restaurant", but the "super-accommodating owner" serves up some of the most "authentic" Mexican fare in these parts, and at "bargain prices."

Taqueria Mexico 21 | 8 | 16 | $14
24 Charles St. (bet. Moody & Prospect Sts.), Waltham, 781-647-0166

■ "It's all about the food" at this "always busy" "dive" in Waltham, a "true diamond in the rough" thanks to its "down-home", "traditional" Mexican cooking and "awesome fruit shakes"; the servers are "proud of their establishment", though sometimes they get "overwhelmed" by the crowds, but still, the result is an "*excelente*" meal at a "cheap" price.

Taranta 24 | 20 | 24 | $40
210 Hanover St. (Cross St.), 617-720-0052; www.tarantarist.com

■ "Not your run-of-the-mill" "red-sauce" factory in the North End, this "adorable" "gem" of a triplex thrills the

Boston | F | D | S | C |

taste buds with "highly imaginative" Southern Italian dishes that "reach the heights" (like its "surreal" spaghetti with sea urchin and bottarga); appreciative admirers attest that "everything is made with care", and only enhancing the "lovely" dining experience is the "knowledgeable" staff that's always "ready to help."

Tasca
24 | 21 | 20 | $25

1612 Commonwealth Ave. (Washington St.), Brighton, 617-730-8002; www.tascarestaurant.com

■ For "a delicious way to spend an evening", "bring friends" and "sample" the "bountiful selection" of "intensely flavorful" tapas offered at this "cute", "romantic" Spanish tavern that aficionados assert is even "better than most of its better-known competitors"; the "courteous" service adds to the "inviting" ambiance ("where else in Brighton are you going to feel like you're sipping drinks in Madrid?"), so "don't let the college-ish location" "throw you" off the track when you're seeking a "simply marvelous adventure."

Taverna Toscana
▽ 23 | 15 | 20 | $29

63 Salem St. (bet. Stillman & Wiget Sts.), 617-742-5233

■ Look for the "scrumptious" platters of antipasti in the window to find this "super little" Italian trattoria "hidden" off the North End's "main drag"; the handful of surveyors who've supped on its "homemade food like mom used to make" (notably "fabulous pastas") praise this "underrated" "secret" as a "standout in a neighborhood full of standouts"; to boot, the staff is "welcoming" and the prices are a "steal" (you "may even have the place all to yourself").

Teatro
– | – | – | E

177 Tremont St. (bet. Avery & Boylston Sts.), 617-778-6841; www.teatroboston.com

Mistral has always had an element of the theatrical in its see-and-be-seen scene, so perhaps it's no surprise that chef-partner Jamie Mammano chose to locate his new venture in the heart of the Theater District; the beautifully restored 15-ft.-high ceiling with ornate gilt moldings creates a most dramatic backdrop for a concise playbill of Northern Italian fare (the antipasti for two has been garnering applause from the moment the curtain was raised).

Temple Bar
16 | 21 | 17 | $26

1688 Mass Ave. (bet. Martin & Shepard Sts.), Cambridge, 617-547-5055; www.templebarcambridge.com

◪ The "cool bar scene" at this "sleek" watering hole near Porter Square makes some respondents "wish we were still single", since it's such a "fun" "place to go for a drink and a bite after work"; though even habitués concede that the New American menu is "just not interesting", that doesn't much matter when the point here is "people looking at each other."

Boston

| | F | D | S | C |

Ten Tables — | — | — | E
597 Centre St. (bet. Pond & Spencer Sts.), Jamaica Plain, 617-524-8810

In the teeny space that was last occupied by Perdix, this new 10-table bistro is carrying on its predecessor's tradition of offering a limited though creative New American menu; owner Krista Kranyak (the former Perdix manager) has kept the open-kitchen layout intact but now takes reservations, a policy likely to endear this eatery to Jamaica Plain neighbors and hungry gourmands from afar.

TERRAMIA 26 | 17 | 23 | $41
98 Salem St. (Parmenter St.), 617-523-3112

■ "Go next door if you want spaghetti and meatballs", but if you're seeking "inventive" Italian fare in the North End, this "outstanding" ristorante "should be on everyone's short list"; even though you're "scrunched" into a "cramped" "phone booth–sized" storefront, it's more than worth the squish to tuck into "incredible homemade pastas" and other "expertly" prepared dishes ("what they do with pork – oh my!"); "we love it – no matter how crowded."

Thai Basil 21 | 12 | 18 | $21
132 Newbury St. (bet. Clarendon & Dartmouth Sts.), 617-578-0089; www.thaibasil-boston.com

◪ Combine "good-quality ingredients", a "talented" chef and a "friendly" staff and what you get is "flavorful" Thai cooking delivered "quickly"; though the "basement" digs are a "downer", fans frequent this Back Bay "staple" for "solid" "standards" offered at prices so "reasonable" that it's a veritable "bargain" in this upscale neighborhood.

Thai Village ▽ 18 | 10 | 19 | $21
592 Tremont St. (Upton St.), 617-536-6548

◪ "Tasty Thai tingles tongues" at this tiny "neighborhood storefront" that satisfies South End residents in search of "consistently good" and "fresh" Siamese food; it's relatively "inexpensive" (at least compared with other Tremont Street spots), and the staff is "friendly and attentive", but those who quibble that the atmosphere "isn't all that congenial" suggest it's "better for takeout", while outright opponents sniff "had better."

1369 Coffee House ⌀ 16 | 15 | 17 | $8
1369 Cambridge St. (bet. Hampshire & Springfield Sts.), Cambridge, 617-576-1369
757 Mass Ave. (bet. Inman & Prospect Sts.), Cambridge, 617-576-4600

◪ "Filled with intellectuals, would-be revolutionaries and students", these "laptop-laden" coffeehouse "hangouts" in Central and Inman Squares attract both "young and aging hipsters", who "grab a cup of joe", order a "creative sandwich, soup" or calzone and "just chill"; the "witty",

Boston | F | D | S | C |

"counterculture" staff delivers "service with a smile, and a nose ring" (though some detect an "occasional holier-than-thou attitude"), making them "funky, punky", "laid-back places" that are also the No. 1 Bang for the Buck in Boston.

33 Restaurant & Lounge ☻ | 15 | 24 | 17 | $42 |
33 Stanhope St. (bet. Berkeley & Clarendon Sts.), 617-572-3311; www.33restaurant.com

◪ "What an amazing space!" swoon the "dressed-up" "Euro" scenesters squeezed into this "too-trendy", late-night newcomer in the Back Bay, whose "fabulous" details include "changing color panels in the bar", maple ceilings and "cool" peekaboo bathrooms (a "must"-see); the menu is a "blend" of two cuisines – classic French and traditional Italian – an "overambitious" concept that gourmands caution results in "uneven" execution; equally as "erratic" is the service, which "ranges from acceptable to clueless."

Tim's Tavern ⌀ | 20 | 4 | 14 | $13 |
329 Columbus Ave. (Dartmouth St.), 617-437-6898

◪ If you're looking to wrap your mouth around a "real hamburger" – "big, juicy" and one of the "best in town" – this "seedy" "little dive bar" is "the place"; rub elbows "with the regulars at the bar (if you dare)", but if you feel "intimidated", head to the back, where the South End's "ethnic and economic groups mix" over "bargain treats."

Tokyo | ▽ 21 | 14 | 19 | $24 |
307 Fresh Pond Pkwy. (Lakeview St.), Cambridge, 617-876-6600

◪ "Pretty good sushi" and a "bountiful lunch buffet" (offered daily) make this Fresh Pond standby a "favorite with many regulars", at least among those who live or work nearby; the fare is "consistently good and "there's never a wait" for a table, but naysayers note "there are better Japanese restaurants elsewhere."

Tom Shea's | 18 | 18 | 17 | $37 |
122 Main St./Rte. 133 (Rte. 22), Essex, 978-768-6931

◪ "Ask for a table near the window" or, better yet, out on the patio at this "quaint" Essex seafood house that boasts a "wonderful view" of the Ipswich River; some North Shore neighbors name it an "old favorite" on a summer afternoon or when taking "out-of-town visitors", as it does a "good job" with "fresh fish" and other "traditional" New England fare; admittedly, however, the "location is much better than the food", while youngsters yap that "you'll be dining with the blue hairs."

TOP OF THE HUB ☻ | 20 | 26 | 20 | $49 |
Prudential Ctr., 800 Boylston St. (Ring Rd.), 617-536-1775; www.selectrestaurants.com

◪ "Pamper yourself" on "a special occasion" or "impress a visitor" with a "picture-perfect evening" at this "classy"

Boston

F | D | S | C

"landmark" on "top of the world" at the Prudential Tower; "definitely go on a clear night", when the "breathtaking view" from its 52nd-floor perch is "worth every cent", though know that the "amazing" vista "upstages the decent" New American menu; P.S. insiders "go up only for cocktails" in the lounge to "get intoxicated" on the panorama.

Torch   22 | 21 | 20 | $43
26 Charles St. (Beacon St.), 617-723-5939;
www.bostontorch.com

▼ When you're "planning a romantic evening with your significant other" – "a first date, an anniversary or other special occasion" – consider this "dark", "beautiful" Beacon Hill boîte; devotees are "lit up" by the "savory" New French fare, but dissenters who caution about a "very limited menu", "jammed together" tables and "uneven" service (from "accommodating" to "inattentive" to "snooty") deem it a "big disappointment."

Tosca   25 | 23 | 24 | $42
14 North St. (Mill St.), Hingham, 781-740-0080;
www.eatwellinc.com

■ "One of the few" places on the South Shore to achieve the "perfect blend of neighborhood-y and sophisticated" atmosphere, this "smashing" Northern Italian ristorante is "consistently good from start to finish"; the "top-notch" menu ("interesting yet comfortable"), "rustic" Tuscan-style interior (with exposed beams, imported tiles and wood floors) and "excellent" service make it "worth the ride to Hingham", even if some find it "far too noisy" in the "barn"-like space.

TRATTORIA A SCALINATELLA   26 | 23 | 25 | $48
253 Hanover St., 2nd fl. (bet. Cross & Richmond Sts.),
617-742-8240

■ Get "as romantic as two people can get in a public place" at this "intimate" cocoon "hidden one story up from the hubbub of Hanover Street"; "superb in every way", it pairs "fabulous", "gourmet" Italian fare (including "homemade pastas that taste like heaven") with an "exceptional wine list" and a "first-class" staff well versed in "old-country hospitality", making for a "special treat" in the North End.

Trattoria Il Panino   20 | 16 | 17 | $29
295 Franklin St. (Broad St.), 617-338-1000
11 Parmenter St. (Hanover St.), 617-720-1336
www.ilpanino.com

▼ When you want something "more adventurous than red sauce but don't want to lay out big bucks", these "reliable" Italian trattorias in the Financial District and the North End may fill the bill; they're widely "popular" (so "try to go at an off time") for their "giant portions" of "surprisingly tasty" dishes (notably the "superb lobster ravioli"), though the

Boston

F | D | S | C

decor is "nothing special", but detractors declare they "wouldn't go out of their way" for this "generic" grub.

Trattoria Pulcinella 23 | 17 | 19 | $39
147 Huron Ave. (Concord Ave.), Cambridge, 617-491-6336
■ "Why go to the North End" when you can visit instead this "secret" near Fresh Pond ask the Cambridge cognoscenti about this "quaint" trattoria where you'll "feel like you're in the movie *Big Night*"; as one of the "only real date restaurants in the area", it's an easy choice for a "romantic" dinner of "sublime" Italian fare proffered with "old-country" service, even if cheapskates charge "seriously overpriced."

Tremont 647 22 | 18 | 20 | $40
647 Tremont St. (W. Brookline St.), 617-266-4600
■ You'll "immediately feel like a regular" at this "playful yet sophisticated" South End "charmer" where chef-owner Andy Husbands' "adventurous" New American "creations" are a "delight" for "both epicurean and plebian palates"; though meat 'n' potato types can't "figure out what the fuss is all about" (whining there are "too many flavors on one plate"), the faithful just urge "run, don't walk", to get in on the "funky" "fun"; P.S. the weekend "pajama brunch is a hoot."

Trio ∇ 20 | 23 | 19 | $37
174 Lincoln St. (bet. Beach & Kneeland Sts.), 617-357-8746; www.trioboston.com
■ Set in one of Boston's "hippest neighborhoods", this "quiet", "elegant" "loft-style place" in the Leather District morphs into the "trendy" Ultra Lounge after hours, so "eat early before the crowd" "starts swarming"; fans "would definitely return for more" of the "very good" New American fare, but critics conclude the "bar hops, the food falls short."

TROQUET 26 | 21 | 25 | $48
140 Boylston St. (bet. S. Charles & Tremont Sts.), 617-695-9463
■ A "must" for "anyone who loves wine", this "charming" French bistro in the Theater District is an "oenophile's delight", "perfectly matching" "fabulous" plates (including an "exquisite cheese course") with "flights of wine"; owners Chris and Diane Campbell are "wonderful hosts", and their "unpretentious", "savvy" staff is "truly interested" in helping "diners enjoy a good evening"; even "Bacchus would be proud."

Truc S 24 | 20 | 23 | $48
560 Tremont St. (Clarendon St.), 617-338-8070
■ With chef Phillip Wang now manning the stove, this "chic" South End French bistro continues to "charm" with a "limited" yet well-executed menu that could "make anyone a Francophile"; the petite space, appointed with "robin's egg–blue walls", antique tin ceilings and an enclosed

Boston

| F | D | S | C |

greenhouse room, provides a "serene" backdrop for a "romantic" dinner, while the "solicitous" service adds to the "lovely" ambiance; if a minority maintains it "doesn't reach the heights", partisans proclaim it "truly a treat."

Tsunami | 22 | 14 | 18 | $25 |

10 Pleasant St. (Beacon St.), Brookline, 617-277-8008

■ From the "chopsticks in little wooden boxes" to the stylish "cushions in the booths", "they add all the right touches" at this small, often "overlooked gem" to make it "more than your standard Brookline sushi experience"; with "creative, fresh" fish preparations and other "satisfying" Japanese fare delivered by "personable" people, it makes for an "inviting", "casual" "alternative."

Tullio's Restaurant & Grotto | 21 | 15 | 20 | $24 |

150 Hancock St. (bet. Neponset Circle & W. Squantum St.), North Quincy, 617-471-3400

■ South Shore surveyors who "don't want to travel to the North End" for an Italian meal select this "friendly" "little" "neighborhood" place in North Quincy, where the basics are "all done right"; the "wonderful wood-oven pizzas" and "fresh pastas" lead reviewers to rave "oh, mama, is this food good!", so who cares that it's a bit of a "hole in the wall"?

Turner Fisheries | - | - | - | E |

Westin Copley Place, 10 Huntington Ave. (bet. Dartmouth & Stuart Sts.), 617-424-7425; www.westin.com

Fin fans would "swim upstream to eat" at this "dependable" Back Bay seafood house at the Westin Copley Place, long known for making one of the "best chowders in Beantown"; even those who "resist going to hotel restaurants" will be "surprised and delighted" by its "excellent fish" dishes, now showcased in "gorgeously" renovated surroundings.

Tuscan Grill | 24 | 18 | 20 | $40 |

361 Moody St. (bet. Spruce & Walnut Sts.), Waltham, 781-891-5486

☑ Regulars "always have a wonderful experience" at this "true" Tuscan grill, an "attractively" "rustic", "lively" "star of Waltham" renowned for its "terrific", "lusty" Northern Italian fare, particularly such items from the wood-burning grill as the "unbelievable" spit-roasted pork loin; the "wonderful tastes help make up for the lack of elbow room" and the "unbearable" "noise", and at least you can avoid the "North End hassle."

Tu y Yo | 22 | 13 | 21 | $19 |

858 Broadway (Powderhouse Circle), Somerville, 617-623-5411

■ "Broaden your notion of Mexican food and try" the "authentic" "country-style" dishes "made with love" from "*tia*'s or *abuela*'s secret family recipes" at this Somerville "find"; amigos who "thank them for refusing to serve

Boston　　　　　　　　　　　　F | D | S | C

burritos" ("no Tex-Mex here") are "enchanted" by the "distinctively" "flavorful" cooking that isn't easily "found elsewhere in Boston"; what's more, the staff is as "cheerful" as the colorful room.

29 Newbury　　　　　　　　　　18 | 17 | 16 | $37
29 Newbury St. (bet. Arlington & Berkeley Sts.), 617-536-0290
◪ "Sit outside" and "people-watch" amid all the "cell phones a'ringing" at this "sleek", "see-and-be-seen" Back Bay cafe; true believers who feel that it has "withstood the test of time" remain satisfied with the "tasty, inventive" New American fare and "fun drinks", but those who think that it's "coasting" on its reputation frown that the food is "not so memorable" anymore and complain too about "service with a snicker."

224 Boston Street　　　　　　　21 | 19 | 21 | $32
224 Boston St. (bet. Andrew Sq. & Mass Ave.), Dorchester, 617-265-1217
◪ A "delightful", "more upscale alternative in an area full of pubs and take-out joints", this "cozy" "neighborhood" "find" in Dorchester is an "oasis" for "original" New American dishes served in a "warm, unpretentious" setting; it pleases a "hip, relaxed crowd", even if nitpickers suggest that the menu "needs revamping" and grumble that "service runs the gamut."

Typhoon ●　　　　　　　　　▽ 18 | 16 | 16 | $23
725 Boylston St. (bet. Exeter & Fairfield Sts.), 617-859-8181
◪ Indecisive diners will appreciate the wide "mix of choices" offered at this Back Bay Pan-Asian where the extensive options run from "creative sushi" and Mongolian sizzling beef to Saigon-style skewers and Thai curries; though armchair travelers applaud it as a "nice change from the run-of-the-mill", critics who charge "change is not always for the better" complain that this "little-bit-of-everything" approach gets "confusing."

Uncle Pete's Hickory Ribs ⌀　　25 | 11 | 20 | $17
309 Bennington St. (Chelsea St.), East Boston, 617-569-7427
■ Dig into the "best barbecue in the area" at this "family-owned" shack in East Boston, where the "finger-licking" vittles are often "served up by Uncle Pete himself"; it's "nice to see" a chef-owner who "really cares" about slow-smoking his "Flintstone-sized ribs" and "delicious" pulled pork just right (the "low cost is just a bonus"); sure this grub is "messy", but it's so "wickedly good"; P.S. make sure you get a side of the "out-of-this-world Asian slaw."

Union Oyster House　　　　　18 | 18 | 16 | $31
41 Union St. (bet. W. Hanover & North Sts.), 617-227-2750; www.unionoysterhouse.com
◪ Reputedly the oldest restaurant in Boston (and the oldest in continuous operation in the U.S.), this "true-blue"

Boston F | D | S | C

"landmark" near Faneuil Hall has been a local "tradition for centuries"; though it's "loaded with tourists", you "can't beat the oysters" (served by folks who must've "been working here since Kennedy was a regular"), but savvy insiders advise just "stick to the raw bar" and "don't spoil" the "historic" experience by ordering from the "classic" seafood-slanted New England menu.

Upper Crust 22 | 11 | 15 | $13
20 Charles St. (Beacon St.), 617-723-9600
286 Harvard St. (Beacon St.), Brookline, 617-739-8518
www.theuppercrustpizzeria.com

■ "Upper Crust? – try Perfect Crust" cheer connoisseurs who crow that "at last" "amazing" pizza can be had on Beacon Hill and in Brookline; the menu offers a choice of "straightforward and innovative" toppings, so a pie purist and a "food snob" can "both be happy" (a "feel-good meal if ever there were one"), but "don't tell anyone because it's already hard enough to get a seat."

UpStairs on the Square – | – | – | VE
(fka UpStairs at the Pudding)
91 Winthrop St. (JFK St.), Cambridge, 617-864-1933;
www.upstairsonthesquare.com

The former UpStairs at the Pudding has relocated to this dramatically over-the-top space in the heart of Harvard Square, where the casual Monday Club Bar downstairs serves lighter meals while the upstairs Soirée Room pulls out all the stops with creative New American fare; co-owners Mary-Catherine Deibel and Deborah Hughes have brought along their longtime chef, Steve Olsen, and hired Amanda Lydon (ex Metro, Truc) to join him at the stove.

Vault *S* – | – | – | E
105 Water St. (Liberty Sq.), 617-292-9966

Reinventing itself yet again, this Financial District magnet for power suits now features multiregional Italian fare – think slow-roasted pork, Tuscan black cabbage with caramelized onions, warm pecorino pudding – courtesy of new chef-partner Carmen Quagliata; the bar menu has also been revamped, with upscale munchies, though the extensive wine list and clubby decor remain.

Veggie Planet ⊄ 23 | 11 | 14 | $14
Club Passim, 47 Palmer St. (Church St.), Cambridge,
617-661-1513; www.veggieplanet.net

◪ "Thank goodness there's a truly veggie restaurant in Harvard Square" laud loyalists of this "new wave" pizza joint housed at folk music Club Passim; the kitchen "thinks outside the box" with "unusual combos" that are certainly "fabulous" for "vegetarians" "but still delicious enough for carnivores"; service, however, can be "slow" in the "dreary" "basement" digs.

Boston | F | D | S | C |

Via Lago | 21 | 9 | 16 | $15 |
1845 Mass Ave. (Bedford St./Rte. 225), Lexington, 781-861-6174; www.vialagocatering.com

☑ "Gourmet items" such as "tasty" create-your-own sandwiches and pastas, "terrific salads, hot specials" "and even better desserts" make up the "varied", largely American menu at this "creative" cafe, an "oasis among Lexington's food outlets"; it makes for a "quick lunch" or "take-out dinner", but it has "all the comforts of a cafeteria", so regulars recommend "skipping the dreary dining area" and having a "picnic" instead "on the Battle Green."

Via Matta ⑤ | 22 | 22 | 22 | $51 |
79 Park Plaza (Arlington St.), 617-422-0008

☑ "Can't afford Radius?" – this "trendy" new Back Bay "hot spot" run by the same team is the "next best thing"; "off to a good start", it's a "modern" Italian "scene" that appeals with "sparkling" dishes brought to table by a "professional" crew in an "elegant" space adorned with artwork by a Russian set designer; yes, it's still a "lot of money for spaghetti" and such, and the "deafening" "noise" "puts the 'din' in 'dining'" here, but "how can you complain when there are all these beautiful people around?"

Vicki Lee Boyajian | 21 | 14 | 14 | $18 |
1019 Great Plain Ave. (Chestnut St.), Needham, 781-449-0022

☑ "Part bakery, part cafe", this "lovely" "ladylike" "lunch spot" in Needham garners applause for its "desserts par excellence"; it's a place for suburbanites to "meet" for "delicious coffee" and "yummy baked goods", to partake of "gourmet" New American soups, salads and sandwiches or to pick up "prepared foods to take out", but opponents feel that it's "way too impressed with itself", not to mention that it's "overpriced"; N.B. no dinner.

Victoria ● | ▽ 18 | 8 | 19 | $18 |
1024 Mass Ave. (New Market Sq.), 617-442-5965

■ "Catering to the local police", city officials and residents of the South End, this "old-style" American diner in New Market Square is "nice to have" around for heaping portions of "good", "basic" greasy-spoon grub, slung "fast" (and "always with a smile") at "inexpensive" prices.

Viet Hong ⌀ | ▽ 21 | 8 | 18 | $13 |
182 Brighton Ave. (bet. Allston St. & Harbor Ave.), Allston, 617-254-3600

☑ Asian admirers in Allston attest that this "family-run" storefront, in all its "spartan splendor", is a "neighborhood favorite" for "great cheap eats"; the majority maintains that it's a "true find" for Vietnamese fare such as ginger-braised fish and crispy squid, but detractors complain about "spotty" execution and caution that "share-a-table is the rule" here.

Boston   F | D | S | C

Viet's Café   21 | 14 | 19 | $18
303 Broadway (Mass Ave.), Arlington, 781-641-2388
■ At this Vietnamese "favorite" in Arlington, the "solid" dishes are full of "crisp, clean flavors"; along with "fresh, traditional offerings", the menu features more "unusual" dishes, all served by "lovely", "helpful" folks in a "comfy" room with a "restful" ambiance; even if it's "unremarkable", it "fills a niche in the area", so locals don't "need to go into the city" to get a pho fix.

Villa Francesca ◐   18 | 16 | 16 | $32
150 Richmond St. (Commercial St.), 617-367-2948
■ "Sit by the window for a good view of the street" action at this "traditional" Italian, an "old-style" charmer that's a suitable place to "take out-of-town visitors" for a classic North End experience; the familiar dishes are "ordinary but enjoyable", though modernists maintain it's just another "tired" "touristy" joint, with "tight seating" to boot.

Village Fish   19 | 10 | 16 | $26
22 Harvard St. (Webster St.), Brookline, 617-566-3474
■ "Big portions" of "fresh fish" "cooked simply", along with "tasty" pastas "served right in the pan", "keep the crowds coming back" to this Brookline Italian seafood house; fans give the thumbs up to the "casual", "neighborhoody" atmosphere and "affordable" tabs, but critics crab that "everything comes in just a little below expectation."

Village Smokehouse   18 | 14 | 16 | $23
1 Harvard St. (Washington St.), Brookline, 617-566-3782
■ "Life, liberty and ribs are what makes America great" proclaim patriots partial to this "friendly" Brookline BBQ shack where the "reliably good" babybacks are cooked "before your eyes" in an "open pit" (the "chicken is nothing to sneeze at either"); "bring a caravan of carnivores" when y'all have a "hankering for smoked meats", though some barbecue connoisseurs conclude "ok, but no real draw."

Village Sushi & Grill   ▽ 23 | 19 | 21 | $23
14 Corinth St. (Birch St.), Roslindale, 617-363-7874
■ Check out this "wonderful addition" to Roslindale "if you're in the neighborhood" for its "enormous selection" of traditional and "innovative" sushi and "delectable" Korean specialties; "simply designed with blond woods and bamboo", it's "owned by the same folks as JP Seafood Cafe", and the "friendly" staff here takes the "same care with the food"; maki in Rozzie? – "progress indeed."

Vin & Eddie's   ▽ 25 | 19 | 23 | $40
1400 Bedford St./Rte. 18 (bet. Rtes. 58 & 139), Abington, 781-871-1469
■ "In business since 1955" and long a "family favorite", this "warm and inviting" ristorante in Abington is "good all

get updates at zagat.com

Boston | F | D | S | C |

around", from its "large" menu of "traditional" Northern Italian food, paired with one of the "best wine lists on the South Shore" (each bottle is also available by the glass), to its "well-spaced tables" to its "accommodating" service; the decor's somewhat "dark and aged, but that's what gives it its charm."

Vinny's at Night ⌀ | 24 | 8 | 19 | $24 |
76 Broadway (Hathorn St.), Somerville, 617-628-1921

■ Though the "entrance through a convenience store" in Somerville feels a bit "surreal", just make your way past the "shelves of chips" to this "real find" of a trattoria that's "reminiscent of the old North End"; settle in and let the "kind, efficient" servers bring you "out-of-this-world" Southern Italian food ("like eating your nonna's cooking"), starting with the antipasti (a "perfect way to begin"), following with the "to-die-for roast pork with vinegar peppers" and ending with a "wonderful" tiramisu – *mangia, mangia!*

V. Majestic ∅ | ▽ 23 | 5 | 17 | $12 |
164 Brighton Ave. (Harvard Ave.), Allston, 617-782-6088

■ "If it's what's on the plate that matters to you, then you're in the right place" say supporters of this Allston "hole-in-the-wall" that turns out "fabulous" Vietnamese food; the kitchen has "great success with grilled dishes and soups" (and an Asian pizza too), and the service is "speedy", so in spite of the "linoleum" surroundings, "at these prices" "why ever cook for yourself again?"

Vox Populi | 16 | 18 | 17 | $34 |
755 Boylston St. (bet. Exeter & Fairfield Sts.), 617-424-8300

◪ A "key stop on the Y.O.M. (yuppies on the make) trail", this "cool, hip restaurant/bar is where cool, hip Bostonians congregate"; expect to ogle "lots of beautiful people" meeting and greeting "after work" (this is a "pickup place if ever there was one"), so while the New American menu is "acceptable", "who goes here for the food?"

Walden Grille | 17 | 14 | 16 | $30 |
24 Walden St. (Main St.), Concord, 978-371-2233; www.waldengrille.com

◪ Set in an 1800s firehouse in "historic" Concord, this "cozy", relaxing bistro with a "neighborhood feeling" sure "beats the chains" as a "convenient" place to stop in for an "intimate lunch or dinner"; staunch supporters swear the "varied" New American menu is "almost always quite good", but skeptics sniff "nothing to write home about."

Warren Tavern | 15 | 18 | 16 | $23 |
2 Pleasant St. (Main St.), Charlestown, 617-241-8142; www.warrentavern.com

◪ "Paul Revere bellied up to the bar" (as did George Washington) at this "dark and cozy" "colonial tavern"

subscribe to zagat.com

Boston | F | D | S | C |

(circa 1780) in Charlestown; infused with an "olde Boston feel", it's a "great place to take out-of-towners" for a "cup of grog" and "plain" New England fare "with no fanfare"; it's also, surprisingly, a "big singles spot" that draws a "lively crowd of townies", but contemporary critics complain that given the "sub-par" grub, "history only gets you so far."

Washington Square Tavern | 23 | 19 | 20 | $28 |

714 Washington St. (Beacon St.), Brookline, 617-232-8989

■ Dubbed the "*Cheers* of Brookline", this "hopping" "local hangout" "tries to be a friendly neighborhood pub, a yuppie hangout and a creative New American bistro" all at once and "somehow succeeds on all counts"; the "kitchen does it right" with its "fantastic seasonal" dishes ("if you can't get a seat, have dinner and meet new friends at the bar") and the vibe is "friendly", so besides the "noise", the "only problem is it's so nice that people linger" – which means an "even longer wait for a table."

Wayside Inn | 16 | 23 | 20 | $34 |

Wayside Inn, 72 Wayside Inn Rd. (Rte. 20), Sudbury, 978-443-1776; www.wayside.org

☑ "Go back in time" (to 1716) and "dine beside the blazing hearth" at this "historic landmark", a "charming inn" in Sudbury that's just the place to "take your out-of-town mother-in-law for Sunday dinner"; with seven fireplaces in seven rustically elegant rooms and a staff attired in "period garb", it's a "tourist favorite", though "adventurous eaters should steer clear" of the "unexceptional" Yankee fare that was "probably already tired in colonial days."

West Side Lounge ● | 22 | 22 | 20 | $30 |

1680 Mass Ave. (Shepard St.), Cambridge, 617-441-5566

■ At this "*Sex and the City*–esque" lounge near Porter Square, the "swanky" yet "comfortable" scene "without the attitude" lures a "crowd that's older and hipper" than you might expect "in this neighborhood"; they come for "fabulous cocktails" mixed at the mahogany bar and nibble on "interesting" American dishes delivered by "pleasant" servers, and when they open up the front windows to the street in the summer, the breeze is as "cool" as the setting.

West Street Grille | 19 | 18 | 17 | $30 |

15 West St. (bet. Tremont & Washington Sts.), 617-423-0300

☑ "Escape the crush of Downtown Crossing" at this "total package" that's both a "quiet" retreat for a "weekday lunch" and a "lively happy-hour" haunt for the "after-work crowd"; the New American menu takes an "imaginative approach to comfort food", "at a price that won't send you to the poorhouse", but the cognoscenti counsel "go to drink and flirt, not to eat."

Boston F | D | S | C

White Rainbow ▽ 20 | 19 | 21 | $44
65 Main St. (Rogers St.), Gloucester, 978-281-0017; www.whiterainbowrestaurant.com

Combining "elegance and fine food", this "cozy place for a special occasion" features a "surprisingly complex and well-executed" menu of updated Continental fare ("not the deep-fried seafood standards" prevalent in Gloucester); loyalists laud the romantic, old-world surroundings, but frugal gourmands gripe "too expensive" for what you get.

White Star Tavern ● 17 | 14 | 15 | $25
565 Boylston St. (bet. Clarendon & Dartmouth Sts.), 617-536-4477

"Meet friends" for "drinks and a nosh after work" at this "hip" Back Bay watering hole where the New American "bar menu" features an "inventive take on the usual", at a "range of prices to suit all pockets"; it's an especially "cool" scene "in the summer", when you can "people-watch" from the sidewalk tables, but foes feel that at any time of year the "forgettable" fare "defines average."

Wisteria House 17 | 9 | 14 | $19
264 Newbury St. (bet. Fairfield & Gloucester Sts.), 617-536-8866

Daring diners who've discovered this Asian alternative "tucked away downstairs on Newbury Street" give an approving nod to its "adventurous" menu of "very good" Taiwanese specialties (it also features "typical" Chinese dishes and sushi); the helpful staff is more than happy to give guidance, so go ahead and "try things not normally found at other restaurants."

Wonder Spice Cafe 22 | 16 | 18 | $19
697 Centre St. (Burroughs St.), Jamaica Plain, 617-522-0200

"Follow your nose" to this "hidden treasure" in Jamaica Plain, where "everything smells good"; the "deliciously exotic" Southeast Asian menu pairing Cambodian and Thai dishes features "enough choices to please most palates", but chile-heads counsel "order the spicier entrees and you'll be perspiring in no time" (a good thing); not only is it a "great place for carnivores and vegetarians" alike, but you'll be "served caringly" at a very "reasonable price."

Woodman's ⊅ 21 | 9 | 10 | $23
125 Main St./Rte. 133 (Willow Ct.), Essex, 978-768-6057; www.woodmans.com

"When that fried seafood urge comes on", there may be "nothing better" than this "rustic" New England "shack" in the small coastal town of Essex, which "allegedly invented the fried clam" more than 85 years ago; it's entirely "no frills" – you sit at a "picnic table", sip "beer or wine out of a plastic cup" and chow down on "huge portions" of "classic" finny fare fresh from the fry-o-later – but for

subscribe to zagat.com

Boston | F | D | S | C |

generations of nostalgic North Shore natives, it has been a must-stop "on the way to or from the beach."

Woody's Grill & Tap ▽ | 18 | 11 | 15 | $17 |
58 Hemenway St. (Westland Ave.), 617-375-9663
■ "Awesome brick-oven pizzas" attract a mixed crowd of "young college" kids, Sox fans and Symphony subscribers to this "homey" "neighborhood joint" in the Fenway, where the "thin-crust" pies are served up by "great people"; yes, it's a "bear trying to park", but the "creative" toppings make it worth driving a few circles around the block.

Wright Catch at Uncommon Grounds | - | - | - | I |
575 Mt. Auburn St. (bet. Bigelow & Dexter Aves.), Watertown, 617-924-9625
What do you get when you cross a funky coffeehouse with a traditional New England seafood joint? – at this small, casual Watertown spot, you get java and pastries in the morning, sandwiches at midday and broiled or fried seafood with some Italian influences in the evening; it makes for an odd combo, perhaps, but if you're looking to chase your clams with an espresso, you've come to the right place.

WuChon | 23 | 11 | 17 | $21 |
290 Somerville Ave. (Union Sq.), Somerville, 617-623-3313
■ "Where the Koreans get Korean food", this kimchi kitchen in Somerville is "not afraid to spice it up"; the "vast" menu of "authentic homestyle" dishes can be "daunting", but the "friendly" servers will "help you with your selections"; besides, with so many tempting choices, you'll have "lots of reasons to go back", "uninspired" decor notwithstanding.

Yama | 22 | 15 | 19 | $26 |
245 Washington St./Rte. 16 (Rte. 9), Wellesley, 781-431-8886
◪ Maki mavens in Wellesley praise the "wide variety of well-prepared sushi" offered at this "unassuming" "pearl"; kudos also go to the "courteous" staff, since "special orders don't upset them", but "don't forget to BYO" ("time to get a liquor license" to accommodate "busy suburbanites").

Yangtze River | 16 | 13 | 16 | $21 |
21-25 Depot Sq. (Mass Ave.), Lexington, 781-861-6030
◪ Longtime loyalists of this spacious Chinese in suburban Lexington claim that it still "hits the spot" after all these years, but more discerning types deride the "standard", "predictable" "flavors that haven't changed since the '70s" ("won ton whatever"), as well as the "tired" digs.

YANKS | 25 | 25 | 23 | $51 |
717 Hale St./Rte. 127 (2nd Ave.), Beverly, 978-232-9898; www.yanksrestaurant.com
◪ Among the "tops on the North Shore" for "fine dining", this "handsome" "class act" in "out-of-the-way" Beverly

Boston | F | D | S | C |

Farms can "stand up to any Downtown heavyweight"; the room's "clean lines", which radiate "city style", provide a "sleek" backdrop for the "rich flavors" of chef Olivier Rigaud's "exceptional" American cooking; "worth the drive" and "worth every penny", "save this one for a special night", even if a few sensitive sorts detect some "attitude."

Zabaglione ▽ | 25 | 13 | 21 | $38 |
10 Central St. (Market St.), Ipswich, 978-356-5466

☑ "Everything is fresh and cooked right in front of you" in the open kitchen at this "tiny" Ipswich "jewel", which wins acclaim for preparing some of the "best gourmet" Italian fare on the North Shore; fans say it "obviously focuses on getting it right", from the "fresh ingredients" to the "fine presentations" to the "nice wine list"; the only downside: it's rather "like eating in a closet."

Zaftigs Delicatessen | 19 | 15 | 17 | $19 |
335 Harvard St. (bet. Babcock & Stedman Sts.), Brookline, 617-975-0075; www.zaftigs.com

☑ Need "comfort food" to "satisfy your soul"? – head to Brookline to this Jewish-style deli that's "popular" for "delicious" "breakfasts served all day" long; given a menu that includes some "inventive" "gourmet" dishes and walls adorned with zany local artwork, this definitely ain't your grandma's deli, which only dismays purists who kvetch that this city remains "starved for the mythical" kosher deal; still, "expect long waits on the weekend."

Zebra's Bistro & Wine Bar | 21 | 19 | 20 | $38 |
21 North St. (Rte. 109), Medfield, 508-359-4100; www.zebrasbistro.com

☑ "Surprisingly trendy for the suburbs", this "delightful" New American bistro in Medfield appeals with a "limited but interesting" menu (sushi too) and "comfortable" wine bar with an ever-changing rotation of labels; though some are left "disappointed" by the experience, enthusiasts just exclaim "what a find" in MetroWest!

Zen 320 | – | – | – | M |
320 Washington St. (Holden St.), Brookline, 617-713-4320; www.zen320.com

The name suits the ambiance at this Brookline newcomer where the banquettes draped in cream-colored fabrics and set against a backdrop of dark walls give it a serene air; the Pan-Asian menu emphasizes Japanese (the long list of sushi choices takes pride of place) and Korean specialties, along with a selection of Thai dishes.

Zon's | 19 | 21 | 17 | $25 |
2 Perkins St. (Centre St.), Jamaica Plain, 617-524-9667; www.zonsjp.com

☑ Delivering "comfort food with a boomer sensibility" (think ground sirloin topped with Stilton, mac 'n' cheese made

Boston F | D | S | C |

with farfalle, farmhouse cheddar and fontina), this "hip" Jamaica Plain storefront could be dubbed "mom's New American kitchen"; with scarlet walls, exposed brick and dim lighting, the "small space" feels almost "sexy", while the staff is "funky and friendly" (if occasionally "spacey – this is JP, after all"), but the unimpressed conclude "not as interesting as you'd hope."

ZuZu! – | – | – | M |
474 Mass Ave. (Brookline St.), Cambridge, 617-492-9181; www.mideastclub.com
"Share a bunch of maza" at this "upscale" annex of the Middle East nightclub, a "cheery" bar and bistro that provides Central Square with an "interesting" "change of pace"; after a post-*Survey* menu update, the appetizers are still inspired by that part of the world, though the entrees now include more Eclectic dishes.

Cape Cod

| F | D | S | C |

ABBA
26 | 19 | 22 | $45

89 Old Colony Way (bet. Old Tote & West Rds.), Orleans, 508-255-8144

■ Chefs Erez Pinhas and Pry Grasinc may well run the "only Israeli-Thai kitchen in America", and together they've created a "cool", "citified" space that's a "rare find on the Cape"; their "inventive" menu tweaks Mediterranean flavors with Asian accents ("finally, fusion that actually works"), and it's presented by an "enthusiastic" staff in a room filled with original artwork; despite the "small" digs, admirers "love this hidden jewel of Orleans" but beg "let's keep it a secret."

ABBICCI
26 | 23 | 23 | $45

43 Main St./Rte. 6A (Willow St.), Yarmouth Port, 508-362-3501

■ "After days of Cape quahogs, check out this bright bit of Italy" in Yarmouth Port, where the "delectable" dishes with Mediterranean flourishes are "consistently" among the "best" in the area; "when you walk into this former captain's house", you might "think it'll be stuffy", but instead the design is "witty" and the ambiance "sophisticated", adding to a "delightful evening"; seating in the "intimate rooms" may be "cheek by jowl", but that's just "*amore*."

Academy Ocean Grill
24 | 20 | 23 | $42

2 Academy Pl. (Orleans Rd.), Orleans, 508-240-1585

◪ "Another real winner" courtesy of "fabled" chef-owner Christian Schultz, this shingled house in Orleans provides a "warm and cozy" haven for "discriminating palates" that appreciate a "truly excellent experience" "every time"; "only top-drawer foods are allowed in his kitchen", from which he prepares "mouthwatering", seafood-slanted Continental classics and Eclectic creations that are served by an "attentive", "friendly" crew; skeptics, however, suggest "there are many more fish in the sea."

Adrian's
19 | 18 | 16 | $26

Outer Reach Resort, 535 Rte. 6 (near Pilgrim Heights Nat'l Seashore Park), North Truro, 508-487-4360; www.adriansrestaurant.com

◪ Perched high on a hill in North Truro, this "bustling", "family-run place that likes families" has long been a "favorite"; take in an "excellent view" of the bay from the terrace (a popular spot for breakfast) while tucking into "terrific pizzas" from the wood-fired oven, "good" Italian pastas or "fresh fish"; the "welcoming owners" are "most

Cape Cod

| | F | D | S | C |

personable", even if the "college-kid" staff "doesn't quite get it", so though it's "not great", it makes for a "nice place on a summer evening."

Aesop's Tables   17 | 20 | 16 | $37
316 Main St. (Bank St.), Wellfleet, 508-349-6450

◪ Oozing "lots of charm", this "rambling" 1805 house in Wellfleet continues to satisfy loyalists with its Traditional American dinners; a growing contingent, however, feels that it has "gone downhill", citing "disappointing" cooking and service that's "lacking", but even though the dining room has "seen better days", "Cape Codders in-the-know" still repair to the "relaxing", "dimly lit" tavern upstairs for cocktails and a "casual" bite.

Alberto's Ristorante   20 | 18 | 19 | $36
360 Main St. (Barnstable Rd.), Hyannis, 508-778-1770; www.albertoscapecod.com

◪ "Striking a neat balance between the self-consciously upmarket" spots on Route 6A and the "family-friendly" joints on Route 28, this "old-school" Northern Italian on Hyannis' Main Street offers "reliable", "authentic" dishes paired with "reasonably priced wines"; the service is generally "good" and adherents enjoy the live piano music, but detractors who deem the fare "basic" and the decor "tired" consider it a "fallback at best."

Aqua Grille   19 | 19 | 18 | $32
14 Gallo Rd. (Coast Guard Rd.), Sandwich, 508-888-8889; www.aquagrille.com

◪ The "well-designed" "decor is what makes it unique on the Cape" say surveyors about this "stylish" Sandwich spot that "feels more like a city restaurant than a waterfront" grill, though as it's anchored "right on the canal" it boasts a most "picturesque" "view of the sun setting" over the marina; while nobody complains about the "attractive" surroundings, the consensus on the New American menu is "so-so."

Ardeo   19 | 18 | 17 | $23
23 Whitespath Rd. (Station Ave.), South Yarmouth, 508-760-1500

◪ It's "nice to have a little Mediterranean flair in South Yarmouth" say appreciative admirers of this "refreshing change from the basic Cape Cod" offerings; the owners obviously "take pride in their products" and their kitchen turns out "interesting" Middle Eastern specialties; though some dishes are occasionally "off the mark", it still adds up to a "fine family value."

Bee-Hive Tavern   19 | 17 | 20 | $22
406 Rte. 6A (Quaker Meetinghouse Rd.), East Sandwich, 508-833-1184

■ "Summer or winter, it's busy as a beehive" at this "quaint New England–style" "family place" in East Sandwich;

get updates at zagat.com

Cape Cod

| F | D | S | C |

"rustic and "homey", it's a "good" pick for Traditional American "comfort food", whether you're "taking the kids" or having an "old ladies' lunch"; the eats may be "basic", but with a "friendly" staff and "value"-oriented prices, it may be the "only restaurant on the Cape that has a wait on a Tuesday night – in February."

Belfry Bistro ⑤ — 21 | 23 | 20 | $45
Belfry Inne, 8 Jarves St. (bet. Main St. & Rte. 6A), Sandwich, 508-888-8550; www.belfryinn.com

"Located in an old church" in Sandwich, where the "stained glass is as beautiful as the presentations on the plate", this "unique" New American–Eclectic bistro turns out "creative" dishes that worshipers hail as a "spiritual experience for the palate"; despite the "heavenly" setting, however, devil's advocates declare that the execution is "inconsistent" (a "few entrees need a retreat").

BRAMBLE INN — 27 | 25 | 25 | $52
2019 Main St./Rte. 6A (Williams Dr.), Brewster, 508-896-7644; www.brambleinn.com

Chef-owner Ruth Manchester "continues to surprise and delight" guests with her "sumptuous" prix fixe dinners, "highly inventive" New American–Eclectic "seasonal offerings" that are just about the best "gourmet food to be found anywhere on the Cape"; "perfect for a romantic evening", it's set in a "charming" 1861 inn in Brewster, where a "knowledgeable" staff proffers "attentive" service; "what a gem!"

Brazilian Grill — 18 | 10 | 21 | $25
680 Main St. (Stevens St.), Hyannis, 508-771-0109

Brandishing "swords laden" with a "great selection" of "delicious" "grilled meats", "enthusiastic" servers circle the room of this "big surprise in Hyannis", carving "all-you-can-eat" Brazilian BBQ tableside until you beg them to stop; even if the food quality can "vary" and the decor is "not tops", this churrascaria is an "incredible value."

Bubala's by the Bay — 18 | 15 | 16 | $26
183 Commercial St. (Court St.), Provincetown, 508-487-0773

Take in a "great show" out on the patio of this "kitschy" Eclectic seafood house where you can "watch the world go by" on Provincetown's "main drag" while tucking into your meal; though the service is "up and down", regulars say the eats are "better than you'd expect from the diner-style interior", but critics carp there are "too many better restaurants in town" to "stand in line" here.

Cafe Edwige/Edwige at Night — 24 | 16 | 20 | $41
333 Commercial St. (bet. Freeman & Standish Sts.), Provincetown, 508-487-2008

"As good as ever" (better, in fact), this "funky", "friendly" cafe in the center of Provincetown is "full of charm";

Cape Cod

F | D | S | C

whether you come for a "superb" breakfast (the "best in town") or a "stupendous" dinner (no lunch is served), the New American cooking is "inventive, fresh and delicious in every way"; of course it's "hectic in season", but in this town, what isn't?

Cape Sea Grille

25 | 21 | 20 | $42

31 Sea St. (off Rte. 28), Harwich Port, 508-432-4745; www.capeseagrille.com

Cherished as a "favorite splurge" for a "sophisticated" dining experience, this "beautifully appointed" Harwich Port "treat" set in a "quaint country house" may be "as good as any swanky joint in Boston"; providing a "welcome escape from all the rustic fried foods on the Cape", it features an "exceptional", "innovative" New American menu ("who needs a view with a meal like this?"); be forewarned, however, that the service can be "slower than midsummer traffic on Route 28."

Captain Linnell House

23 | 26 | 23 | $48

137 Skaket Beach Rd. (bet. Rte. 6A & West Rd.), Orleans, 508-255-3400; www.linnell.com

"Get dressed up" for dinner and visit this "lovely" "former sea captain's house" in Orleans for a "romantic" "special evening" "enhanced" by "elegant surroundings" appointed with period furniture ("in the summer, you can wander around in the garden" replete with a gazebo); loyalists laud the "diverse" menu of "delectable gourmet" American seafood selections brought to table by a "professional" staff, but trendoids dismiss this "old-fashioned" dowager as "blue-hair city."

Chapoquoit Grill

23 | 18 | 20 | $29

410 W. Falmouth Hwy./Rte. 28A (Brick Kiln Rd.), West Falmouth, 508-540-7794

"Don't tell anyone about this" "always jumping" "gem" "hidden" in the "middle of nowhere" in West Falmouth, because it "doesn't take reservations" and it's "already too crowded"; credit its "marvelous" pizzas and "fantastic", New American fare prepared with "flair", "cheerful" service and the "right prices"; "get here early" or "be prepared to wait" (it's "worth" it).

Chart Room

20 | 19 | 18 | $32

1 Shore Rd. (County Rd.), Cataumet, 508-563-5350

"Hundreds of boats are moored right outside" this "old-fashioned summer place" quartered in a rustic barge overlooking Cataumet's marina, adding to its appropriately "nautical" feel; "guests from out of town" get a "real Cape Cod experience" here while munching on "amazing lobster rolls" and other "traditional", "nothing fancy" New England seafood specialties; landlubbers, though, crab that this time warp is "stuck in the '70s."

get updates at zagat.com

Cape Cod F | D | S | C

Chatham Bars Inn 22 | 26 | 21 | $48
Chatham Bars Inn, 279 Shore Rd. (Seaview St.), Chatham, 508-945-0096; www.chathambarsinn.com

■ Evoking a "wonderful feeling of long-ago luxury", this "grand lady on the hill" – a "captivating" "beauty" set in a tranquil resort perched high on a bluff "overlooking the ocean" in Chatham – "makes you remember why you sit in traffic to get to the Cape"; along with the "exceptional view", patrons are served "well-prepared" Eclectic dishes by a "formal" staff, making for a "sophisticated culinary experience"; N.B. jacket required.

Chatham Squire 16 | 13 | 16 | $26
487 Main St. (bet. Chatham Bars Ave. & Seaview St.), Chatham, 508-945-0945; www.thesquire.com

☒ "Where else can you find fishermen and trust fund babies" having "rowdy fun" together "over beers and burgers" than at this "basic watering hole" in Chatham, a "hangout" as "comfortable" as an "old pair of shoes"; regardless of the "spotty" service, the Traditional American menu is "dependable", but "you may be better off playing the lottery" than "trying to get a table" here on summer weekends.

CHESTER 27 | 23 | 24 | $52
404 Commercial St. (bet. Dyer & Washington Sts.), Provincetown, 508-487-8200; www.chesterrestaurant.com

☒ "Polished and elegant", this Greek Revival–style mansion in Provincetown "always impresses"; "everything is well thought out and well done", from the "luscious" New American fare to the "appealing" decor to the "impeccable" service; the "owners are most gracious hosts" and "they know their wines" too (the "super-fabulous" list caters to "all tastes and budgets"), so even if a few find this "gem" a bit too "precious", most just "rave" "simply irresistible."

CHILLINGSWORTH 26 | 25 | 25 | $64
2449 Main St./Rte. 6A (Foster Rd.), Brewster, 508-896-3640; www.chillingsworth.com

■ Dining at this "gracious" "grande dame" in Brewster is "like visiting your rich Yankee aunt", "with her finest china and linens" setting the stage for a "memorable meal"; served with "style and grace" by a "knowledgeable" staff, the prix fixe New French courses add up to a "sumptuous feast" ("though the wine prices may require a second mortgage"); it's an ideal "special-occasion destination" – just "sit up straight, remember those manners" and you'll be treated to a "divine" evening.

Christian's 16 | 18 | 18 | $33
443 Main St. (bet. Chatham Bars Ave. & Shore Rd.), Chatham, 508-945-3362; www.christiansrestaurant.com

☒ "Ask to be seated upstairs" near the "entertaining piano bar" advise adherents of this "friendly" Chatham landmark

Cape Cod | F | D | S | C |

where most of the dishes and cocktails are "cleverly named" after famous movies; former friends, however, who warn that it has "gone downhill", cite "heavy, mediocre" Traditional American grub and suggest "there are much better places" in town to choose among.

Clancy's of Dennisport | 18 | 17 | 17 | $26 |
8 Upper County Rd. (bet. Rtes. 28 & 134), Dennisport, 508-394-6661; www.clancysrestaurant.com

◪ "*Erin Go Braugh,* but never will Erin go hungry" at this tavern "overlooking the Swan River" in Dennisport, where "good, plain" Traditional American food is served with Irish charm; "there's something for everyone" on the menu, which may explain why the "casual" room is "always a mob scene" in season, but still, the unimpressed yawn "boring."

Contrast Bistro | 19 | 16 | 15 | $30 |
605 Rte. 6A (bet. Antonelli Circle & New Boston Rd.), Dennis, 508-385-9100; www.contrastbistro.com

◪ "Quirky" and "funky", this cozy, colorful bistro in Dennis offers a "different spin on the norm" with its "inventive" Eclectic creations (alongside "comfort food" like meatloaf and chicken pot pie); detractors may deride the "uneven quality" of the dishes and the spotty service, but the addicted urge just "save room" for the "yummy desserts", especially the "unbelievably good 'coma-inducing chocolate cake' that lives up to its name."

Coonamessett Inn | 19 | 21 | 20 | $36 |
311 Gifford St. (Jones Rd.), Falmouth, 508-548-2300

◪ "Take your mother-in-law" to this Cape "classic", a "charming" inn overlooking "beautiful" Jones Pond in Falmouth; it's a "quiet", "pleasant" place for an "elegant Sunday brunch" or "traditional" New England–style lunch or dinner (the menu is "at its best when it sticks to its Yankee roots"); chic-seekers, however, who find it "unimaginative", dismiss it as a "mainstay for the over-70 crowd."

Dancing Lobster | 19 | 19 | 16 | $43 |
373 Commercial St. (Johnson St.), Provincetown, 508-487-0900

◪ "Watch the boats come in as you dine" on the deck "overlooking Provincetown Harbor" at this Italian "favorite" that draws a "fun crowd of tourists and locals"; the "varied menu" includes "lots of seafood", served by a "friendly" staff, but opponents report that it "needs to try harder to get back the old zing" (too tired to tango, "this lobster has now slipped into a comfortable waltz").

Dan'l Webster Inn | 20 | 23 | 20 | $38 |
Dan'l Webster Inn, 149 Main St. (bet. Rtes. 6A & 130), Sandwich, 508-888-3622; www.danlwebsterinn.com

◪ At this "traditional" colonial-style inn in the "quaint village of Sandwich", the "romantic glass conservatory"

Cape Cod   F | D | S | C

"overlooking the pretty garden" boasts the "perfect ambiance for that summer dinner" "when you're looking for a more formal Cape Cod experience"; the negative, though, nag that the "classic" Continental menu isn't "up to the surroundings" and want to know what's with all the "blue-hair" tour groups stopping here.

Dolphin   22 | 14 | 20 | $27
3250 Main St./Rte. 6A (Braggs Ln.), Barnstable, 508-362-6610

☑ "No wonder it's filled with locals" – this "cheerful", Barnstable "institution" (since 1954) offers one of the "best overall values on the Cape"; though the "basic", never-changing Traditional American menu may "not be very exciting" (the "typical lobster this and chowder that"), the "homestyle" cooking is "consistently" "good" and the atmosphere "pretty relaxing."

Eclectic Cafe   ▽ 21 | 20 | 21 | $36
606 Main St. (bet. Basset Ln. & Sea St.), Hyannis, 508-771-7187

☑ "Hidden amid a sea of tourist traps" in downtown Hyannis, this teeny "jewel" is "hard to find but worth the search"; the intrepid who "love" it praise the Eclectic fare – the "menu is always a surprise", daring to be "different without going over the edge" – and "lovely" garden dining, but foes "don't even bother."

Esther's   ▽ 23 | 24 | 21 | $40
186 Commercial St. (Court St.), Provincetown, 508-487-7555; www.estherlives.com

■ Whether you sit in one of the "handsome" dining rooms upstairs "overlooking" busy Commercial Street, the deco-inspired piano bar downstairs (a "gorgeous surprise") or the European-like outdoor cafe (where the "people-watching can't be beat"), this "beautifully renovated" Victorian house is a "welcoming" haven in Provincetown; the "excellent" New American menu nearly matches the "great scene", making this one a definite "up-and-comer."

Fazio's Trattoria   22 | 11 | 21 | $27
294 Main St. (Center St.), Hyannis, 508-775-9400; www.fazio.net

☑ "Be prepared to wait at this bustling", family-run trattoria in Hyannis, where the "homemade" country-style food that comes out of the "open kitchen" is "consistently" "excellent" and "very reasonably priced"; as befits the site's original incarnation as a bakery, the breads and desserts are especially "wonderful", making diners "forget all about" the nondescript digs; though a few shrug "ok", most cheer "what a great find!"

Finely JP's   21 | 8 | 18 | $33
554 Rte. 6 (Castanga Dr.), Wellfleet, 508-349-7500

☑ "Forget the decor and just enjoy every tasty morsel" at this "convivial", "unpretentious" "little gem" in Wellfleet,

Cape Cod   F | D | S | C

where the "creative" kitchen turns out "delicious" New American food in the "equivalent of a trailer park" setting; as long as you don't "judge a book by its cover", this is a neighborhood "winner"; P.S. it's a "tremendous bargain on Thursday nights in the off-season", when a $10.95 prix fixe dinner is available.

Fishmonger's Cafe 19 | 16 | 19 | $28
56 Water St. (Luscombe Ave.), Woods Hole, 508-540-5376; www.fishmongerscafe.com

■ "Sit by the window and watch the boats go by" at this funky New American seafood cafe, a "marginally crunchy-sprouty" joint ("who knew a fishmonger could come up with so many vegetarian entrees?") "right on the water"; the "imaginative", "wholesome" dishes are "prepared with care", making it perhaps the "best choice in Woods Hole", though, frankly, the "competition isn't that tough."

Five Bays Bistro 25 | 20 | 21 | $44
825 Main St. (Wianno Ave.), Osterville, 508-420-5559

☒ Like a bit of "SoHo on Cape Cod", this "contempo-chic" bistro set in an Osterville storefront is both "fancy and fun"; the "fabulous", "ambitious" Eclectic menu attracts a "way preppy and perfectly coifed" clientele ("watch out for all the BMWs in front"), but if you "can ignore the Lily Pulitzer crowd" (and "way too much noise"), the eating is "yummy with a capital Y."

Flume 17 | 10 | 16 | $26
13 Lake Ave. (Rte. 130), Mashpee, 508-477-1456

☒ "To get a good home-cooked meal", Mashpee "locals" head to this "rustic", "laid-back" spot run by Wampanoag elder Earl Mills Sr., whose old-fashioned New England menu is "nothing fancy" but does reflect some "interesting" "Portuguese and Native American influences"; detractors, however, "don't understand" its enduring appeal.

Front Street 25 | 19 | 22 | $49
230 Commercial St. (Masonic Pl.), Provincetown, 508-487-9715; www.frontstreetrestaurant.com

■ Whether you opt for one of the "ever-changing" dishes on the modern Continental menu or an "all-time" Italian "favorite", it's "always a special evening" at this "excellent" Victorian house in Provincetown, where the staff "does everything right"; "nobody makes a better rack of lamb", though the "tea-smoked duck" is so "fantastic" that "you almost forget you're eating" in a "cramped" "dungeon" in a "town known for its spectacular views."

Gina's by the Sea 20 | 14 | 16 | $33
134 Taunton Ave. (Chapin Beach Rd.), Dennis, 508-385-3213

☒ Gina's is the name and "garlic is the game" at this "always jammed" Italian "joint" "nestled in the sand dunes" near Dennis' Chapin Beach; a rustic throwback to the '30s, it's a

Cape Cod

F | D | S | C

"cozy" ("be prepared to wait and wait") "family restaurant" with "nice-sized portions" of "generally good" food (insiders always "stick with the outstanding specials"), though the perplexed are puzzled by its "inexplicable popularity."

Impudent Oyster   22 | 16 | 19 | $36
15 Chatham Bars Ave. (Main St.), Chatham, 508-945-3545
☑ "Informal" and "friendly" compared to other options in "tony" Chatham, this "busy" seafood bistro is a "delightful place" to dine on a "great piece of fish" at a "good value"; boosters swear that the kitchen "executes everything well" (try the "excellent mussels, a specialty"), but note that the tables are "much too close together" and it can get very "loud", "so save your sweet nothings till after you leave."

INAHO   26 | 21 | 21 | $36
157 Main St./Rte. 6A (bet. Minden & Sandyside Lns.), Yarmouth Port, 508-362-5522
■ "Far and away" among the "best on the Cape", this slice of Japanese "serenity" tucked into a "charming" "old captain's house" in Yarmouth Port is a "blessing" for "super-fresh" sushi the "way it should be" ("tastes right off the boat"); not only does it feature "quite a variety of exciting offerings", but the "efficient" staff is "extremely helpful"; loyalists who have been coming here "for years" have "never once had a bad meal."

Karoo Kafe   – | – | – | I
338 Commercial St. (Center St.), Provincetown, 508-487-6630
For something different and eminently affordable, visit this "wonderful" change of pace in Provincetown that's part sandwich shop and part South African cafe; the menu offers standard deli fare, but armchair travelers take a fast-food safari by ordering "exotic, intensely flavored" specialties from the chef-owner's homeland, such as "savory" samosas and shrimp with peri-peri sauce; note, though, that with only 10 seats, it's mostly for takeout.

L'Alouette   25 | 20 | 24 | $40
787 Main St./Rte. 28 (Julien Rd.), Harwich Port, 508-430-0405
■ It's "easy to miss" this "hidden jewel" in Harwich Port as "traffic whizzes by on busy Route 28", which may explain why it remains "one of the Cape's best-kept secrets"; owned by a "husband-and-wife team", it achieves the "perfect marriage of classic French cuisine and Cape Cod seafood", turning out "incredible", "artfully presented" dishes; habitués who simply swoon "*oui, oui, oui*" bet that "once you visit, you'll return often."

Landfall   18 | 22 | 19 | $33
2 Luscombe Ave. (Water St.), Woods Hole, 508-548-1758
☑ Set right "on the water" near the Martha's Vineyard Steamship Authority in Woods Hole, this seafood house is

Cape Cod   F | D | S | C

a "reliable" spot to take visitors for a "traditional" "Cape Cod dining experience"; the cottage-like quarters, built from wood salvaged from historic shipwrecks, feature an aptly nautical motif ("old lobster buoys, mounted fish"), though the grub – "as you'd expect in such a touristy place" – is "nothing to write home about."

Lobster Pot   18 | 13 | 16 | $31
321 Commercial St. (Standish St.), Provincetown, 508-487-0842; www.ptownlobsterpot.com

☑ "Fish you want, fish they got" – "plainly but properly cooked" – at this "no-frills" seafood shack, a "staple on any Provincetown visit" (at least for those who believe that "not every meal has to be an adventure"); both dining rooms allow a "nice view of the harbor", but cynics wonder if "they use the same trap to catch both the lobsters and the tourists", and warn "they get you in and out so quickly you wonder if you've had a chance to eat what you ordered."

Lorraine's   22 | 17 | 18 | $35
463 Commercial St. (Bangs St.), Provincetown, 508-487-6074; www.lorrainesrestaurant.com

■ "Come hungry" to this Provincetown "favorite" that "year after year" dishes out "inspired, nontraditional" Mexican food (its "succulent" roast duckling is known throughout the town); quartered in a '30s building constructed in part from an old schooner, it boasts a "beautiful view of the tide" through its multitude of windows, along with one of the largest collections of tequila in New England; N.B. it plans to move shortly down the road to 133 Commercial Street.

Martin House   22 | 24 | 22 | $51
157 Commercial St. (Atlantic Ave.), Provincetown, 508-487-1327

■ "On a cool, windy Cape evening", "cozy" up at this "quaint" 18th-century Provincetown house and "enjoy the fireplaces" (all five of them) while sampling "serious", "imaginative" New American cooking that "changes with the seasons" and draws inspiration from near and far; enhanced by a "lovely" interior and "accommodating" service, the dining experience is always "special."

Mews   25 | 24 | 24 | $47
429 Commercial St. (Lovetts Ct.), Provincetown, 508-487-1500; www.mews.com

■ If the "beautiful" "view" of the harbor "doesn't make you woozy, the king-sized martinis certainly will" remark respondents about this "welcoming" "destination" in Provincetown that features "gorgeous sunset" watching and the "best vodka bar in 100 miles" (60-plus brands); whether you opt for a "casual", light meal in the upstairs cafe or a "quieter, more romantic" dinner in the beach-level fine-dining room, you'll be treated to "luscious", "inventive" New American fare; "all is well" here.

get updates at zagat.com   **167**

Cape Cod | F | D | S | C |

Misaki
▽ 28 | 18 | 24 | $28

379 W. Main St. (Pitchers Way), Hyannis, 508-771-3771

■ "Sushi with a smile" is "just what the Cape needed" cheer the connoisseurs who've discovered this "neat" little place off the beaten path in Hyannis; "when the ingredients practically swim in the backyard", you can "expect" "excellent" raw fish "done right", and the prices are a "bargain compared with other Japanese restaurants" in the area.

Naked Oyster Bistro & Raw Bar ⌀
24 | 22 | 21 | $39

20 Independence Dr. (Rte. 132), Hyannis, 508-778-6500; www.nakedoyster.com

■ One of the "best raw bars this side of the canal" lurks in this "New York–swank" Hyannis "meeting place" that "doesn't look like much from the outside" (it's "tucked in a nondescript building"); inside, the menu showcases "lots of seafood choices", all "fresh" and "outrageously good" and paired with a "delightful selection of wines by the glass."

Napi's
19 | 21 | 18 | $33

7 Freeman St. (Commercial St.), Provincetown, 508-487-1145

■ "So many cuisines, so well done" laud loyalists of the "imaginative" Eclectic menu featured at this "reliable" "institution", which "mixes" many different influences (it's even "fun for your vegetarian friends"); the "funky" decor is "appealing" too, with an "interesting" collection of paintings and sculptures (the owners are art collectors), and there's even "free parking – a rarity in Provincetown."

Nauset Beach Club
24 | 18 | 18 | $44

222 Main St. (Beach Rd.), East Orleans, 508-255-8547; www.nausetbeachclub.com

☑ "Exquisite" Northern Italian cuisine entices enthusiasts to this "private" "little hideaway" in East Orleans that's "not your typical Cape Cod restaurant", a "great relief" to adventurous appetites seeking "ingenious" pastas and "fresh seafood to die for"; the drawbacks, however, are "tight seating (you'll get to know your neighbors)" and a host of service complaints ranging from "snooty" to "hostile."

Ocean House
24 | 23 | 22 | $43

Depot St. (Upper County Rd.), Dennisport, 508-394-0700; www.oceanhouserestaurant.com

☑ "So close to the water" "you'll think you're on a cruise" rhapsodize "romantics" about this airy, elegant bistro in Dennisport that boasts an "incredible view of Nantucket Sound" through its endless windows; the "adventurous chef" prepares "outstanding" New American fare with "flair", but some grumps grouse that "you're mostly paying for the amazing" setting; N.B. there's live jazz nightly in the oceanfront lounge.

Cape Cod

| | F | D | S | C |

Paddock | 21 | 20 | 21 | $38 |
West End Rotary, 20 Scudder Ave. (Main St.), Hyannis, 508-775-7677; www.paddockcapecod.com

☑ "On the Cape forever", this "old-time" standby "near the Melody Tent" "never fails to please" veterans, because the "owners are always on the scene" to "make them feel at home"; the food is probably "better than you'd expect" – "solid" New England classics along with more "imaginative" dishes – but dissenters who deem it "only ordinary" suggest "there are better places to eat in Hyannis."

Penguins Sea Grill & Steakhouse | 25 | 18 | 23 | $35 |
331 Main St. (Ocean St.), Hyannis, 508-775-2023

■ "Fresh seafood is the name of the game, but they can cook a fillet just as well" at this "pretty" surf 'n' turf house in Hyannis, where everything is made from scratch, from the breads to the desserts; the "well-balanced menu" suits "all tastes", and the service is "very good", making for an "always enjoyable" dinner that's "far better" than you'd "expect" "from its name."

Polcari's | 16 | 15 | 16 | $23 |
Cape Cod Mall, Rte. 132 (Airport Rd.), Hyannis, 508-790-3800
See review in Boston Directory.

Red Inn | 21 | 26 | 21 | $49 |
15 Commercial St. (Province Lands Rd.), Provincetown, 508-487-7334; www.theredinn.com

■ Situated "at the very end of the Cape", "where the Pilgrims first landed", this "fantastic restoration" of an 1805 inn in Provincetown boasts such "unbeatable views" of the harbor and the lighthouse that a meal is "sure to be a hit"; while you "watch the waves" from the "warm", "beautiful" dining rooms full of old-world charm, you'll be served "wonderful" Eclectic fare by an "accommodating" staff.

Red Pheasant | 24 | 22 | 23 | $49 |
905 Rte. 6A (Elm St.), Dennis, 508-385-2133; www.redpheasantinn.com

■ "Delicious, delightful, de-lovely" sums up this "quaint", "very New England" "gem" set in a 200-year-old barn in Dennis that's particularly "inviting" if you nab a seat "next to the fireplace"; wherever your table, you'll be treated to an "inventive" New American menu "filled with interesting choices" and delivered by an "informed, approachable" staff; a "real comfort zone", it provides a "perfect escape from all the clam shacks and lobster shanties" around.

REGATTA OF COTUIT AT THE CROCKER HOUSE | 27 | 26 | 24 | $56 |
4631 Falmouth Rd./Rte. 28 (Rte. 130), Cotuit, 508-428-5715

■ For the "best dining on the Cape, bar none", "don't miss this Regatta" urge fans of this "lovely", intimate mansion

Cape Cod F | D | S | C |

in Cotuit that "pampers" with "sublime modern" American cuisine (the buffalo tenderloin is "outstanding") delivered with "European-style professional" service in "candlelit" rooms made even more "romantic" by the live nightly piano music; despite "terrifying prices", it's "worth every penny" to indulge in such a "memorable" "special-occasion" meal.

Ristorante Barolo 23 | 19 | 22 | $38 |
1 Financial Pl., 297 North St. (Sea St. ext.), Hyannis, 508-778-2878
■ "Tucked away" in the "most unsuspecting locale" (a nondescript Hyannis office building), this "unpretentious" ristorante is "worth the search" for "killer" Northern Italian cooking that's "worth every calorie"; to boot, the dining room is "pleasant" and the service "experienced"; sure, it's "hard to find", but at least that "keeps out the riffraff" (aka "tourists").

Roadhouse Cafe 21 | 21 | 19 | $35 |
488 South St. (Sea St.), Hyannis, 508-775-2386; www.roadhousecafe.com
■ "Complete with a romantic piano bar", this "comfortable", "friendly" Hyannis "roadhouse" "gets better every year – by staying the same"; expect "hefty portions" of "succulent seafood" and "hearty" Italian-style entrees, served by a "hospitable" staff in two "charming", antique-filled dining rooms, a more casual lounge or the bistro, which features "great Monday night jazz."

RooBar 20 | 17 | 17 | $34 |
285 Main St. (Cahoon Ct.), Falmouth, 508-548-8600
586 Main St. (Bassett Ln.), Hyannis, 508-778-6515
www.theroobar.com
☑ "Great appetizers", "exotic pizzas" and "fantastic martinis" are all on the "interesting menu" at these "creative" Eclectic bistros, whose "funky", "big-city cool" ambiance is "not normally found on the Cape"; it makes for a "happening bar scene" with "good people-watching", even if the dishes can be "erratic" and the "music so loud you'd think you were at a rock concert"; N.B. a new branch is scheduled to open soon in Chatham.

Ross' Grill 22 | 22 | 19 | $40 |
237 Commercial St. (bet. Gosnold St. & Masonic Pl.), Provincetown, 508-487-8878
■ "Tiny" but appointed with windows all around that allow for a "great view of the bay", this upscale, "happening" haunt in Provincetown has plenty of "local color"; not only does it appeal with "reliably good" New American cooking, but it features an "excellent" selection of "wines by the glass" (75), though even supporters are "turned off" by the "no-reservations policy" ("what does it take to get in here? – more seats, please").

Cape Cod   F | D | S | C

Sal's Place   19 | 17 | 17 | $39
99 Commercial St. (bet. Cottage & Mechanic Sts.), Provincetown, 508-487-1279

☑ "Don't tell mama" that this Provincetown "classic" dishes up stick-to-the-ribs Southern Italian food just like she used to make; instead, "go hungry" (the "portions are huge"), sit out on the patio "right on the bay" (the "inside is rather dreary") and "tackle" its famous steak pizzaiola ("incredibly delicious"); boosters only hope that this "tasty" red-sauce "tradition lives on", though the dismayed dismiss it as "acceptable" but "average."

Siena   – | – | – | M
Mashpee Commons, Rtes. 28 & 151, Mashpee, 508-477-5929; www.siena.us

Bob Calderone (ex the late Anago in Boston's Back Bay) has taken his toque to the Cape to launch this spacious, contemporary Italian ristorante at Mashpee Commons; the menu starts with such family-friendly basics as brick-oven pizzas and an array of pastas, but the chef's city pedigree really comes through in his select list of sophisticated entrees, while pastry chef Liz Miles (ex Lumière) confects her sweet finales.

Sosumi Asian Bistro   ∇ 21 | 21 | 16 | $32
14 Chatham Bars Ave. (Main St.), Chatham, 508-945-0300

☑ "How refreshing" to find this "wonderfully funky addition to stuffy downtown Chatham", where the "very fresh" sushi and "imaginative" Asian Fusion fare, all "beautifully presented", make for a "nice break from the ubiquitous American seafood on the Cape"; while most appreciate the "creative" menu ("so good we wish this place were in Boston"), critics contend that the "unresponsive" staff can be "slow" or downright "rude."

Stir Crazy   ∇ 23 | 10 | 22 | $22
626 MacArthur Blvd. (bet. Barlows Landing Rd. & Williams Ave.), Pocasset, 508-564-6464

■ "Why go to Boston for Asian food when you have such a delight on the Upper Cape?" wonder the lucky locals who've stumbled across this "well-kept secret" hidden in a Pocasset strip mall; sure, it's just a "little hole-in-the-wall", but you get a "warm welcome" and an "authentic" (if "limited") selection of "amazing" Cambodian "home cooking" at "bargain" prices.

Terra Luna   21 | 18 | 20 | $39
104 Shore Rd. (Rte. 6A), North Truro, 508-487-1019

■ "You don't expect food this sophisticated way out in North Truro" marvel enthusiasts of this "delightful", "rustic" "bungalow" that attracts an "incredibly varied crowd without the nuttiness of P-town"; the "solid" Mediterranean menu delivered by a "hip, friendly" crew makes for a "nice

Cape Cod | F | D | S | C |

change of pace" in this "land of fried seafood", though tightwads gripe that it's "too pricey for what you get."

Twenty-Eight Atlantic | 24 | 26 | 25 | $48 |
Wequassett Inn, 2173 Orleans Rd./Rte. 28 (Pleasant Bay Rd.), Chatham, 508-432-5400; www.wequassett.com

■ Set in an 18th-century sea captain's house overlooking Pleasant Bay, the "elegant" yet "relaxing" Wequassett Inn in Chatham pairs "luxe" appointments with a "spectacular" setting that affords one of the "best water views" on the Cape; chef Bill Brodsky's "fantastic", "stunningly presented" New England specialties do their best to match the "gorgeous surroundings", while the "sophisticated" service team contributes to the "exceptional experience."

Vining's Bistro | 22 | 16 | 17 | $34 |
Gallery Bldg., 595 Main St. (Seaview St.), Chatham, 508-945-5033; www.viningsbistro.com

☑ Perhaps "you wouldn't think" that a dining experience in Chatham could be so "inventive", but insiders bet that the "ever-changing" Eclectic menu at this "cozy", "sleeper" will "bring you back again and again"; the "gourmet" dishes that emerge from the open kitchen are "flavorful and original", but be forewarned about some "attitude" ("this place definitely doesn't want kids" present).

Martha's Vineyard

| F | D | S | C |

Alchemy
22 | 19 | 20 | $52

71 Main St. (bet. School & Summer Sts.), Edgartown, 508-627-9999

☑ "Even cynical folks from New York" are pleasantly pleased by the "combination of island-casual and sophistication" achieved at this "modern bistro" in Edgartown, where the "chic crowd" makes it a "happening" (and "noisy") spot for prime "people-watching"; the "upstairs bar is a great place to hang out", while the dining room downstairs "beautifully presents" "delicious", seafood-slanted New American fare, but service can be "uneven" and some deem it "too pricey for what you get."

Artcliff Diner ⊘
22 | 13 | 17 | $16

39 Beach Rd. (Main St.), Vineyard Haven, 508-693-1224

■ A "hole-in-the-wall with class", this "salty joint" near the Vineyard Haven ferry docks is far more "gourmet" than you'd expect; the "surprisingly good" Traditional American eats are "flavorful (and appropriately arty)" and "always served with a smile", which means it's usually packed with "locals", so "get there early for breakfast" (it "makes getting out of bed worth it") or "late for lunch."

Atria
25 | 23 | 23 | $57

137 Main St. (Pine St.), Edgartown, 508-627-5850

■ Fans fall for the "fabulous" "fine dining" that makes this "lovely" "experience" "one of the best in Edgartown"; the "marvelous", daily changing New American bill of fare, influenced by the flavors of Asia and the Mediterranean, is presented in an interior of "understated elegance" and out in the lovely rose garden, making for a "great place for a romantic dinner" (accompanied by live music nightly); just don't forget the platinum card – the prices are "exorbitant", "even for the Vineyard."

Balance
23 | 19 | 20 | $55

57 Circuit Ave. (Narragansett St.), Oak Bluffs, 508-696-3000; www.balancerestaurant.com

☑ For "city eating in a beach town", join the "hip" throngs at this "hot" Oak Bluffs "nightspot" with "big buzz"; not only is it perhaps the "best place on the island for stargazing", but it provides an "excellent meal after a long day of biking on the Vineyard"; groupies "love" the "great vibe" and "innovative, well-presented" New American dishes, but foes find it "hard to get past all the noise and chaos" and bet it "wouldn't make it off the island at these prices."

get updates at zagat.com

Martha's Vineyard | F | D | S | C |

Beach Plum Inn | 22 | 24 | 22 | $57 |
Beach Plum Inn, 50 Beach Plum Ln. (North Rd.), Menemsha, 508-645-9454; www.beachpluminn.com

◪ Boasting a "picture-perfect" setting overlooking the sea, with a "stunning view" of the sunset, this "casually elegant" country inn in Menemsha is a "serene" oasis for a "romantic" BYO dinner; though the "fresh" New England seafood specialties are "thoughtfully prepared", the disappointed lament that the food "doesn't quite match the wonderful location."

Black Dog Tavern | 17 | 16 | 15 | $27 |
21 Beach St. ext. (Vineyard Haven Harbor), Vineyard Haven, 508-693-9223; www.theblackdog.com

◪ Among some vacationers, a "trip to the Vineyard isn't complete" without a stop at this "rustic", "way too hectic" Vineyard Haven "institution" whose "picturesque location" near the ferry docks is hard to beat; if you "stick to the basics" on the American menu, you could have a "fun time" and see what all the "hype" is about, but opponents sneer that the "best thing" about this "tourist doghouse" is the "tacky T-shirts" for sale.

Cafe Moxie | 21 | 14 | 18 | $40 |
48 Main St. (Center St.), Vineyard Haven, 508-693-1484; www.cafemoxie.com

■ "Local art hangs on the walls" at this "pleasant" storefront bistro in Vineyard Haven, which "dedicated fans" frequent for its "interesting", "consistently" "well-executed" New American selections and a "BYO policy" that helps "keep the costs down."

Chesca's | 23 | 18 | 21 | $41 |
38 N. Water St. (Winter St.), Edgartown, 508-627-1234

◪ Thanks to its "wonderful" Italian cooking (notably pastas packed with "potent flavors" and "excellent" seafood), "warm and fuzzy feel" and "amenable" service, not to mention its "good price-value" ratio, this "unpretentious" trattoria in Edgartown is always "crowded"; while there's usually a "wait for a table", the "rocking chairs outside" on the porch help ease the ordeal, but the "noise spoils the entire experience" for some.

Coach House | 22 | 23 | 21 | $47 |
Harbor View Hotel, 131 N. Water St. (bet. Cottage & Thayer Sts.), Edgartown, 508-627-7000; www.harbor-view.com

◪ Blessed with an "amazing view of Edgartown Harbor and the lighthouse", this "lovely" destination mixes "island" informality with an "old-world charm from the era of grand hotels"; admirers say that the "consistently good" seafood specialties and "gracious" service add up to a "fine" dining experience, but detractors feel that though it "has all the pieces, it's just not that special" ("not bad, not great").

Martha's Vineyard | F | D | S | C |

Daggett House | 20 | 21 | 18 | $26 |
Daggett House, 59 N. Water St. (bet. Daggett & Morse Sts.), Edgartown, 508-627-4600; www.thedaggetthouse.com

■ "Three cheers for the waffles and granola" prepared at this "charming, historical" American tavern (billed as the first on the Vineyard) applaud adherents who know that it features one of the "best breakfasts on the island" ("good, hearty food for not an outrageous price"); the quarters are "cozy", replete with a beehive fireplace, but even better is a table out on the patio "overlooking Edgartown Harbor", where the view is "breathtaking" and you can "watch the boats heading out"; N.B. no lunch or dinner.

Home Port | 19 | 13 | 17 | $37 |
512 North Rd. (Basin Rd.), Menemsha, 508-645-2679

☑ For "fish so fresh it could almost jump onto your plate", as well as "lobster any way you like it", schools of fin fans are hooked on this "no-frills", "family-style" "favorite" in Menemsha, where the "plates come fast and furious" and the "cordial" crew works hard to keep up (it's a "madhouse in season"); frugal sorts, however, are dismayed by the "sticker shock", quipping you "feel like you're paying for dinner and a show" – which you are "if you count" the real lure here: the "fantastic sunsets."

Ice House | 24 | 20 | 22 | $47 |
688 State Rd. (North Rd.), West Tisbury, 508-696-3966

☑ Regarded as the "most creative eatery on the Vineyard", this hot table with a cool name is a "sweet little" house up in West Tisbury that's "popular with islanders and summer folks alike"; the "inventive" New American menu, based on "local fish and produce", keeps getting "better and better", and though tabs are predictably "high", the "BYO policy helps keep the cost in line"; even if a few deem it "overrated", there are plenty of pleased patrons just "trying to get a table outside" in the garden.

Ipanema | – | – | – | E |
52 Beach Rd. (Main St.), Vineyard Haven, 508-693-8383

"Some coconut here, some lime zest there" and the "tasty" result is "interesting", "excellent" Brazilian food at this Vineyard Haven BYO eatery that makes diners "giddy" with excitement; as befits its "beautiful" harborside location, it features a "great variety of skillfully prepared seafood", delivered by a staff that "tries hard to please."

Jimmy Seas Pan Pasta | 26 | 12 | 18 | $32 |
32 Kennebec Ave. (off Post Office Sq.), Oak Bluffs, 508-696-8550

■ "Don't eat for a week before you come" to this "no-nonsense" "garlic heaven" in Oak Bluffs, which brings a "little bit of Boston's North End to the island"; the family-style portions are "huge (sometimes overwhelming)",

get updates at zagat.com   **175**

Martha's Vineyard | F | D | S | C |

especially the "paradisaical" pastas served right "in the pan"; there's "always a long wait" to get in, because the "incredible", "ultra-fresh" Italian cooking "brings diners back" again and again – just remember the "breath mints."

Lambert's Cove Country Inn | 22 | 22 | 23 | $44 |
Lambert's Cove Rd. W. (State Rd.), West Tisbury, 508-693-2298; www.lambertscoveinn.com

■ "Off the beaten path" "in the middle of the Vineyard woods", this "elegant country inn" (circa 1790) in West Tisbury has the "feel of a private home" ("like eating in Laura Ashley's house"); it's a tranquil, romantic retreat that cossets with "excellent" service and a daily changing menu of "delicious" New American fare; though "hard to find", it's "worth the trip", but better "bring your own wine – this is a dry town."

Lattanzi's | 21 | 17 | 20 | $31 |
Old Post Office Sq., 19 Church St. (Main St.), Edgartown, 508-627-8854; www.lattanzis.com

■ "Actually two restaurants" side by side, this Edgartown Italian in Old Post Office Square is the site of a "white-tablecloth" ristorante that specializes in "fine", traditional Tuscan-style dishes (including "delicious" handmade pastas) and a "casual", family-friendly pizzeria (open summers only) with "superb" pies and sandwiches baked in a "wood-fired" stone oven; either way, "when the weather's not great", it'll "warm you up", and it's "not too expensive."

Le Grenier | 24 | 16 | 21 | $47 |
96 Main St. (bet. Church St. & Colonial Ln.), Vineyard Haven, 508-693-4906; www.legrenierrestaurant.com

☑ "Arguably the island's most serious" classic French establishment, this long-standing BYO "favorite" where "nothing ever changes" is moored opposite the Steamship Authority docks in Vineyard Haven; "discerning palates" find all the traditional standards here – from "delicious" escargots to steak au poivre to profiterole au chocolat – served by a "fine" staff; just "bring your own bubbly" to ensure a "romantic" evening.

L'ETOILE | 26 | 27 | 25 | $74 |
Charlotte Inn, 27 S. Summer St. (Davis Ln.), Edgartown, 508-627-5187

■ "Go with someone special" to this "magical" "haven" in Edgartown, the "posh" dining room of the "exquisitely appointed" Charlotte Inn; "start your evening off" with a couple of "cocktails in the library bar", then move on to the "Monet-inspired garden room", an "elegant" setting for "gourmet" French cuisine that's the "best on the island"; "everyone should go at least once", because this "over-the-top" ("on every level") experience guarantees a "wow" of a "celebration."

Martha's Vineyard | F | D | S | C |

Lola's | 21 | 20 | 20 | $38 |
15 Beach Rd. (near State Beach), Oak Bluffs, 508-693-5007; www.lolassouthernseafood.com

☑ "Have a blast at this happening" Southerner in Oak Bluffs, a "funky", "festive" joint where "you always feel as if a party's going on"; not only is it "live music central", but you'll be fed "tons" of "tasty" vittles ("wonderful interpretations" of Cajun-Creole cooking) by folks who "want you to be happy"; rebels, however, mystified about its "popularity", charge "they must be getting back for the Civil War."

Newes from America | 18 | 18 | 16 | $23 |
Kelley House, 23 Kelley St. (N. Water St.), Edgartown, 508-627-4397; www.kelley-house.com

■ Set in a 1742 inn near the waterfront in Edgartown, this "lively" English-style pub is appropriately adorned with maritime artifacts; it's a "friendly" "drinking spot for townies and sailors" that's particularly "homey" in the "off-season", when a "roaring fire" makes the quarters even "cozier"; the American menu offers "traditional favorites", while the "rack of beers" is a "great gimmick", as are the "rude bar maids" (just part of the "experience").

Opus | ▽ 23 | 21 | 18 | $61 |
Winnetu Inn & Resort, 31 Dunes Rd. (Katama Rd.), Edgartown, 508-627-3663; www.winnetu.com

☑ "Fish dishes reign supreme" in the "open, airy" dining room at the Winnetu Inn, which boasts an "awesome location right off" South Beach, with "lovely" ocean views to match; fans say the "creative" New England fare is "infused with flavor" and the ambiance "wonderful", but critics feel that though the menu is "solid", it's "not up to the setting", while the tone is "pretentious for the Vineyard."

Outermost Inn | ▽ 22 | 24 | 21 | $57 |
Outermost Inn, 81 Lighthouse Rd. (State Rd.), Aquinnah, 508-645-3511; www.outermostinn.com

■ "If you like ocean views and salt air breezes, you won't want to be anywhere else but here" swoon supporters of this "romantic" inn nestled above the cliffs of Aquinnah, "one of the more special spots on the island"; also "part of the package" are the "prix fixe" American dinners, which show "freshness and imagination", and the attention of co-owner Hugh Taylor (James' brother), a "charming host"; just remember to "bring your own best wine."

Park Corner Bistro | ▽ 23 | 17 | 21 | $52 |
20H Kennebec Ave. (Circuit Ave.), Oak Bluffs, 508-696-9922

☑ A "little gem in the Bluffs" remark respondents who've "discovered" this "great find", an "intimate" "hideaway" with a rustic European look and "ample choices" of "flavorful", "well-presented" New American dishes brought to table by a "pleasant" staff; though the lukewarm deem

---

get updates at zagat.com   **177**

Martha's Vineyard

F | **D** | **S** | **C**

it "somewhat disappointing", devotees insist that this "wonderful" "nook" is "just what the Vineyard needs" and definitely "worth a visit."

Sweet Life Cafe
24 | 23 | 22 | $51

63 Circuit Ave. (bet. Narragansett & Pequot Aves.), Oak Bluffs, 508-696-0200

☑ "Out in the garden" "under the stars", "life is indeed sweet" at this oh-so-"romantic" cafe set in a "lovely" Victorian house in Oak Bluffs; the New American–New French menu comes "highly recommended", the "wine list is well chosen" and the service is "solicitous" without being "overbearing"; "surrounded by tiny lights and candles" that sparkle "on summer evenings", starry-eyed supporters are entirely content, even if a few sigh "if only the food were as good as its aspirations."

Theo's
▽ 20 | 20 | 21 | $56

Inn at Blueberry Hill, 74 North Rd. (bet. Old Farm Rd. & Tea Ln.), Chilmark, 508-645-3322; www.blueberryinn.com

☑ The smitten find their thrill at the Inn at Blueberry Hill, a "remote, peaceful" "treasure" up-island in Chilmark that's "worth the little extra effort" required to find it; set amid 56 acres of woodland, it's a "quaint" BYO retreat in which to partake of "fresh fish" and "creative" New American dishes, though dissenters conclude "pleasant and pretty, but not too exciting", and "expensive for what it is."

Zapotec
20 | 14 | 16 | $30

14 Kennebec Ave. (Atlantic Ave.), Oak Bluffs, 508-693-6800

■ "Quite a happy surprise", this bright Southwestern cantina in Oak Bluffs is "one of the best" options for "casual" eating "on the Rock"; "order a pitcher of sangria" to wash down the "tasty" food, "simply done but pleasing to the palate"; though "there are no frills here", the menu provides a "welcome respite from the standard Vineyard seafood" picks and "your wallet won't take a severe beating."

Zephrus
- | - | - | E

Mansion House Hotel, 9 Main St. (Beach St.), Vineyard Haven, 508-693-3416; www.zephrus.com

Though the Tisbury Inn was destroyed in a fire (and is being rebuilt as the Mansion House Hotel at press time), this "sophisticated" New American "favorite" in Vineyard Haven has reopened and continues to "put it all together" with a "nice combination of menu, ambiance and service"; satisfied surveyors cite "consistent quality", while penny-pinchers point out that the "BYO" policy "lowers the check."

Nantucket

| F | D | S | C |

American Seasons
25 | 22 | 23 | $54

80 Centre St. (W. Chester St.), 508-228-7111;
www.americanseasons.com

■ At this "delightful" Nantucket "jewel", the "unique" menu spans "four corners of the country" – from the Pacific Coast and the Wild West to Down South and New England; even those "wary of this gimmick" take their hats off to "gifted chef" Michael LaScola, who "expertly prepares" "imaginative", "delectable" New American selections; consider too the "fabulous" list of boutique wines and the "extremely accommodating" service, and it's easy to see why admirers cherish this "special place."

Arno's
19 | 16 | 17 | $29

41 Main St. (Union St.), 508-228-7001

■ "There's something for everyone" on the "reliable" New American menu at this "down-home family place" beloved for its "fabulous breakfasts"; "during the summer", there's "always a crowd waiting to get in the door" in the mornings, but that's to be expected with its "perfect location" on Main Street and "good-value" prices.

Black Eyed Susan's ⊘
24 | 14 | 20 | $32

10 India St. (Centre St.), 508-325-0308

☑ "Funky" and "unpretentious", this storefront is a "small joint with big flavors", and it packs them in with its "super breakfasts" and "original without being silly" New American dinners; adherents appreciate that you can "bring your own wine", though the wary warn about "atrocious lines" and add that it's "so cramped you might eat your neighbor's food by mistake"; N.B. no lunch.

Bluefin
24 | 18 | 20 | $41

15 S. Beach St. (Harbor View Way), 508-228-2033;
www.nantucketbluefin.com

■ A "cool clientele" patronizes this equally "cool room" near Downtown for a "crowd-pleasing menu" of "surprisingly tasty" New American fare as well as "ultra-fresh sushi" ("try the tuna sashimi pizza") presented by an "eager-to-please" staff; "you'll see locals in here all summer, which means it's an impressive" "find."

BOARDING HOUSE
26 | 23 | 23 | $57

12 Federal St. (India St.), 508-228-9622;
www.boardinghouse-pearl.com

■ Run by Seth and Angela Raynor (of the hugely popular Pearl), this "long-standing" "happening place" Downtown

Nantucket F | D | S | C

pulls in the "who's who" of Nantucket for some of the "best" fine dining on the island; devotees "love this place" for its "exceptional" New American menu and "dictionary-sized", award-winning wine list, not to mention its "inviting", "romantic" ambiance and "lovely" service; it's "difficult to get reservations", but keep trying because a "fabulous" dinner is a "sure thing" here.

Brant Point Grill   23 | 24 | 22 | $59
White Elephant Hotel, 50 Easton St. (Harbor View Way), 508-228-2500

◪ Overlooking "scenic" Nantucket Harbor, this "beautiful" dining room at the White Elephant Hotel is blessed with a "treasure of a location" (anticipate a "breathtaking" view of the sailboats and yachts bobbing about); however, for every respondent who "loves the deck" dining ("what a way to watch the sun set") and is content with the "non-threatening" Traditional American surf 'n' turf menu, another dismisses the "nothing special" food at "outrageous prices", as well as the "spotty" service.

Centre Street Bistro ⌀   ▽ 25 | 16 | 19 | $31
Meeting House, 29 Centre St. (bet. Chestnut & India Sts.), 508-228-8470

■ Chef-owners Ruth and Tim Pitts "turn out consistently great" New American dishes "year-round" at their "tiny", "quaint" bistro Downtown; it's a "favorite" pick for breakfast (on weekends), lunch and dinner (the prix fixe deal is "fantastic") served by "eager" folks at "reasonable prices" (for the island); P.S. in the summertime, opt for the pretty patio, which feels much less "cramped."

CHANTICLEER   26 | 26 | 23 | $74
9 New St. (Milestone Rd.), Siasconset, 508-257-6231; www.thechanticleerinn.com

■ Like its "stupendous wine cellar", this "very French, very fabulous and very expensive" Siasconset "classic" seems to "improve with age"; given the prices, it may be a "once-a-decade experience", but a "most memorable" meal at this "romantic" grande dame is a "must for lovers of all ages"; the staff is "professional" and "attentive", and even if a few find it "pretentious", most just sigh "perfection."

Cioppino's   ▽ 23 | 19 | 22 | $42
20 Broad St. (bet. Centre & Federal Sts.), 508-228-4622; www.cioppinos.com

◪ Perhaps the "friendliest" restaurant on Nantucket, this "small gem" Downtown is run by the "warmest" owners; followers swear that after one bite of the cioppino, you'll know why "they named the place" after their signature seafood stew; "you'll be smacking your lips" over the kitchen's other "excellent" Mediterranean dishes too, though some find it all rather "run-of-the-mill."

Nantucket

| F | D | S | C |

Club Car
| 21 | 17 | 18 | $52 |

1 Main St. (Easy St.), 508-228-1101;
www.theclubcar.com

☒ "Stuck in a time warp", this "island landmark" at the foot of Main Street remains a "standby" for "(very) rich", "old-school" Continental fare; the "disappointed", however, lament that it has "lost some of its glamour", "slipping in quality over the years" (though still "overpriced"), but concede that the "rowdy bar", set in an railroad car (circa 1875) "attached to the side of the restaurant", is a "fun" place "filled with locals and tourists."

COMPANY OF THE CAULDRON
| 26 | 24 | 26 | $59 |

5 India St. (bet. Centre & Federal Sts.), 508-228-4016;
www.companyofthecauldron.com

■ "Prix fixe but not pre-fab", this "eclectic" Downtown dining room in the heart of the Historic District "marches to its own beat", serving exclusively a set New American menu that changes daily and is offered at only two seatings nightly; as long as the "evening's fare is to your tastes, you'll be rewarded" with a "glorious", "seriously" gourmet meal made even more "romantic" by the live harp music (on some nights); it's definitely "worth rubbing elbows" in these "close quarters" for such a "sublime" experience.

DeMarco
| ▽ 25 | 18 | 23 | $50 |

9 India St. (bet. Centre & Federal Sts.), 508-228-1836

■ All rustic charm, this long-standing Downtown ristorante quartered in a 19th-century sea captain's house is a warm haven appointed with beamed ceilings, original pine floors, white stucco walls and a crackling fireplace; it's one of the "best choices on the island" for "authentic" Northern Italian dishes, especially *boscaiola* ("badly cut pasta") in a wild mushroom sauce.

Fifty-Six Union
| 21 | 19 | 21 | $53 |

56 Union St. (E. Dover St.), 508-228-6135

■ Removed from all the Downtown "hustle and bustle", this "friendly" "find" is a "comfortable" place where the "owners' presence in the dining room is noticeable"; the "innovative" Eclectic menu is "always good", while "some items are outstanding", such as the "amazing curried mussels" and "incredible" butterscotch brownie sundae; though it doesn't reach the "level of A-1 restaurants" on the island, at least its prices are "less than stratospheric."

Fog Island Cafe
| 20 | 12 | 16 | $18 |

7 S. Water St. (India St.), 508-228-1818; www.fogisland.com

■ "On one of the Grey Lady's typical foggy days", morning mavens make tracks for this "relaxing" "almost-diner" where the "interesting breakfast selections" ("catch those fresh cinnamon buns!") "make waking up early to avoid the lines a real pleasure"; offering all-day dining year-round,

Nantucket   F D S C

it's also handy for a "quick" lunch or dinner Downtown, when the New American menu has a "healthy twist to it"; to boot, it's "one of the few nice places in town where you won't have to empty your wallet."

Galley on Cliffside Beach   22 | 26 | 21 | $60
54 Jefferson Ave. (off N. Beach St.), 508-228-9641

◪ "Sand, surf, sunset" "and the eyes of the one you love" – what more could you want ask those enamored by this "romantic" "beauty" where the "breathtaking" setting "overlooking postcard-famous Cliffside Beach" is "totally memorable"; a "knowledgeable" staff turns out Continental specialties that "blend interesting and straightforward ingredients", and even if some connoisseurs complain that the menu is "just ok", "location, location, location is all that counts" to others.

Jared's   17 | 20 | 21 | $35
Jared Coffin House, 29 Broad St. (Centre St.), 508-228-2400; www.jaredcoffinhouse.com

◪ For a taste of "auld Nantucket", visit the "period" Jared Coffin House, which offers two options: "old-style" New England fine dining at Jared's upstairs and Traditional American pub fare at the "casual" Tap Room downstairs, which features a "real tavern feel"; the disgruntled may declare that this "tired-looking" institution is "resting on its laurels", but at least you won't have to "increase your equity line to pay for a meal."

Le Languedoc   25 | 22 | 23 | $53
Le Languedoc Inn, 24 Broad St. (bet. Centre & Federal Sts.), 508-228-2552; www.lelanguedoc.com

■ "Classic" French fare teamed with "amazing wines" and "terrific" service is the winning combination that has made this "lovely" destination a "perennial favorite"; the upstairs dining room is "not too Nantucket", but insiders suggest "meet and eat with the locals at the cafe" – it's "like a club for those in-the-know", with the same "delicious" cooking.

Nantucket Lobster Trap   20 | 12 | 16 | $39
23 Washington St. (Coffin St.), 508-228-4200; www.nantucketlobstertrap.com

◪ Better "wear your bib" advise adherents before "chowing down" at this "old-fashioned" seafood shack, a "no-nonsense", "unpretentious" pick for a "very informal" dinner "with the locals"; "stick to the boiled lobster and steamed mussels or clams" and "you're in for a delicious meal", though critics who crab about "offensively overpriced" grub insist "trap is the operative word."

ÒRAN MÓR   26 | 23 | 23 | $65
2 S. Beach St. (Whalers Ln.), 508-228-8655

■ "Not to be missed", this "intimate" Downtown hideaway is so "serene" "you feel like you're having a private dinner

Nantucket

F | D | S | C

at home", though bets are chef Peter Wallace can trump you in the kitchen; his "fabulous" Eclectic menu, spotlighting organic ingredients and the "freshest seafood", "satisfies lots of different tastes", and it's "expertly delivered" by an "attentive" staff in a "warren of rooms"; if you can tear yourself away from the "stunning view of the harbor", it's a perfect place to "gaze into someone's eyes."

PEARL
26 | 25 | 24 | $67

12 Federal St. (India St.), 508-228-9701;
www.boardinghouse-pearl.com

■ It may be "easier to have dinner at the White House" than to score a reservation at this hot, hot "gem" where chef-partner Seth Raynor creates plenty of "culinary excitement" in an "ultra-modern" Downtown space; "expansive glass tanks" full of "tropical fish" set the "underwater-chic" backdrop for "glamorous" dining on "delectable" New French dishes that marry "Asian tastes" with "local flavors"; despite reports of service with an "attitude", "if you can get in, don't miss" this "fabulous experience."

Sconset Café ≠
∇ 24 | 13 | 20 | $39

8 Main St. (Post Office Sq.), Siasconset, 508-257-4008;
www.sconsetcafe.com

■ "Take a bottle of wine" to this "great little" BYO "find" out in Siasconset, an "unassuming, relaxing" oasis for "delicious", "high-quality" New American breakfasts (in season only), lunches and dinners (try the grilled New Zealand lamb loin); it's a "very good value for Nantucket", making it a "definite repeat" for most visitors.

SeaGrille
22 | 15 | 21 | $41

45 Sparks Ave. (bet. Hooper Farm & Sanford Rds.),
508-325-5700; www.theseagrille.com

■ "Straightforward seafood" (the quahog "chowder alone is worth the flight from Boston") plus New England specialties spun with a "creative twist" lure locals and visitors alike to this "consistently good" "family restaurant" set in a "likeable" "mid-island" location ("read: easy parking"); both the menu and atmosphere are "kid-friendly", and the prices "affordable" (at least "by Nantucket standards"), which explains why this "sure thing" is "where the year-round folks go."

Sfoglia ≠
∇ 24 | 21 | 22 | $47

130 Pleasant St. (bet. Boyers Way & Warren St.),
508-325-4500

■ "Luscious, rustic" Italian "home cooking" prepared "with pride" by a husband-and-wife team that "takes care of its customers with gusto" draws foodies "off the usual tourist path" to this "small and soulful" "island favorite"; "using as many local ingredients as possible", the chef-owners turn out "outstanding" fare (notably "heartbreakingly

Nantucket   F | D | S | C

beautiful breads" and "hearty" handmade pastas) brought to mismatched communal tables by "well-meaning" servers; in short, it's a "true find."

Straight Wharf   25 | 24 | 24 | $55
6 Harbor Sq. (Straight Wharf), 508-228-4499

■ "Overlooking the harbor", this "elegant" seafood house is a "classy" splurge for an "intensely Nantucket" experience that's "still great after all these years"; whether you dine inside the high-ceilinged interior or out on the patio, you'll be served "superlative" fish dishes by an "enthusiastic" staff; note that despite the "blue-blazer" dinner crowd, the "bar scene can turn quite rambunctious."

Summer House   22 | 24 | 21 | $60
17 Ocean Ave. (Magnolia Ave.), Siasconset, 508-257-9976; www.thesummerhouse.com

◨ "Fall in love with Nantucket" all over again at this airy Siasconset summer house that's "beautiful in its simplicity"; even "if you can't splurge for the full treatment", you can take in the "spectacular views" from its "breathtaking" oceanfront setting by having "drinks and sandwiches at poolside" (at lunch only); "if the chef is on", the seafood-centric New American fare "can be great", but naysayers gripe that the "unimpressive", "overpriced" menu is "simply not up to snuff."

Sushi by Yoshi   ▽ 24 | 11 | 15 | $37
2 E. Chestnut St. (Main St.), 508-228-1801; www.sushibyyoshi.com

■ For "fresh and delicious" "sushi by the sea", set sail to Nantucket's only Japanese restaurant; aside from raw fish, the menu includes a limited selection of cooked traditional dishes, such as noodles, tempura and teriyaki; the modest quarters are very "tiny", however, so "get there early (and BYO)" or opt for takeout.

TOPPER'S   28 | 28 | 27 | $85
The Wauwinet, 120 Wauwinet Rd. (2 mi. north of Polpis Rd.), 508-228-8768; www.wauwinet.com

■ "Take the love of your life or your dearest friends" to the "luxurious" Wauwinet inn for a "perfect" dining experience; chef Chris Freeman "makes wonderful use of fine New England ingredients" to create "heavenly" New American dishes that are accompanied by a "superb wine list" and brought to table by a staff that's "at your beck and call" without being "in your face"; whether you sit amid "old-world elegance" inside or out on the "gorgeous" terrace, this is an "incredible" "treat not to be missed."

21 Federal   25 | 24 | 23 | $59
21 Federal St. (bet. Chestnut & India Sts.), 508-228-2121; www.21federal.net

◨ "Classic" and "understated" in a "very New England" way, this "Nantucket institution" Downtown continues to

Nantucket F | D | S | C |

be "one of the standard-bearers on the island" for "top-notch" New American cuisine and a "knockout wine list"; a "longtime favorite" "bastion" for the "see-and-be-seen" crowd, it also "satisfies" with its "sophisticated" ambiance and "gracious" service (naturally, this "elegance" comes at an "eye-popping price"), even if a minority of dissenters finds it a "tad stuffy."

WEST CREEK CAFE   26 | 24 | 25 | $55 |
11 W. Creek Rd. (bet. Orange & Pleasant Sts.), 508-228-4943

■ Chef Jaime Hurley's "exciting" New American cooking at this "cozy, adorable" "hideaway" is moving it into the "top ranks" of Nantucket's restaurants; admirers "praise the constantly evolving menu" (it changes weekly, yet there are "no mistakes"), "comfortable" environs and the "warm" service that gives it the feel of a "local hangout"; "maybe because it's not in town", it's "one of the best-kept secrets on the island", but it's "definitely worth the short ride from Main Street."

Woodbox ⊄   ▽ 23 | 22 | 22 | $52 |
Woodbox Inn, 29 Fair St. (Charter St.), 508-228-0587; www.woodboxinn.com

◪ "Step back into history" at this "charming" "colonial" dowager set in the island's oldest inn (circa 1709); amid low beamed ceilings, pine-board floors, brick fireplaces and antique tables, traditionalists dine on "fine" Continental fare, starting with the "best popovers anywhere" and proceeding to familiar standards such as beef Wellington, rack of lamb and crème brûlée; rebels, however, who dismiss the "uninteresting" menu and "dark" setting, charge that the colonists wouldn't believe these "high prices."

Indexes

**CUISINES
LOCATIONS
SPECIAL FEATURES**

Indexes list the best of many within each category.

All restaurants are in Boston unless otherwise noted (C=Cape Cod; M=Martha's Vineyard; N=Nantucket).

get updates at zagat.com 187

Cuisine Index

CUISINES

Afghan
Helmand

American (New)
Alchemy/M
American Seasons/N
Aqua
Aqua Grille/C
Ariadne
Arno's/N
Aspasia
Atria/M
Aujourd'hui
Aura
Azure
Baker's Best
Balance/M
Bay Tower
Belfry Bistro/C
Black Eyed Susan's/N
blu
Bluefin/N
Boarding House/N
Bramble Inn/C
Bristol Lounge
B-Side Lounge
Cafe Edwige/C
Cafe Moxie/M
Cape Sea Grille/C
Central Kitchen
Centre Street Bistro/N
Chapoquoit Grill/C
Chester/C
Clio
Club Cafe
Company of Cauldron/N
Daedalus
Dalia's Bistro
Deluxe Town
Devlin's
Elbow Room
Esther's/C
Excelsior
Fava
Federalist
Finely JP's/C
Fishmonger's Cafe/C
flora
Fog Island Cafe/N
Franklin Cafe
Franklin Cape Ann
Full Moon

Gardner Museum
Gargoyles on Sq.
Grafton Street Pub
Grapevine
Green St. Grill
Hamersley's Bistro
Harvest
Icarus
Ice House/M
Independent
Indigo
Intrigue Cafe
Isabella
Jer-Ne
J's at Nashoba
Lambert's Cove/M
Laurel
Lucy's
Lyceum B&G
Martha's Galley
Martin House/C
Meritage
Mews/C
Nightingale
Ocean House/C
Olio
On the Park
Orleans
Park Corner/M
Pravda 116
Prose
Redline
Red Pheasant/C
Red Raven
Red Rock Bistro
Regatta of Cotuit/C
Ross' Grill/C
Sage
Salts
Sconset Café/N
Scoozi
Seasons
Second St. Cafe
75 Chestnut
Sherborn Inn
Sidney's Grille
Sister Sorel
Stephanie's
Summer House/N
Sweet Life Cafe/M
Temple Bar

Cuisine Index

Ten Tables
Theo's/M
Top of the Hub
Topper's/N
Tremont 647
Trio
29 Newbury
21 Federal/N
224 Boston St.
UpStairs on Square
Vicki Lee Boyajian
Vox Populi
Walden Grille
Washington Sq.
West Creek Cafe/N
West Side Lounge
West Street Grille
White Star Tavern
Zebra's Bistro
Zephrus/M
Zon's

American (Traditional)

Aesop's Tables/C
Andover Inn
Artcliff Diner/M
Asgard
Audubon Circle
BARCODE
Barker Tavern
Bee-Hive Tav./C
Bella's
Black Cow
Black Dog Tav./M
Black Sheep Cafe
Blue Cat Cafe
Blue Plate Express
Boston Beer Works
Brant Point Grill/N
Brenden Crocker's
Cafe Fleuri
Café Suisse
Cambridge Common
Captain Linnell Hse./C
Charley's
Charlie's Sandwich
Chart House
Chatham Squire/C
Cheers
Cheesecake Factory
Christian's/C
Clancy's/C
Colonial Inn
Coolidge Corner

Copley's Grand
Daggett House/M
Dakota's
Dalya's
Deluxe Town
Devlin's
Dodge St. B&G
Dolphin/C
Doyle's Cafe
eat
Firefly
Flash's
Geoffrey's Cafe
Good Life
Green Dragon
Grill 23 & Bar
Halfway Cafe
Harry's
Hartwell House
Harvard Gardens
Ironside Grill
Jacob Wirth
James's Gate
Jared's/N
Joe's American B&G
John Harvard's
Johnny D's
Johnny's Lunch.
Landing
Lucky's
Maddie's Sail
Margo Bistro
Mike's
Miracle of Science
Mr. & Mrs. Bartley's
New Bridge Cafe
Newes from America/M
News
Not Your Average Joe's
Oak Room
Oceana
Other Side Cosmic
Outermost Inn/M
Parish Cafe
Plaza III
Rosebud Diner
Silvertone B&G
Skellig
Sorella's
Sound Bites
South St. Diner
Spinnaker
Stars on Hingham
Stars on Huntington

get updates at zagat.com 189

Cuisine Index

Sunset Grill
Tim's Tavern
Via Lago
Victoria
Yanks

Argentinean
Tango

Asian
Grasshopper

Asian Fusion
Abba/C
Ambrosia
Blue Ginger
Epiphany
Pearl/N
Sosumi Asian/C

Barbecue
Bison County BBQ
Blue Ribbon BBQ
East Coast Grill
Jake's Boss BBQ
Jake's Dixie
Linwood Grill
New Bridge Cafe
New Jang Su
Pit Stop BBQ
Redbones BBQ
Uncle Pete's
Village Smokehse.

Brazilian
Brazilian Grill/C
Buteco
Cafe Belo
Café Brazil
Ipanema/M
Midwest Grill
MuQueCa

Cajun
Bob the Chef's
Lola's/M
Magnolia's

Californian
Baja Betty's
California Pizza Kit.
Caliterra B&G
Picante Mexican
Purple Cactus

Cambodian
Carambola
Elephant Walk

Stir Crazy/C
Wonder Spice

Caribbean
Green St. Grill

Chinese
(Dim sum specialists are noted)
Big Fish
Buddha's Delight
Café China
Changsho
Chau Chow City (dim sum)
Chef Chang's Hse.
Chef Chow's Hse.
China Pearl (dim sum)
Chinatown Seafood
Dynasty (dim sum)
Eastern Pier
East Ocean City
Emperor's Garden (dim sum)
Golden Temple
Grand Chau Chow
House of Zen
Imperial Seafood (dim sum)
Joy Luck Café
Jumbo Seafood
King Fung
Kowloon
Lotus Blossom
Mary Chung
New Shanghai (dim sum)
Ocean Wealth
Peach Farm
Peking Cuisine
P.F. Chang's
Royal East
Shangri-La
Sichuan Garden
Taiwan Cafe
Yangtze River

Coffeehouses
Cafe Pamplona
Caffe Paradiso
Caffe Vittoria
flour bakery & café
Hi-Rise Bread
1369 Coffee House
Wright Catch

Coffee Shops/Diners
Artcliff Diner/M
Charlie's Sandwich
Deluxe Town

Cuisine Index

Harry's
Johnny's Lunch.
Mike's
News
Rosebud Diner
South St. Diner
Stars on Hingham
Victoria

Colombian
El Cafetal

Continental
Academy Ocean/C
Andover Inn
Cafe Escadrille
Club Car/N
Dan'l Webster Inn/C
Front Street/C
Galley on Cliffside/N
Hartwell House
Locke-Ober
Raffael's
White Rainbow
Woodbox/N

Creole
Lola's/M
Rouge

Cuban
Chez Henri
El Oriental de Cuba
Naked Fish

Delis
B & D Deli
Milk St. Cafe
Rubin's
S&S
Zaftigs

Dessert
Bristol Lounge
Cafe Fleuri
Caffe Paradiso
Caffe Vittoria
Cheesecake Factory
Finale
flour bakery & café
Hi-Rise Bread
Mr. Crepe
Vicki Lee Boyajian

Dominican
Merengue

Eclectic
Academy Ocean/C
Anam Chara
Belfry Bistro/C
Blue Room
Bramble Inn/C
Bubala's/C
Centre Street Café
Chatham Bars/C
Christopher's
Claremont Cafe
Contrast Bistro/C
Cuchi Cuchi
Delux Cafe
Dish
Eclectic Cafe/C
EVOO
Fifty-Six Union/N
Fire & Ice
Five Bays Bistro/C
Glenn's Rest.
Marché
Metropolis Cafe
Mount Blue
Mr. Crepe
Napi's/C
Òran Mór/N
Red Inn/C
RooBar/C
Saint
Sonsie
Stone Soup
Vining's Bistro/C
ZuZu!

English
Cornwall's
Edwardian Tea Rm.

Eritrean
Asmara

Ethiopian
Addis Red Sea
Asmara

French
Brasserie Jo
Cafe Fleuri
Caffe Umbra
Chanticleer/N
Elephant Walk
Garden of Eden
Hungry i
Jasmine Bistro
L'Alouette/C

Cuisine Index

Le Grenier/M
Le Languedoc/N
Le Lyonnais
Le Soir
L'Etoile/M
Maison Robert
Mistral
No. 9 Park
Pigalle
Ritz-Carlton Din. Rm.
Silks
33 Restaurant

French (Bistro)

Aquitaine
Aquitaine Bis
Beacon Hill Bistro
Cassis
Chez Henri
Coriander
Craigie St. Bistrot
Hamersley's Bistro
Les Zygomates
Sandrine's
Sel de la Terre
Troquet
Truc

French (New)

Ambrosia
Bomboa
Chillingsworth/C
Clio
Julien
L'Espalier
Lumière
Mantra
Pearl/N
Radius
Spire
Square Café
Sweet Life Cafe/M
Torch

German

Jacob Wirth

Greek

Aegean
Demos
Ithaki

Hamburgers

Audubon Circle
Cambridge Common
Charley's
Christopher's
Johnny's Lunch.
Miracle of Science
Mr. & Mrs. Bartley's
Sunset Grill
Tim's Tavern

Hungarian

Jasmine Bistro

Indian

Ajanta
Akbar India
Bhindi Bazaar
Bombay Bistro
Bombay Classic
Bombay Club
Bukhara
Cafe of India
Diva Indian
Indian Cafe
Indian Club
India Pavilion
India Quality
Kashmir
Kebab Factory
Kebab-N-Kurry
Mantra
New Mother India
Passage to India
Punjab
Punjabi Dhaba
Rangoli
Saffron
Shalimar of India
Shanti
Tanjore

Irish

Asgard
Burren
Desmond O'Malley's
Doyle's Cafe
Grafton Street Pub
Grand Canal
Green Dragon
James's Gate
Matt Murphy's
Skellig

Italian

(N=Northern; S=Southern)
Abbicci/C
Abbondanza
Adrian's/C
Alberto's Rist./C (N)
Al Dente

subscribe to zagat.com

Cuisine Index

Alloro
Amelia's Tratt.
Anchovies
Angelo's
Antico Forno
Antonia's
Antonio's
Appetito
Armani Cafe
Artichokes Rist.
Artu
Assaggio
Bacco
Bella's
Bertucci's
Bistro 5 (N)
Bluestone Bistro
Bocelli's
Bricco
Bridgeman's (N)
Café Louis
Cafe Marliave
Caffe Umbra
Caliterra B&G
Cantina Italiana (S)
Carlo's Cucina
Carmen
Centro
Chesca's/M
Ciao Bella
Circolo (N)
Daily Catch (S)
Dancing Lobster/C
Davide Rist. (N)
Davio's (N)
Delfino
DeMarco/N (N)
Dom's (N)
Donatello
Euno
Fazio's Trattoria/C
Figlia
Figs
Filippo Rist.
Five North Sq.
Florentina
Florentine Cafe
Front Street/C
Galleria Umberto (S)
Giacomo's
Gina's by the Sea/C
Giuseppe's (S)
Greg's (S)
Gusto

G'Vanni's
Il Capriccio (N)
Il Moro
Jimmy Seas/M
Joe Tecce's
La Campania
La Famiglia Giorgio
La Groceria
La Summa (S)
Lattanzi's/M
Limoncello
L'Osteria
Lucca (N)
Maggiano's
Mamma Maria (N)
Margo Bistro
Marino Rist.
Massimino's
Maurizio's
Monica's
Mother Anna's
Nauset Beach/C (N)
No. 9 Park
Out of the Blue
Pagliuca's
Paolo's Tratt.
Papa Razzi
Pellino's (N)
Piattini
Piccola Venezia
Piccolo Nido
Polcari's/C
Pomodoro
Ponte Vecchio
Porcini's
Prezza
Raffael's
Red Sauce
Rist. Barolo/C (N)
Rist. Fiore
Rist. Lucia
Rist. Marcellino (S)
Rist. Toscano (N)
Riva
Roadhse. Cafe/C
Sage (N)
Sal's Place/C (S)
Saporito's (N)
Saraceno
Serafina Rist. (N)
Sfoglia/N
Siena/C
Siros
Sorento's

get updates at zagat.com 193

Cuisine Index

Stellina
Sweet Basil
Taranta (S)
Taverna Toscana
Teatro (N)
Terramia
33 Restaurant
Tosca (N)
Tratt. a Scalinatella
Tratt. Il Panino
Tratt. Pulcinella
Tullio's Rest.
Tuscan Grill (N)
Vault
Via Matta
Villa Francesca
Village Fish
Vin & Eddie's (N)
Vinny's at Night (S)
Zabaglione

Jamaican
Rhythm & Spice

Japanese
(Sushi specialists are noted)
Apollo Grill (sushi)
Bisuteki
Blue Fin (sushi)
Bluefin/N (sushi)
Cafe Sushi (sushi)
Fugakyu (sushi)
Ginza (sushi)
Gyuhama (sushi)
Inaho/C (sushi)
JP Seafood Cafe (sushi)
Kaya
Misaki/C (sushi)
Mr. Sushi (sushi)
Nara (sushi)
New Ginza (sushi)
Oga (sushi)
Oishii (sushi)
Osushi (sushi)
Roka
Sakurabana (sushi)
Sapporo
Shabu-Zen
Shilla (sushi)
Shogun (sushi)
Sosumi Asian/C (sushi)
Suishaya (sushi)
Sushi by Yoshi/N (sushi)
Takeshima (sushi)
Tokyo (sushi)

Tsunami (sushi)
Village Sushi (sushi)
Yama (sushi)
Zen 320 (sushi)

Korean
Apollo Grill
JP Seafood Cafe
Kaya
New Jang Su
Sapporo
Seoul Food
Shilla
Suishaya
Village Sushi
WuChon
Zen 320

Lebanese
Phoenicia

Malaysian
Penang
Pinang

Mediterranean
Abba/C
Aigo Bistro
Ardeo/C
Aspasia
Bar 10
Caffe Bella
Casablanca
Central Kitchen
Cioppino's/N
Dalia's Bistro
Dalya's
Gallia
Il Moro
Ithaki
Kouzina
Limbo
Oleana
Olives
Paolo's Tratt.
Red Fez
Rialto
Rustic Kit.
Sabur
Savannah Grill
Scutra
Terra Luna/C

Mexican
Baja Betty's
Baja Mexican
Casa del Rey

Cuisine Index

Casa Mexico
Casa Romero
Cilantro
El Pelón Taqueria
El Sarape
Forest Cafe
La Paloma
Lorraine's/C
Olé, Mexican
Picante Mexican
Plaza Garibaldi
Purple Cactus
Sol Azteca
Tacos El Charro
Tacos Lupita
Taqueria la Mex.
Taqueria Mexico
Tu y Yo

Middle Eastern

Cafe Barada
Cafe Jaffa
Helmand
Istanbul Cafe
Karoun
Middle East
Red Fez
Sepal
Skewers
Sound Bites
Sultan's Kitchen
ZuZu!

Moroccan

Argana
Enormous Room
Tangierino

New England

Amrheins
Anthony's Pier 4
Beach Plum Inn/M
Bee-Hive Tav./C
Boston Sail Loft
Chart Room/C
Clam Box
Coonamessett Inn/C
Copley's Grand
Durgin Park
Fireplace
Flume/C
Harvest
Henrietta's Table
Jared's/N
Jasper White's
Jimmy's Harborside
Opus/M
Paddock/C

Parker's
SeaGrille/N
75 Chestnut
Sherborn Inn
Tom Shea's
Twenty-Eight Atlantic/C
Union Oyster Hse.
Warren Tavern
Wayside Inn
Woodman's
Wright Catch

Nuevo Latino

Betty's Wok
Bomboa

Pan-Asian

Bernard's
Betty's Wok
Billy Tse
Blue Ginger
Island Hopper
Jae's
Kowloon
Ma Soba
No. 1 Noodle
Soya's
Typhoon
Wisteria House
Zen 320

Persian

Lala Rokh

Pizza

Adrian's/C
Antico Forno
Bertucci's
Bluestone Bistro
California Pizza Kit.
Cambridge, 1.
Emma's Pizzeria
Figs
Galleria Umberto
Lattanzi's/M
Not Your Average Joe's
Papa Razzi
Pizzeria Regina
Real Pizza
Santarpio's
Tullio's Rest.
Upper Crust
Veggie Planet
Woody's Grill

Polish

Cafe Polonia

get updates at zagat.com

Cuisine Index

Polynesian
Kowloon

Portuguese
Atasca
Casa Portugal
Neighborhood Rest.
O Cantinho
O'Fado
Rest. Cesaria
Sunset Cafe

Pub Food
Black Cow
Boston Beer Works
Burren
Cambridge Common
Charley's
Cheers
Christopher's
Coolidge Corner
Cornwall's
Desmond O'Malley's
Doyle's Cafe
Good Life
Halfway Cafe
James's Gate
John Harvard's
Johnny D's
Lucky's
Matt Murphy's
Miracle of Science
New Bridge Cafe
Newes from America/M
Paolo's Tratt.
Skellig
Sunset Grill
Tim's Tavern

Puerto Rican
El Coqui

Russian
Cafe St. Petersburg

Salvadoran
Tacos Lupita

Seafood
Academy Ocean/C
Alchemy/M
Anthony's Pier 4
Atlantica
Atlantic Fish Co.
Azure
Back Eddy
Barking Crab
Beach Plum Inn/M
Big Fish
Boston Sail Loft
Bubala's/C
Captain Linnell Hse./C
Captain's Wharf
Chart House
Chart Room/C
Chinatown Seafood
Clam Box
Coach House/M
Court House
Daily Catch
Dancing Lobster/C
Dolphin/C
Dolphin Seafood
East Coast Grill
Eastern Pier
East Ocean City
FIFTY SEVEN
Finz
Fishmonger's Cafe/C
Giacomo's
Grand Chau Chow
Grillfish
Grill 23 & Bar
Home Port/M
Impudent Oyster/C
Jasper White's
Jimmy's Harborside
JP Seafood Cafe
Jumbo Seafood
KingFish Hall
L'Alouette/C
Landfall/C
Legal Sea Foods
Lobster Pot/C
Maddie's Sail
McCormick & Schmick's
Morse Fish
Naked Fish
Naked Oyster/C
Nantucket Lobster/N
No Name
Oceana
Ocean Wealth
Out of the Blue
Peach Farm
Penguins Sea Grill/C
Roadhse. Cafe/C
SeaGrille/N
Skipjack's
Straight Wharf/N
Tom Shea's

196 subscribe to zagat.com

Cuisine Index

Turner Fisheries
Union Oyster Hse.
Village Fish
Woodman's
Wright Catch

South African
Karoo Kafe/C

Southern
Bob the Chef's
House of Blues
Lola's/M
Magnolia's
Pit Stop BBQ
Redbones BBQ
Rouge

Southwestern
Cottonwood Cafe
Masa
Zapotec/M

Spanish
Azafran
Dalí
Flash's
Iruna
Solea Rest.
Taberna de Haro
Tapeo
Tasca

Steakhouses
Abe & Louie's
Bisuteki
Bonfire
Bugaboo Creek
Capital Grille
FIFTY SEVEN
Fleming's Prime
Frank's Steak
Grill 23 & Bar
Hilltop Steak
Jimmy's Steer Hse.
Morton's of Chicago
Oak Room
Palm
Penguins Sea Grill/C
Plaza III
Stockyard

Swiss
Café Suisse

Tapas (Specialties)
Azafran
Cuchi Cuchi
Dalí
Flash's
Solea Rest.
Taberna de Haro
Tangierino
Tapeo
Tasca

Tex-Mex
Anna's Taqueria
Boca Grande
Border Cafe
Cactus Club
Fajitas & 'Ritas
José's

Thai
Amarin
Bamboo
Bangkok Basil
Bangkok Bistro
Bangkok Blue
Bangkok City
Bangkok Cuisine
Brown Sugar Cafe
Erawan of Siam
Great Thai Chef
Green Papaya
House of Siam
Jamjuli
Khao Sarn
King & I
Kowloon
Lam's
Montien
9 Tastes
Rod Dee
711 Grill
Spice Thai
Tantawan
Thai Basil
Thai Village
Wonder Spice

Tibetan
House of Tibet

Tunisian
Baraka Cafe

Turkish
Istanbul Cafe
Sultan's Kitchen

Vegetarian
Buddha's Delight
Christopher's

Cuisine Index

Country Life
Grasshopper
Other Side Cosmic
Sepal
Veggie Planet

Venezuelan
La Casa de Pedro

Vietnamese
Buddha's Delight
Dong Khanh
Lam's
Pho Hoa
Pho Lemon Grass
Pho Pasteur
Pho République
Saigon
711 Grill
Viet Hong
Viet's Café
V. Majestic

Location Index

LOCATIONS

BOSTON

Allston/Brighton
Bamboo
Bangkok Bistro
Bluestone Bistro
Cafe Belo
Café Brazil
Carlo's Cucina
Devlin's
Elbow Room
El Cafetal
Grasshopper
Jasmine Bistro
Pho Pasteur
Rangoli
Saigon
Stockyard
Sunset Grill
Tasca
Viet Hong
V. Majestic

Back Bay
Abe & Louie's
Ambrosia
Armani Cafe
Atlantic Fish Co.
Aujourd'hui
Azure
Baja Mexican
Bangkok Blue
BARCODE
Bar 10
Bertucci's
Bhindi Bazaar
Blue Cat Cafe
Bomboa
Bonfire
Brasserie Jo
Bristol Lounge
Cactus Club
Cafe Jaffa
Café Louis
California Pizza Kit.
Capital Grille
Casa Romero
Charley's
Ciao Bella
Clio
Copley's Grand
Cottonwood Cafe
Davio's
Excelsior
Fire & Ice
Firefly
Flash's
Geoffrey's Cafe
Grill 23 & Bar
Gyuhama
Island Hopper
Joe's American B&G
Kashmir
Kaya
Kebab-N-Kurry
La Famiglia Giorgio
Laurel
Legal Sea Foods
L'Espalier
Marché
Morton's of Chicago
Oak Room
Osushi
Other Side Cosmic
Palm
Papa Razzi
Parish Cafe
Pho Pasteur
Piattini
Ritz-Carlton Din. Rm.
Saffron
Saint
Scoozi
Skipjack's
Sonsie
Stephanie's
Tapeo
Thai Basil
33 Restaurant
Top of the Hub
Turner Fisheries
29 Newbury
Typhoon
Via Matta
Vox Populi
White Star Tavern
Wisteria House

Beacon Hill
Antonio's
Artu
Beacon Hill Bistro

get updates at zagat.com 199

Location Index

Cheers
Federalist
Figs
Harvard Gardens
Hungry i
Istanbul Cafe
King & I
Lala Rokh
Ma Soba
No. 9 Park
Phoenicia
Rist. Toscano
75 Chestnut
Torch
Upper Crust

Charlestown
Figs
Ironside Grill
Olives
Paolo's Tratt.
Tangierino
Warren Tavern

Chelsea/ East Boston/Revere
Billy Tse
Bisuteki
Cafe Belo
New Bridge Cafe
Plaza Garibaldi
Santarpio's
Uncle Pete's

Chinatown/Leather Dist.
Apollo Grill
Big Fish
Buddha's Delight
Chau Chow City
China Pearl
Dong Khanh
Dynasty
East Ocean City
Emperor's Garden
Epiphany
Ginza
Grand Chau Chow
Imperial Seafood
Jumbo Seafood
King Fung
Les Zygomates
News
New Shanghai
Ocean Wealth
Peach Farm
Peking Cuisine
Penang
Pho Hoa
Pho Pasteur
Shabu-Zen
South St. Diner
Suishaya
Taiwan Cafe
Trio

Downtown/ Financial District
Aqua
Cafe Fleuri
Cafe Marliave
Café Suisse
Caliterra B&G
Country Life
Dakota's
Fajitas & 'Ritas
Good Life
Julien
Legal Sea Foods
Limbo
Locke-Ober
Maison Robert
Mantra
Margo Bistro
Milk St. Cafe
Nara
Parker's
Radius
Sakurabana
Silvertone B&G
Spire
Sultan's Kitchen
Tratt. Il Panino
Vault
West Street Grille

Faneuil Hall
Bay Tower
Bertucci's
Cheers
Durgin Park
Green Dragon
KingFish Hall
McCormick & Schmick's
Naked Fish
Pinang
Pizzeria Regina
Plaza III
Rustic Kit.
Seasons
Union Oyster Hse.

Location Index

Fenway/Kenmore Square
Audubon Circle
Boston Beer Works
Brown Sugar Cafe
Buteco
Cafe Belo
Cornwall's
El Pelón Taqueria
Gardner Museum
India Quality
Linwood Grill
Rod Dee
Sorento's
Woody's Grill

Jamaica Plain
Bukhara
Centre Street Café
Doyle's Cafe
El Oriental de Cuba
Jake's Boss BBQ
James's Gate
JP Seafood Cafe
Purple Cactus
711 Grill
Sorella's
Tacos El Charro
Ten Tables
Wonder Spice
Zon's

North End/North Station
Al Dente
Alloro
Antico Forno
Artu
Assaggio
Bacco
Billy Tse
Boston Beer Works
Bricco
Caffe Paradiso
Caffe Vittoria
Cantina Italiana
Carmen
Daily Catch
Davide Rist.
Dom's
Euno
Filippo Rist.
Five North Sq.
Florentine Cafe
Galleria Umberto
Giacomo's
Grand Canal
G'Vanni's
Joe's American B&G
Joe Tecce's
La Famiglia Giorgio
La Summa
Limoncello
L'Osteria
Lucca
Mamma Maria
Massimino's
Maurizio's
Monica's
Mother Anna's
Pagliuca's
Piccola Venezia
Piccolo Nido
Pizzeria Regina
Pomodoro
Prezza
Rist. Fiore
Rist. Lucia
Sage
Saraceno
Taranta
Taverna Toscana
Terramia
Tratt. a Scalinatella
Tratt. Il Panino
Villa Francesca

South End/Roxbury/Dorchester/Mattapan
Addis Red Sea
Anchovies
Aquitaine
Bob the Chef's
Caffe Umbra
Charlie's Sandwich
Claremont Cafe
Club Cafe
Delux Cafe
Dish
flour bakery & café
Franklin Cafe
Gallia
Garden of Eden
Giacomo's
Grillfish
Hamersley's Bistro
House of Siam
Icarus
Jae's
Masa
Merengue

get updates at zagat.com   **201**

Location Index

Metropolis Cafe
Mike's
Mistral
Morse Fish
Nightingale
On the Park
Pho Hoa
Pho République
Pit Stop BBQ
Red Fez
Rest. Cesaria
Rouge
Shanti
Sister Sorel
Thai Village
Tim's Tavern
Tremont 647
Truc
224 Boston St.
Victoria

Symphony
Bangkok City
Bangkok Cuisine
Betty's Wok
Shanti
Stars on Huntington

Theater District
blu
California Pizza Kit.
FIFTY SEVEN
Finale

Fleming's Prime
Jacob Wirth
Jer-Ne
Legal Sea Foods
Maggiano's
McCormick & Schmick's
Montien
P.F. Chang's
Pho Pasteur
Pigalle
Pravda 116
Teatro
Troquet

Waterfront/South Boston
Amrheins
Anthony's Pier 4
Aura
Barking Crab
Boston Sail Loft
Cafe Polonia
Chart House
Daily Catch
Eastern Pier
Intrigue Cafe
Jimmy's Harborside
Lucky's
Meritage
No Name
Oceana
Sel de la Terre

CAMBRIDGE

Central Square
Asgard
Asmara
Atasca
Baraka Cafe
Bertucci's
Bisuteki
Central Kitchen
Centro
Cuchi Cuchi
Enormous Room
Good Life
Green St. Grill
India Pavilion
La Groceria
Mary Chung
Middle East
Miracle of Science
Picante Mexican

Rhythm & Spice
Royal East
Salts
Shalimar of India
Sidney's Grille
Spinnaker
1369 Coffee House
ZuZu!

East Cambridge
Ajanta
Boca Grande
California Pizza Kit.
Cheesecake Factory
Court House
Davio's
El Coqui
Helmand
Papa Razzi
Second St. Cafe

Location Index

Fresh Pond
Aspasia
Full Moon
Hi-Rise Bread
Jasper White's
José's
Real Pizza
Tokyo
Tratt. Pulcinella

Harvard Square
Bertucci's
Bombay Club
Border Cafe
Cafe of India
Cafe Pamplona
Cafe Sushi
Caffe Paradiso
Cambridge Common
Cambridge, 1.
Casablanca
Casa Mexico
Chez Henri
Craigie St. Bistrot
Daedalus
Dolphin Seafood
Finale
Fire & Ice
Grafton Street Pub
Harvest
Henrietta's Table
Hi-Rise Bread
House of Blues
House of Zen
Iruna
John Harvard's
Johnny's Lunch.
Mr. & Mrs. Bartley's
9 Tastes
Penang
Pho Pasteur
Redline
Rialto
Roka
Sandrine's
Shilla
Skewers
Spice Thai

Tanjore
UpStairs on Square
Veggie Planet

Inman Square
Akbar India
Argana
Café China
Casa Portugal
East Coast Grill
Magnolia's
Midwest Grill
MuQueCa
O Cantinho
Oleana
Olé, Mexican
Punjabi Dhaba
S&S
Sunset Cafe
1369 Coffee House

Kendall Square
Amelia's Tratt.
Atasca
Black Sheep Cafe
Blue Room
B-Side Lounge
Emma's Pizzeria
Florentina
Legal Sea Foods

Porter Square
Anna's Taqueria
Blue Fin
Boca Grande
Cafe Barada
Changsho
Christopher's
Elephant Walk
Forest Cafe
Frank's Steak
Giuseppe's
Indian Club
Kaya
Marino Rist.
Passage to India
Seoul Food
Temple Bar
West Side Lounge

NEARBY SUBURBS

Arlington/Belmont/ Winchester
Azafran
Blue Plate Express

Blue Ribbon BBQ
Bombay Classic
Edwardian Tea Rm.
flora

Location Index

Full Moon
Jimmy's Steer Hse.
Mr. Sushi
Not Your Average Joe's
Olé, Mexican
Prose
Punjab
Rist. Lucia
Scutra
Shangri-La
Tango
Viet's Café

Brookline/Chestnut Hill

Anam Chara
Anna's Taqueria
Aquitaine Bis
Baja Betty's
B & D Deli
Bangkok Basil
Bernard's
Bertucci's
Boca Grande
Bombay Bistro
Buddha's Delight
Cafe St. Petersburg
Capital Grille
Captain's Wharf
Charley's
Cheesecake Factory
Chef Chang's Hse.
Chef Chow's Hse.
Chinatown Seafood
Coolidge Corner
Daily Catch
Dalia's Bistro
Fajitas & 'Ritas
Figs
Fireplace
Fugakyu
Ginza
Golden Temple
Indian Cafe
Jae's
Kaya
Khao Sarn
Legal Sea Foods
Lucy's
Matt Murphy's
Mr. Sushi
Oishii
Papa Razzi
Pho Lemon Grass
Pho Pasteur
Rod Dee
Rubin's
Sichuan Garden
Sol Azteca
Taberna de Haro
Takeshima
Tsunami
Upper Crust
Village Fish
Village Smokehse.
Washington Sq.
Zaftigs
Zen 320

Lexington

Hartwell House
Via Lago
Yangtze River

Newton/Needham

Amarin
Appetito
Ariadne
Baker's Best
Bertucci's
Blue Ribbon BBQ
Fava
Figlia
Indigo
Jamjuli
Johnny's Lunch.
Joy Luck Café
Karoun
Kouzina
Lam's
Le Soir
Lumière
No. 1 Noodle
Not Your Average Joe's
Peking Cuisine
Red Sauce
Sapporo
Shogun
Skipjack's
Sol Azteca
Soya's
Sweet Basil
Vicki Lee Boyajian

Quincy/Braintree

Bertucci's
Bugaboo Creek
El Sarape
Fajitas & 'Ritas
Hilltop Steak
Joe's American B&G

Location Index

La Paloma
Legal Sea Foods
Pizzeria Regina
Raffael's
Red Sauce
Siros
Tullio's Rest.

Roslindale/Dedham
Delfino
Gusto
Halfway Cafe
Isabella
Joe's American B&G
Village Sushi

Somerville/Medford
Anna's Taqueria
Antonia's
Bertucci's
Bistro 5
Bocelli's
Burren
Cafe Belo
Dalí
Diva Indian
eat
EVOO
Gargoyles on Sq.
Great Thai Chef
House of Tibet
Independent
Johnny D's
Kebab Factory
Mr. Crepe
Neighborhood Rest.
Orleans
Out of the Blue
Picante Mexican
Redbones BBQ
Rosebud Diner

Sabur
Savannah Grill
Sound Bites
Tacos Lupita
Taqueria la Mex.
Tu y Yo
Vinny's at Night
WuChon

Watertown/Waltham
Aegean
Bertucci's
Bison County BBQ
Bugaboo Creek
Carambola
Deluxe Town
Demos
Erawan of Siam
Green Papaya
Greg's
Halfway Cafe
Il Capriccio
Jake's Dixie
La Campania
La Casa de Pedro
Naked Fish
New Ginza
New Mother India
Not Your Average Joe's
Porcini's
Red Sauce
Rist. Marcellino
Sepal
Skellig
Solea Rest.
Stellina
Tantawan
Taqueria Mexico
Tuscan Grill
Wright Catch

OUTLYING SUBURBS

North of Boston
Abbondanza
Andover Inn
Angelo's
Artichokes Rist.
Black Cow
Border Cafe
Brenden Crocker's
Bugaboo Creek
Cassis
China Pearl
Cilantro

Circolo
Clam Box
Daily Catch
Dodge St. B&G
Donatello
Finz
Franklin Cape Ann
Glenn's Rest.
Grapevine
Hilltop Steak
Il Moro
Ithaki

Location Index

Joe's American B&G
Kowloon
Landing
Legal Sea Foods
Lyceum B&G
Maddie's Sail
Naked Fish
O'Fado
Pellino's
Polcari's
Ponte Vecchio
Red Raven
Red Rock Bistro
Stone Soup
Tom Shea's
White Rainbow
Woodman's
Yanks
Zabaglione

South of Boston
Atlantica
Back Eddy
Barker Tavern
Bella's
Bridgeman's
Caffe Bella
Casa del Rey
Coriander
Joe's American B&G
Martha's Galley
Mount Blue
Not Your Average Joe's
Olio
Papa Razzi
Pizzeria Regina
Red Sauce
Riva
Saporito's
Siros
Square Café

Cape Cod
Abba
Abbicci
Academy Ocean
Adrian's
Aesop's Tables
Alberto's Rist.
Aqua Grille
Ardeo
Bee-Hive Tav.
Belfry Bistro

Stars on Hingham
Tosca
Vin & Eddie's

West of Boston
Aegean
Aigo Bistro
Amarin
Blue Ginger
Bugaboo Creek
Cafe Belo
Cafe Escadrille
California Pizza Kit.
Colonial Inn
Dalya's
Desmond O'Malley's
Dolphin Seafood
Figs
Fugakyu
Halfway Cafe
Harry's
John Harvard's
J's at Nashoba
Legal Sea Foods
Le Lyonnais
Lotus Blossom
Naked Fish
New Jang Su
Oga
Oishii
Papa Razzi
Pizzeria Regina
Serafina Rist.
Sherborn Inn
Silks
Skipjack's
Walden Grille
Wayside Inn
Yama
Zebra's Bistro

FAR OUTLYING AREAS

Bramble Inn
Brazilian Grill
Bubala's
Cafe Edwige
Cape Sea Grille
Captain Linnell Hse.
Chapoquoit Grill
Chart Room
Chatham Bars
Chatham Squire
Chester
Chillingsworth

206   subscribe to zagat.com

Location Index

Christian's
Clancy's
Contrast Bistro
Coonamessett Inn
Dancing Lobster
Dan'l Webster Inn
Dolphin
Eclectic Cafe
Esther's
Fazio's Trattoria
Finely JP's
Fishmonger's Cafe
Five Bays Bistro
Flume
Front Street
Gina's by the Sea
Impudent Oyster
Inaho
Karoo Kafe
L'Alouette
Landfall
Lobster Pot
Lorraine's
Martin House
Mews
Misaki
Naked Oyster
Napi's
Nauset Beach
Ocean House
Paddock
Penguins Sea Grill
Polcari's
Red Inn
Red Pheasant
Regatta of Cotuit
Rist. Barolo
Roadhse. Cafe
RooBar
Ross' Grill
Sal's Place
Siena
Sosumi Asian
Stir Crazy
Terra Luna
Twenty-Eight Atlantic
Vining's Bistro

Martha's Vineyard
Alchemy
Artcliff Diner
Atria
Balance
Beach Plum Inn
Black Dog Tav.
Cafe Moxie
Chesca's
Coach House
Daggett House
Home Port
Ice House
Ipanema
Jimmy Seas
Lambert's Cove
Lattanzi's
Le Grenier
L'Etoile
Lola's
Newes from America
Opus
Outermost Inn
Park Corner
Sweet Life Cafe
Theo's
Zapotec
Zephrus

Nantucket
American Seasons
Arno's
Black Eyed Susan's
Bluefin
Boarding House
Brant Point Grill
Centre Street Bistro
Chanticleer
Cioppino's
Club Car
Company of Cauldron
DeMarco
Fifty-Six Union
Fog Island Cafe
Galley on Cliffside
Jared's
Le Languedoc
Nantucket Lobster
Òran Mór
Pearl
Sconset Café
SeaGrille
Sfoglia
Straight Wharf
Summer House
Sushi by Yoshi
Topper's
21 Federal
West Creek Cafe
Woodbox

get updates at zagat.com

Special Feature Index

SPECIAL FEATURES

For multi-location restaurants, the availability of index features may vary by location.

Breakfast
(See also Hotel Dining)
Arno's/N
Artcliff Diner/M
Baker's Best
Black Dog Tav./M
Black Eyed Susan's/N
Cafe Edwige/C
Charlie's Sandwich
Chau Chow City
China Pearl
Claremont Cafe
Deluxe Town
Doyle's Cafe
El Cafetal
El Oriental de Cuba
Emperor's Garden
Fishmonger's Cafe/C
flour bakery & café
Fog Island Cafe/N
Garden of Eden
Geoffrey's Cafe
Hi-Rise Bread
Imperial Seafood
Johnny's Lunch.
Lucy's
Marché
Merengue
Mike's
Milk St. Cafe
Mr. Crepe
MuQueCa
Neighborhood Rest.
On the Park
Park Corner/M
Pomodoro
Real Pizza
Riva
Rosebud Diner
Rubin's
S&S
Sconset Café/N
Second St. Cafe
Sonsie
Sorella's
Sound Bites
South St. Diner
Stars on Hingham
Stone Soup
1369 Coffee House
Vicki Lee Boyajian
Victoria
Wright Catch
Zaftigs

Brunch
Abe & Louie's
Aquitaine
Aquitaine Bis
Argana
Aujourd'hui
Baker's Best
Beacon Hill Bistro
blu
Blue Room
Bob the Chef's
Bombay Club
Brant Point Grill/N
Brasserie Jo
Cafe Fleuri
Caffe Umbra
Casablanca
Centre Street Café
Chillingsworth/C
Clancy's/C
Claremont Cafe
Copley's Grand
Dan'l Webster Inn/C
Deluxe Town
East Coast Grill
Esther's/C
Federalist
Fifty-Six Union/N
Fireplace
Franklin Cape Ann
Full Moon
Harvest
Henrietta's Table
House of Blues
Hungry i
Johnny D's
J's at Nashoba
KingFish Hall
Laurel
Le Languedoc/N
Lola's/M

Special Feature Index

Lyceum B&G
Matt Murphy's
Meritage
Metropolis Cafe
Mews/C
Nightingale
Oceana
Ocean House/C
Olé, Mexican
Opus/M
Red Rock Bistro
Ritz-Carlton Din. Rm.
Rosebud Diner
Rouge
Sabur
S&S
Sel de la Terre
75 Chestnut
Sherborn Inn
Silks
Siros
Sonsie
Sorella's
Spinnaker
Spire
Top of the Hub
Topper's/N
Tremont 647
Turner Fisheries
UpStairs on Square
Veggie Planet
Vicki Lee Boyajian
Washington Sq.
White Rainbow
Zebra's Bistro

Buffet Served
(Check availability)
Ajanta
Akbar India
Amrheins
Bombay Bistro
Bristol Lounge
Bukhara
Cafe Belo
Cafe Fleuri
Cafe of India
Café Suisse
Club Cafe
Colonial Inn
Coonamessett Inn/C
Copley's Grand
Country Life
Diva Indian
Fajitas & 'Ritas
Fire & Ice
India Pavilion
Intrigue Cafe
Jer-Ne
Kashmir
Lola's/M
Maggiano's
MuQueCa
Neighborhood Rest.
Oceana
Ocean House/C
Opus/M
Parker's
Passage to India
Plaza III
Raffael's
Ritz-Carlton Din. Rm.
Shalimar of India
Shanti
Sidney's Grille
Spinnaker
Sunset Grill
Tanjore
Tokyo
Wright Catch
Yangtze River

Business Dining
Ambrosia
Aquitaine
Aquitaine Bis
Aujourd'hui
Azure
Bay Tower
Beacon Hill Bistro
blu
Blue Ginger
Bombay Club
Bristol Lounge
Cafe Fleuri
Café Louis
Capital Grille
Chillingsworth/C
Clio
Copley's Grand
Davio's
Federalist
FIFTY SEVEN
Grapevine
Green Papaya
Grill 23 & Bar
Hamersley's Bistro
Harvest

Special Feature Index

Henrietta's Table
Il Capriccio
Jer-Ne
Julien
Legal Sea Foods
Le Soir
L'Espalier
Locke-Ober
Maison Robert
Mamma Maria
Mantra
Margo Bistro
McCormick & Schmick's
Meritage
Mistral
Morton's of Chicago
No. 9 Park
Oga
Olives
Palm
Pigalle
Plaza III
Prezza
Radius
Rialto
Rist. Toscano
Ritz-Carlton Din. Rm.
Sandrine's
Seasons
Sel de la Terre
Sidney's Grille
Spire
Troquet
Turner Fisheries
Twenty-Eight Atlantic/C
UpStairs on Square
Vault

BYO

Artcliff Diner/M
Black Dog Tav./M
Black Eyed Susan's/N
Cafe Moxie/M
Clam Box
Daily Catch
House of Zen
Ice House/M
Ipanema/M
Lambert's Cove/M
Le Grenier/M
Outermost Inn/M
Sconset Café/N
Skewers
Sushi by Yoshi/N

Sweet Basil
Theo's/M
Tsunami
Yama
Zephrus/M

Catering

Abbondanza
Addis Red Sea
Aigo Bistro
Ajanta
Al Dente
Amelia's Tratt.
Angelo's
Antonia's
Antonio's
Aquitaine
Aquitaine Bis
Artcliff Diner/M
Artu
Asmara
Aspasia
Atria/M
Back Eddy
Baja Betty's
Baker's Best
Balance/M
Bamboo
Bangkok Cuisine
Baraka Cafe
Beach Plum Inn/M
Bernard's
Bistro 5
Bluefin/N
Blue Ribbon BBQ
Bombay Bistro
Bombay Classic
Bombay Club
Bomboa
Bramble Inn/C
Brown Sugar Cafe
Bukhara
Café Louis
Cafe Moxie/M
Cafe of India
Cantina Italiana
Carambola
Carlo's Cucina
Casa Portugal
Centre Street Bistro/N
Changsho
Chanticleer/N
Chez Henri
Chillingsworth/C

Special Feature Index

Cilantro
Claremont Cafe
Davide Rist.
DeMarco/N
Dish
Dolphin/C
Dong Khanh
East Coast Grill
Eastern Pier
Elephant Walk
El Oriental de Cuba
El Pelón Taqueria
Fava
Fireplace
Five Bays Bistro/C
flour bakery & café
Gargoyles on Sq.
Hi-Rise Bread
House of Siam
Il Moro
Indian Club
India Quality
Isabella
Ithaki
Jamjuli
Jasmine Bistro
Jimmy Seas/M
Joy Luck Café
Julien
Kashmir
Kebab Factory
Kebab-N-Kurry
Khao Sarn
King Fung
La Casa de Pedro
La Paloma
La Summa
Legal Sea Foods
L'Espalier
Les Zygomates
Limoncello
Lola's/M
Lorraine's/C
Lotus Blossom
Lumière
Lyceum B&G
Martin House/C
Massimino's
Metropolis Cafe
Midwest Grill
Misaki/C
Mother Anna's
Naked Oyster/C
New Bridge Cafe

New Ginza
New Jang Su
Oishii
Olé, Mexican
Olio
Paolo's Tratt.
Park Corner/M
Passage to India
Peach Farm
Pellino's
Penang
Penguins Sea Grill/C
Pho Lemon Grass
Pho Pasteur
Pho République
Piccolo Nido
Pit Stop BBQ
Prose
Rangoli
Redbones BBQ
Sabur
Saffron
Sakurabana
SeaGrille/N
Second St. Cafe
Sel de la Terre
Seoul Food
Sepal
Shalimar of India
Sichuan Garden
Sister Sorel
Sol Azteca
Sosumi Asian/C
South St. Diner
Stone Soup
Straight Wharf/N
Sultan's Kitchen
Summer House/N
Sunset Cafe
Sushi by Yoshi/N
Sweet Basil
Sweet Life Cafe/M
Tanjore
Tantawan
Taqueria la Mex.
Taqueria Mexico
Taranta
Tasca
Taverna Toscana
Terra Luna/C
Terramia
Thai Basil
Tim's Tavern
Tokyo

get updates at zagat.com 211

Special Feature Index

Top of the Hub
Tosca
Tratt. Pulcinella
Trio
Tu y Yo
Uncle Pete's
Upper Crust
Via Lago
Vicki Lee Boyajian
Viet Hong
Viet's Café
Vinny's at Night
White Rainbow
Wonder Spice
Woodman's
Yama
Yanks
Zabaglione

Child-Friendly

(Besides the normal fast-food places; * children's menu available)

Addis Red Sea
Adrian's/C*
Aegean
Aesop's Tables/C*
Ajanta
Alberto's Rist./C*
Amarin
Amelia's Tratt.
Amrheins*
Angelo's
Anna's Taqueria
Anthony's Pier 4*
Antico Forno
Antonia's
Aqua Grille/C*
Ardeo/C*
Arno's/N*
Artcliff Diner/M
Artichokes Rist.
Artu
Asmara
Atasca
Atlantic Fish Co.*
Back Eddy*
Baja Betty's
Baker's Best
Bamboo
B & D Deli
Barker Tavern
Barking Crab*
Beach Plum Inn/M*

Bee-Hive Tav./C*
Bernard's
Bertucci's*
Betty's Wok
Big Fish
Billy Tse
Bison County BBQ
Bisuteki
Black Cow*
Black Dog Tav./M*
Black Sheep Cafe
Blue Fin
Blue Plate Express*
Blue Ribbon BBQ
Bluestone Bistro*
Boarding House/N*
Bob the Chef's
Boca Grande
Bocelli's*
Border Cafe
Brasserie Jo*
Brazilian Grill/C
Bridgeman's*
Bristol Lounge*
Brown Sugar Cafe
Bugaboo Creek*
Cafe Belo
Cafe Fleuri*
Cafe Jaffa
Cafe Marliave*
Café Suisse*
California Pizza Kit.*
Captain's Wharf*
Casa Mexico
Casa Portugal
Chapoquoit Grill/C
Charley's*
Charlie's Sandwich
Chart House*
Chatham Squire/C*
Cheers*
Cheesecake Factory*
Chesca's/M
China Pearl
Chinatown Seafood
Christopher's*
Cilantro
Cioppino's/N
Clancy's/C*
Coonamessett Inn/C*
Court House*
Daily Catch
Dan'l Webster Inn/C*
Deluxe Town*

Special Feature Index

Demos*
Dolphin/C
Dolphin Seafood*
Doyle's Cafe
Durgin Park
El Coqui*
El Oriental de Cuba
El Sarape
Excelsior
Fazio's Trattoria/C
Figs*
Finz*
Fire & Ice
flour bakery & café
Fog Island Cafe/N*
Frank's Steak*
Full Moon*
Giacomo's
Giuseppe's
Great Thai Chef
G'Vanni's*
Harry's*
Henrietta's Table*
Hilltop Steak*
Hi-Rise Bread*
Impudent Oyster/C*
Inaho/C
Ironside Grill*
Jake's Dixie*
Jasper White's*
Joe's American B&G*
Johnny's Lunch.*
KingFish Hall*
Kouzina*
Landfall/C*
Landing*
La Paloma*
Lattanzi's/M
Legal Sea Foods*
Le Soir
Lobster Pot/C*
Lyceum B&G*
Marché
Marino Rist.*
Matt Murphy's
McCormick & Schmick's*
Merengue
Midwest Grill
Mr. & Mrs. Bartley's*
Nantucket Lobster/N*
Neighborhood Rest.*
New Ginza
New Jang Su
No Name*
Not Your Average Joe's*
O Cantinho
Oceana*
Ocean House/C
O'Fado*
Out of the Blue
Paddock/C*
Papa Razzi*
Penguins Sea Grill/C*
Pho Hoa*
Pho Lemon Grass
Picante Mexican
Pinang
Pit Stop BBQ
Porcini's
Purple Cactus*
Redbones BBQ*
Red Sauce*
Rod Dee
Rosebud Diner
Rubin's*
S&S
Santarpio's
SeaGrille/N*
Second St. Cafe
711 Grill
Shanti
Sichuan Garden
Siena/C
Siros*
Skipjack's*
Solea Rest.
Sorella's*
South St. Diner*
Soya's
Stars on Hingham*
Sunset Cafe*
Tacos El Charro
Tacos Lupita
Taiwan Cafe
Tanjore*
Tapeo
Taqueria la Mex.
Taqueria Mexico*
Tom Shea's*
Tullio's Rest.*
Turner Fisheries*
Uncle Pete's
Union Oyster Hse.*
Upper Crust
Via Lago*
Victoria*
Village Fish
Village Smokehse.*

get updates at zagat.com 213

Special Feature Index

Vin & Eddie's
Vinny's at Night
Wayside Inn*
Woodman's
Wright Catch
WuChon
Yangtze River*
Zaftigs*
Zapotec/M*

Critic-Proof
(Get lots of business despite so-so food)
Anthony's Pier 4
B & D Deli
Barking Crab
Boston Beer Works
Bugaboo Creek
Charley's
Fajitas & 'Ritas
Fire & Ice
Good Life
Hilltop Steak
Marché

Dancing
Burren
Cafe Escadrille
Chatham Bars/C
Cheers
Johnny D's
Mount Blue
Opus/M
Plaza Garibaldi
Raffael's
Rhythm & Spice
Skellig
Spinnaker
Top of the Hub
Tratt. Il Panino
West Street Grille

Delivery/Takeout
(D=delivery, T=takeout)
Ajanta (T)
Akbar India (D, T)
Alberto's Rist./C (T)
Amarin (T)
Amelia's Tratt. (T)
Amrheins (D, T)
Anna's Taqueria (T)
Antico Forno (T)
Antonia's (T)
Antonio's (D, T)

Aquitaine Bis (T)
Artcliff Diner/M (T)
Artu (T)
Atasca (T)
Audubon Circle (T)
Back Eddy (T)
Baja Betty's (T)
Baker's Best (T)
Bamboo (D, T)
B & D Deli (D, T)
Bangkok Basil (D, T)
Bangkok Bistro (D, T)
Bangkok Blue (T)
Bangkok City (D, T)
Bangkok Cuisine (T)
Baraka Cafe (T)
Bella's (T)
Bernard's (D, T)
Billy Tse (D, T)
Blue Ribbon BBQ (T)
Bluestone Bistro (D, T)
Bombay Bistro (T)
Bombay Classic (D, T)
Bombay Club (D, T)
Bridgeman's (T)
Brown Sugar Cafe (D, T)
Bukhara (D, T)
Buteco (T)
Café Brazil (T)
Café China (D, T)
Cafe Jaffa (D, T)
Cafe Marliave (D, T)
Cafe Moxie/M (T)
Cafe of India (D, T)
Cafe St. Petersburg (T)
Cambridge, 1. (T)
Cantina Italiana (T)
Carambola (D, T)
Carlo's Cucina (T)
Casablanca (T)
Casa Portugal (T)
Centre Street Bistro/N (T)
Centre Street Café (T)
Changsho (T)
Chapoquoit Grill/C (T)
Charlie's Sandwich (T)
Chart Room/C (T)
Chau Chow City (T)
Chef Chang's Hse. (D, T)
Chef Chow's Hse. (D, T)
Chez Henri (T)
China Pearl (T)
Chinatown Seafood (D, T)
Cilantro (T)

subscribe to zagat.com

Special Feature Index

Cioppino's/N (T)
Clam Box (T)
Claremont Cafe (T)
Coolidge Corner (D, T)
Country Life (D, T)
Daily Catch (T)
Dish (T)
Dolphin/C (T)
Dolphin Seafood (D, T)
Dong Khanh (T)
East Coast Grill (T)
Eastern Pier (D, T)
East Ocean City (T)
eat (T)
El Cafetal (D, T)
Elephant Walk (D)
El Oriental de Cuba (D, T)
El Pelón Taqueria (D, T)
El Sarape (T)
Emma's Pizzeria (T)
Esther's/C (T)
Fazio's Trattoria/C (T)
Figs (T)
Florentine Cafe (T)
flour bakery & café (T)
Fog Island Cafe/N (T)
Fugakyu (T)
Galleria Umberto (T)
Garden of Eden (D, T)
Ginza (D, T)
Golden Temple (D, T)
Grand Chau Chow (T)
Grasshopper (T)
Great Thai Chef (T)
Gyuhama (D, T)
Helmand (T)
Hi-Rise Bread (T)
House of Siam (T)
House of Tibet (T)
House of Zen (D, T)
Impudent Oyster/C (T)
Inaho/C (T)
Indian Cafe (T)
Indian Club (T)
India Pavilion (D, T)
India Quality (T)
Island Hopper (D, T)
Istanbul Cafe (T)
Ithaki (T)
Jae's (T)
Jake's Dixie (D, T)
James's Gate (T)
Jamjuli (D, T)
Jasmine Bistro (T)

Joy Luck Café (T)
JP Seafood Cafe (D, T)
Jumbo Seafood (D, T)
Kebab Factory (D, T)
Kebab-N-Kurry (T)
Khao Sarn (T)
King & I (D, T)
King Fung (T)
Kouzina (T)
La Casa de Pedro (T)
Lam's (T)
La Paloma (T)
Lattanzi's/M (T)
Legal Sea Foods (T)
Lola's/M (T)
Lotus Blossom (T)
Lucy's (D, T)
Lyceum B&G (T)
Magnolia's (T)
Mary Chung (T)
McCormick & Schmick's (T)
Merengue (D, T)
Midwest Grill (T)
Mike's (T)
Misaki/C (T)
Montien (T)
Mother Anna's (D, T)
Mr. & Mrs. Bartley's (T)
Mr. Crepe (T)
Mr. Sushi (D, T)
MuQueCa (D, T)
Naked Oyster/C (T)
Neighborhood Rest. (T)
New Bridge Cafe (T)
New Ginza (D, T)
New Jang Su (T)
News (D, T)
New Shanghai (T)
Ocean Wealth (T)
Oga (T)
Oishii (D, T)
Olé, Mexican (T)
Out of the Blue (T)
Paddock/C (T)
Paolo's Tratt. (T)
Parish Cafe (T)
Passage to India (D, T)
Peach Farm (T)
Penang (D, T)
Penguins Sea Grill/C (T)
Phoenicia (D, T)
Pho Lemon Grass (D, T)
Pho Pasteur (T)
Pho République (T)

get updates at zagat.com 215

Special Feature Index

Picante Mexican (D, T)
Pinang (D, T)
Pit Stop BBQ (T)
Pizzeria Regina (T)
Punjab (T)
Punjabi Dhaba (T)
Purple Cactus (D, T)
Rangoli (D, T)
Real Pizza (T)
Redbones BBQ (D, T)
Red Rock Bistro (T)
Roadhse. Cafe/C (T)
Rod Dee (D, T)
Rubin's (D, T)
Sabur (T)
Saffron (T)
Saigon (T)
Sakurabana (D, T)
S&S (D, T)
Santarpio's (T)
Saporito's (T)
Sapporo (T)
Sconset Café/N (D)
Second St. Cafe (T)
Seoul Food (T)
Sepal (T)
Shalimar of India (T)
Shanti (D, T)
Sichuan Garden (D, T)
Sister Sorel (T)
Skewers (D, T)
Sol Azteca (D, T)
Sorento's (D, T)
Sosumi Asian/C (T)
Soya's (D, T)
Spice Thai (D, T)
Square Café (T)
Stir Crazy/C (T)
Stone Soup (T)
Suishaya (T)
Sultan's Kitchen (D, T)
Sunset Cafe (T)
Sunset Grill (D, T)
Sushi by Yoshi/N (T)
Sweet Basil (T)
Tacos Lupita (T)
Taiwan Cafe (T)
Takeshima (T)
Tanjore (D, T)
Tantawan (T)
Taqueria la Mex. (D, T)
Taqueria Mexico (T)
Terra Luna/C (T)
Thai Basil (T)
Thai Village (D, T)
Tim's Tavern (T)
Tremont 647 (D, T)
Tsunami (T)
Tullio's Rest. (T)
Tuscan Grill (T)
Tu y Yo (D, T)
224 Boston St. (T)
Uncle Pete's (D, T)
Upper Crust (D, T)
Veggie Planet (T)
Vicki Lee Boyajian (D, T)
Viet Hong (T)
Viet's Café (D)
Village Sushi (T)
Vinny's at Night (T)
V. Majestic (T)
West Side Lounge (T)
Wisteria House (D, T)
Wonder Spice (T)
Woodman's (D)
WuChon (T)
Yama (T)
Zaftigs (D, T)
Zen 320 (D, T)

Dining Alone

(Other than hotels and places with counter service)

Amelia's Tratt.
Anam Chara
Antonia's
Bluefin/N
Blue Plate Express
Cafe Barada
Cafe Jaffa
Chez Henri
Claremont Cafe
Dish
Diva Indian
eat
Fishmonger's Cafe/C
Istanbul Cafe
Kebab Factory
Lucy's
Metropolis Cafe
MuQueCa
Sandrine's
Sister Sorel
Stir Crazy/C
Taranta
Veggie Planet
Wonder Spice

Special Feature Index

Entertainment
(Call for days and times of performances)

Alberto's Rist./C (jazz)
Anam Chara (bands)
Andover Inn (orchestra/piano)
Ardeo/C (jazz piano/keyboard)
Argana (belly dancing)
Atlantica (jazz)
Atria/M (jazz)
Barking Crab (blues/jazz/rock)
Bay Tower (jazz/piano/swing)
Belfry Bistro/C (jazz piano)
blu (jazz band)
Blue Cat Cafe (DJ)
Bob the Chef's (jazz)
Bonfire (band/DJ)
Brant Point Grill/N (jazz)
Bristol Lounge (jazz/piano)
B-Side Lounge (piano)
Bubala's/C (jazz)
Burren (cover bands/Irish)
Café Brazil (Brazilian/guitar)
Cafe Escadrille (band)
Cafe Fleuri (jazz)
Café Louis (blues/jazz)
Cafe Marliave (piano)
Cafe St. Petersburg (piano)
Café Suisse (piano)
Cambridge Common (bands)
Chart Room/C (bass/piano)
Chatham Bars/C (varies)
Chatham Squire/C (varies)
Cheers (DJs/guitar/vocals)
Club Cafe (piano/vocals)
Club Car/N (piano)
Colonial Inn (folk/jazz)
Company of Cauldron/N (harp)
Coonamessett Inn/C (jazz/piano)
Dan'l Webster Inn/C (piano)
Desmond O'Malley's (Irish)
Dodge St. B&G (varies)
Durgin Park (bands)
El Sarape (guitar)
Enormous Room (varies)
FIFTY SEVEN (jazz)
Finz (jazz)
Fireplace (acoustic guitar)
Forest Cafe (guitar)
Franklin Cape Ann (varies)
Frank's Steak (piano)
Glenn's Rest. (blues/jazz)
Good Life (jazz)
Grand Canal (rock bands)
Green Dragon (varies)
Green St. Grill (varies)
Halfway Cafe (acoustic)
Hartwell House (piano)
Hilltop Steak (dinner shows)
House of Blues (blues)
Icarus (jazz)
Independent (varies)
Jake's Dixie (blues)
Jared's/N (keyboard/vocals)
Jimmy's Harborside (piano)
Johnny D's (varies)
Julien (piano)
Karoun (belly dancing)
Kowloon (bands/comedy)
Landfall/C (bands)
Landing ('50s cover bands)
Les Zygomates (jazz)
Limbo (jazz)
Lola's/M (blues/R&B/salsa)
Lorraine's/C (jazz)
Lucky's (bands)
Lyceum B&G (piano)
Maison Robert (jazz)
Matt Murphy's (varies)
Merengue (Latin)
Middle East (bands)
Midwest Grill (Brazilian)
Mount Blue (varies)
Oceana (jazz)
Ocean House/C (jazz)
Paddock/C (organ/piano)
Park Corner/M (jazz duo)
Plaza Garibaldi (Latin)
Polcari's/C (bands)
Raffael's (cover bands)
Red Rock Bistro (varies)
Regatta of Cotuit/C (piano)
Rest. Cesaria (Cape Verdean)
Rhythm & Spice (DJ/reggae)
Roadhse. Cafe/C (jazz/piano)
RooBar/C (band)
Sandrine's (guitar)
75 Chestnut (jazz duo)
Sherborn Inn (jazz)
Siena/C (jazz guitar/sax)
Silks (piano)
Siros (piano)
Skellig (varies)
Spinnaker (DJ)
Sunset Cafe (varies)
33 Restaurant (DJs)
Top of the Hub (jazz)
Tosca (jazz)

get updates at zagat.com   217

Special Feature Index

Tratt. Il Panino (DJ)
Turner Fisheries (jazz)
Veggie Planet (folk)
Warren Tavern (guitar)
Washington Sq. (jazz)
Wayside Inn (drum/fife)
West Street Grille (DJs)
Zebra's Bistro (jazz)

Fireplaces
Abe & Louie's
Academy Ocean/C
Alberto's Rist./C
Andover Inn
Atlantica
Atria/M
Beacon Hill Bistro
Black Dog Tav./M
Black Sheep Cafe
Captain Linnell Hse./C
Chapoquoit Grill/C
Chester/C
Chillingsworth/C
Christian's/C
Christopher's
Colonial Inn
Daggett House/M
Dalya's
Dan'l Webster Inn/C
DeMarco/N
Desmond O'Malley's
Dolphin Seafood
Donatello
Eclectic Cafe/C
Esther's/C
Euno
Finz
Fireplace
Gina's by the Sea/C
Hungry i
James's Gate
Joe's American B&G
Martin House/C
Mews/C
Mistral
Mount Blue
Newes from America/M
Ocean House/C
Oleana
Opus/M
Òran Mór/N
Outermost Inn/M
Palm
Papa Razzi
Piccolo Nido
Porcini's
Red Inn/C
Red Pheasant/C
Red Rock Bistro
Regatta of Cotuit/C
Rist. Fiore
Riva
Roadhse. Cafe/C
Rouge
Saffron
Sherborn Inn
Silks
Siros
Summer House/N
Sunset Cafe
Topper's/N
Tratt. a Scalinatella
Twenty-Eight Atlantic/C
UpStairs on Square
Warren Tavern
Wayside Inn
West Street Grille
White Rainbow

Game in Season
Abbicci/C
Academy Ocean/C
Adrian's/C
Alchemy/M
Al Dente
American Seasons/N
Ariadne
Atria/M
Bay Tower
Belfry Bistro/C
Boarding House/N
Bubala's/C
Cafe Moxie/M
Café Suisse
Cassis
Club Car/N
Coach House/M
Coonamessett Inn/C
Coriander
Daedalus
Eclectic Cafe/C
Elephant Walk
EVOO
Fava
Federalist
Fifty-Six Union/N
Finz
Fireplace

218 subscribe to zagat.com

Special Feature Index

Flume/C
Franklin Cafe
Franklin Cape Ann
Front Street/C
Galley on Cliffside/N
Hungry i
Icarus
Isabella
Lambert's Cove/M
Le Lyonnais
Le Soir
Meritage
No. 9 Park
Olio
Olives
On the Park
Òran Mór/N
Paolo's Tratt.
Park Corner/M
Pellino's
Porcini's
Prezza
Red Inn/C
Red Raven
Red Rock Bistro
Regatta of Cotuit/C
Rist. Fiore
Rist. Lucia
Roadhse. Cafe/C
Saffron
Salts
Sconset Café/N
Seasons
75 Chestnut
Sfoglia/N
Silks
Siros
Sister Sorel
Temple Bar
Terra Luna/C
Torch
Tratt. Pulcinella
Tremont 647
29 Newbury
224 Boston St.
West Side Lounge
White Rainbow
Yanks

Historic Places

(Year opened; * building)
1634 Barker Tavern
1650 Green Dragon*
1660 Daggett House/M*
1716 Wayside Inn
1720 Chart House*
1755 Martin House/C*
1780 Warren Tavern
1790 Chester/C*
1800 DeMarco/N*
1800 Durgin Park*
1805 Aesop's Tables/C*
1805 Red Inn/C*
1805 Terra Luna/C*
1818 Christian's/C*
1826 Union Oyster Hse.
1845 Chatham Squire/C*
1845 Jared's/N*
1847 21 Federal/N*
1850 Dalya's*
1850 Dolphin/C*
1856 Parker's
1860 Franklin Cafe*
1863 Café Louis*
1865 Maison Robert*
1868 Cafe Marliave
1868 Jacob Wirth
1870 Captain Linnell Hse./C*
1875 Club Car/N*
1882 Doyle's Cafe*
1890 Amrheins
1890 Coach House/M*
1890 Rist. Lucia*
1892 Locke-Ober
1897 Cape Sea Grille/C*
1900 Carambola*
1900 Cassis*
1900 Chez Henri*
1900 Dancing Lobster/C*
1900 Fajitas & 'Ritas*
1900 Fava*
1900 Federalist*
1900 Front Street/C*
1901 Morse Fish
1902 Gardner Museum*
1904 Coriander*
1905 Davide Rist.*
1906 UpStairs on Square*
1912 Chatham Bars/C
1912 Copley's Grand
1912 Oak Room
1914 Woodman's
1917 No Name
1919 S&S
1920 Caliterra B&G*
1920 Woodbox/N
1924 B & D Deli
1924 Jimmy's Harborside

get updates at zagat.com 219

Special Feature Index

1926 Pizzeria Regina
1927 Charlie's Sandwich
1927 Ritz-Carlton Din. Rm.
1928 Rubin's
1930 Andover Inn
1930 Centre Street Bistro/N*
1930 Coonamessett Inn/C
1930 Harvard Gardens
1930 Santarpio's
1931 Cantina Italiana
1933 Forest Cafe
1933 Greg's
1935 Clam Box*
1937 Mother Anna's
1938 Frank's Steak
1938 Gina's by the Sea/C
1941 Colonial Inn
1941 Rosebud Diner
1943 Artcliff Diner/M
1946 Harry's
1946 Landfall/C
1946 Maddie's Sail
1947 Deluxe Town*
1947 South St. Diner
1948 Joe Tecce's
1950 Fazio's Trattoria/C*
1950 FIFTY SEVEN
1950 Kowloon

Hotel Dining

Andover Inn
  Andover Inn
Beach Plum Inn
  Beach Plum Inn/M
Beacon Hill Hotel
  Beacon Hill Bistro
Belfry Inne
  Belfry Bistro/C
Boston Harbor Hotel
  Intrigue Cafe
  Meritage
Boston Marriott Long Wharf
  Oceana
Bramble Inn
  Bramble Inn/C
Charles Hotel
  Henrietta's Table
  Rialto
Charlotte Inn
  L'Etoile/M
Chatham Bars Inn
  Chatham Bars/C
Clarion Hotel
  Siros
Cohasset Harbor Inn
  Atlantica

Colonnade
  Brasserie Jo
Coonamessett Inn
  Coonamessett Inn/C
Daggett House
  Daggett House/M
Dan'l Webster Inn
  Dan'l Webster Inn/C
Eliot Suite Hotel
  Clio
Fairmont Copley Plaza
  Copley's Grand
  Oak Room
Four Seasons Hotel
  Aujourd'hui
  Bristol Lounge
Harborside Inn
  Margo Bistro
Harbor View Hotel
  Coach House/M
Howard Johnson Hotel
  Bisuteki
Hyatt Regency Cambridge
  Spinnaker
Inn at Blueberry Hill
  Theo's/M
Jared Coffin House
  Jared's/N
Kendall Hotel
  Black Sheep Cafe
Lambert's Cove Inn
  Lambert's Cove/M
Le Languedoc Inn
  Le Languedoc/N
Le Méridien Hotel
  Cafe Fleuri
  Julien
Lenox Hotel
  Azure
Mansion House Hotel
  Zephrus/M
Millennium Bostonian Hotel
  Seasons
Nine Zero Hotel
  Spire
Omni Parker House
  Parker's
Outermost Inn
  Outermost Inn/M
Outer Reach Resort
  Adrian's/C
Park Plaza Hotel
  Bonfire
  McCormick & Schmick's

Special Feature Index

Radisson Hotel Boston
  FIFTY SEVEN
Radisson Hotel Cambridge
  Bisuteki
Red Inn
  Red Inn/C
Ritz-Carlton Boston
  Ritz-Carlton Din. Rm.
Ritz-Carlton Boston Common
  Jer-Ne
Royal Sonesta Hotel
  Davio's
Seaport Hotel
  Aura
Sherborn Inn
  Sherborn Inn
Stonehedge Inn
  Silks
Summer House
  Summer House/N
Swissôtel Boston
  Café Suisse
University Park Hotel @ MIT
  Sidney's Grille
Wauwinet
  Topper's/N
Wayside Inn
  Wayside Inn
Wequassett Inn
  Twenty-Eight Atlantic/C
Westin Copley Place
  Bar 10
  Osushi
  Palm
  Turner Fisheries
White Elephant Hotel
  Brant Point Grill/N
Winnetu Inn & Resort
  Opus/M
Woodbox Inn
  Woodbox/N
Wyndham Hotel
  Caliterra B&G
XV Beacon Hotel
  Federalist

"In" Places
Alchemy/M
Argana
Armani Cafe
Azure
Balance/M
blu
Caffe Umbra
Cambridge, 1.
Carmen
Clio
East Coast Grill
Enormous Room
Epiphany
Franklin Cafe
Franklin Cape Ann
Ginza
Hamersley's Bistro
Ice House/M
KingFish Hall
Le Soir
Limbo
Lumière
Mantra
Mistral
Nightingale
No. 9 Park
Oleana
Pearl/N
Red Fez
Rouge
Saint
Sonsie
Teatro
33 Restaurant
UpStairs on Square
Via Matta

Jacket Required
(* Tie also required)
Aujourd'hui
Chatham Bars/C
Julien*
Ritz-Carlton Din. Rm.

Late Dining
(Weekday closing hour)
Anchovies (1 AM)
Apollo Grill (4 AM)
Big Fish (2:45 AM)
Brasserie Jo (1 AM)
Caffe Vittoria (1 AM)
Chau Chow City (3 AM)
Club Cafe (1 AM)
Coolidge Corner (1:15 AM)
Dynasty (4 AM)
East Ocean City (4 AM)
Epiphany (1 AM)
Finale (varies)
Franklin Cafe (1:30 AM)
Fugakyu (varies)
Ginza (varies)
Golden Temple (1 AM)
Grand Chau Chow (3 AM)

Special Feature Index

Gyuhama (1:30 AM)
Harry's (1 AM)
Imperial Seafood (3 AM)
Jumbo Seafood (1 AM)
Kaya (varies)
Kowloon (1 AM)
McCormick & Schmick's (varies)
News (4 AM)
Oceana (1 AM)
Ocean Wealth (4 AM)
Orleans (1 AM)
Parish Cafe (1 AM)
Peach Farm (3 AM)
Pho République (1:30 AM)
Suishaya (2 AM)
Sunset Grill (1 AM)
Taiwan Cafe (1 AM)
Top of the Hub (1 AM)

Meet for a Drink

Alchemy/M
Ambrosia
Anam Chara
Aqua
Aqua Grille/C
Asgard
Audubon Circle
Baja Mexican
BARCODE
Bar 10
Black Cow
Blue Cat Cafe
Boarding House/N
Bomboa
B-Side Lounge
Burren
Cactus Club
Casablanca
Chez Henri
Club Cafe
Cottonwood Cafe
Daedalus
Dalí
Davio's
Delux Cafe
Dish
Doyle's Cafe
Enormous Room
Epiphany
Esther's/C
FIFTY SEVEN
Fifty-Six Union/N
Fishmonger's Cafe/C
Flash's
Franklin Cafe
Franklin Cape Ann
Glenn's Rest.
Good Life
Grafton Street Pub
Grill 23 & Bar
Harvard Gardens
Independent
Jake's Dixie
James's Gate
Joe's American B&G
John Harvard's
Johnny D's
Les Zygomates
Limbo
Lucky's
Mantra
Matt Murphy's
Miracle of Science
Mistral
No. 9 Park
Orleans
Pravda 116
Red Fez
Redline
Rhythm & Spice
RooBar/C
Saint
Sel de la Terre
Silvertone B&G
Sister Sorel
Skellig
Solea Rest.
Sonsie
Stephanie's
Tangierino
Temple Bar
33 Restaurant
Top of the Hub
Trio
29 Newbury
21 Federal/N
Via Matta
Vox Populi
West Side Lounge

Noteworthy Newcomers

Aqua
Argana
Ariadne
Azure
Bhindi Bazaar
Black Sheep Cafe
Bocelli's

Special Feature Index

Cafe Polonia
Caffe Umbra
Cambridge, 1.
Carmen
Circolo
Craigie St. Bistrot
Dalia's Bistro
Edwardian Tea Rm.
El Coqui
Enormous Room
Epiphany
Gallia
Giuseppe's
House of Zen
Indigo
Lucy's
Meritage
News
Nightingale
9 Tastes
No. 1 Noodle
Osushi
Pinang
Red Fez
Rest. Cesaria
Rist. Marcellino
Ritz-Carlton Din. Rm.
Rouge
Saint
Savannah Grill
Scutra
Second St. Cafe
Siena/C
Skellig
Soya's
Spire
Tango
Teatro
Ten Tables
33 Restaurant
Twenty-Eight Atlantic/C
UpStairs on Square
Via Matta
Wright Catch
Zen 320

Offbeat

Baraka Cafe
Barking Crab
Bob the Chef's
Brazilian Grill/C
Cafe Belo
Cafe Polonia
Centre Street Café
eat
El Oriental de Cuba
Enormous Room
Galleria Umberto
Green St. Grill
Helmand
Johnny D's
Karoo Kafe/C
Karoun
King Fung
Magnolia's
Martha's Galley
Merengue
MuQueCa
Neighborhood Rest.
On the Park
Penang
Pho République
Pit Stop BBQ
Plaza Garibaldi
Prose
Punjabi Dhaba
Redbones BBQ
Red Raven
Rest. Cesaria
Santarpio's
Shabu-Zen
Tango
Tim's Tavern
224 Boston St.
Uncle Pete's
Victoria
Vinny's at Night

Outdoor Dining

(G=garden; P=patio;
S=sidewalk; T=terrace)
Abe & Louie's (P)
Academy Ocean/C (G, P)
Adrian's/C (T)
Aesop's Tables/C (P)
Alberto's Rist./C (S)
Alchemy/M (P, T)
American Seasons/N (P)
Anam Chara (S)
Andover Inn (P)
Anthony's Pier 4 (T)
Antonia's (S)
Aqua (T)
Aqua Grille/C (T)
Armani Cafe (P)
Asmara (S)
Atasca (P)
Atlantica (P)

get updates at zagat.com 223

Special Feature Index

Atlantic Fish Co. (P)
Atria/M (G, P)
Bacco (T)
Back Eddy (P, T)
Baker's Best (S)
B & D Deli (S)
Bangkok Blue (P)
BARCODE (P)
Barking Crab (T)
Beach Plum Inn/M (P)
Belfry Bistro/C (P)
Bertucci's (P)
Black Cow (T)
Black Dog Tav./M (T)
Black Sheep Cafe (S)
blu (T)
Blue Ginger (P)
Blue Plate Express (P)
Blue Ribbon BBQ (S)
Blue Room (P)
Bluestone Bistro (P)
Bomboa (P)
Boston Beer Works (P)
Bramble Inn/C (G)
Brant Point Grill/N (T)
Brasserie Jo (P)
Bridgeman's (T)
Brown Sugar Cafe (P)
Bubala's/C (P)
Cactus Club (P)
Cafe Barada (S)
Cafe Edwige/C (T)
Café Louis (P)
Cafe Pamplona (P)
Caffe Paradiso (S)
California Pizza Kit. (P, S)
Captain Linnell Hse./C (P)
Casa del Rey (P)
Casa Romero (P)
Centre Street Bistro/N (P)
Chanticleer/N (G)
Charley's (P)
Chart House (P)
Chatham Bars/C (T)
Cheers (P)
Chester/C (G, T)
Chillingsworth/C (P)
Christian's/C (P)
Ciao Bella (P, S)
Cioppino's/N (P)
Clam Box (T)
Clancy's/C (T)
Claremont Cafe (S)
Colonial Inn (P)
Coonamessett Inn/C (T)
Coriander (S)
Cottonwood Cafe (P)
Daggett House/M (G, P)
Daily Catch (P)
Dalya's (T)
Dancing Lobster/C (T)
Davio's (P)
Desmond O'Malley's (P)
Dish (P)
Durgin Park (P)
Eastern Pier (T)
Eclectic Cafe/C (G)
El Pelón Taqueria (S)
Esther's/C (P, T)
Excelsior (S)
FIFTY SEVEN (P)
Fifty-Six Union/N (G, P)
Finale (P)
Finz (T)
Firefly (P)
Fireplace (S)
flour bakery & café (S)
Flume/C (T)
Galley on Cliffside/N (P)
Gallia (S)
Garden of Eden (S)
Gardner Museum (G)
Geoffrey's Cafe (P)
Gina's by the Sea/C (P)
Giuseppe's (P)
Golden Temple (S)
Grapevine (G)
Grillfish (P)
Gusto (P)
Hamersley's Bistro (P)
Hartwell House (G, P)
Harvest (T)
Henrietta's Table (T)
Hi-Rise Bread (P)
Home Port/M (T)
Ice House/M (G)
India Quality (P)
Intrigue Cafe (T)
Ipanema/M (T)
Ironside Grill (P)
Iruna (P)
Jacob Wirth (P)
Jae's (P)
Jared's/N (P)
Jimmy's Harborside (P)
Joe's American B&G (P, T)
John Harvard's (P)

Special Feature Index

Johnny's Lunch. (S)
J's at Nashoba (P)
Karoo Kafe/C (T)
Kashmir (P)
Kebab Factory (P)
La Campania (T)
La Casa de Pedro (P)
La Famiglia Giorgio (P)
Landfall/C (G)
Landing (T)
Lattanzi's/M (P)
Legal Sea Foods (P)
Le Languedoc/N (P)
L'Etoile/M (P)
Linwood Grill (P)
Lola's/M (P)
Maison Robert (T)
Mamma Maria (T)
Martha's Galley (S)
Martin House/C (G)
McCormick & Schmick's (S)
Mr. & Mrs. Bartley's (S)
Mr. Crepe (S)
Nantucket Lobster/N (P)
Neighborhood Rest. (G)
Oleana (G, P)
Olé, Mexican (S)
Olives (P)
Opus/M (T)
Orleans (S)
Other Side Cosmic (T)
Outermost Inn/M (P)
Papa Razzi (P, T)
Parish Cafe (P)
Penguins Sea Grill/C (P)
P.F. Chang's (P)
Pho Pasteur (P)
Piattini (P)
Picante Mexican (P)
Pigalle (S)
Pinang (P)
Plaza III (P)
Polcari's/C (S)
Porcini's (P)
Red Fez (P)
Red Inn/C (T)
Red Rock Bistro (G, P)
Rhythm & Spice (S)
Rist. Fiore (P, T)
Rist. Marcellino (T)
Riva (P)
Rod Dee (S)
Rouge (S)
Rustic Kit. (P)

Saffron (P)
Sal's Place/C (P)
Sapporo (S)
Scoozi (P)
SeaGrille/N (P)
Sherborn Inn (P)
Siena/C (P)
Silks (P, T)
Siros (P)
Sister Sorel (P)
Skipjack's (P)
Sol Azteca (P)
Sorento's (P)
Sound Bites (S)
Stephanie's (P)
Straight Wharf/N (P)
Sweet Life Cafe/M (G)
Taberna de Haro (S)
Tapeo (P)
Taqueria Mexico (S)
1369 Coffee House (S)
33 Restaurant (T)
Tom Shea's (P)
Topper's/N (T)
Tratt. Pulcinella (P)
Tremont 647 (P)
29 Newbury (P)
21 Federal/N (P)
224 Boston St. (G)
Uncle Pete's (S)
Via Matta (P)
Village Sushi (P)
Vox Populi (P)
White Rainbow (G)
White Star Tavern (P)
Wisteria House (S)
Wonder Spice (P)
Woodbox/N (P)
Woodman's (G)
Wright Catch (P)
WuChon (P)
Yangtze River (P)
Yanks (P)
Zebra's Bistro (G)
Zephrus/M (P)

Parking

(V=valet, *=validated)
Abe & Louie's (V)
Al Dente*
Amarin*
Ambrosia (V)
Aquitaine (V)
Armani Cafe (V)

get updates at zagat.com   225

Special Feature Index

Asgard*
Atlantica (V)
Aujourd'hui (V)
Azure (V)
Bacco*
Bar 10 (V)
Bay Tower*
Bertucci's*
Billy Tse (V)
blu*
Blue Cat Cafe (V)
Blue Room*
Bob the Chef's*
Bomboa (V)
Bonfire (V)
Boston Beer Works*
Brasserie Jo (V)
Bricco (V)
Cafe Fleuri (V)
Café Louis (V)
Cafe Marliave*
Café Suisse (V)
Caffe Paradiso*
Caffe Umbra (V)
Caffe Vittoria*
California Pizza Kit.*
Caliterra B&G (V)
Cantina Italiana (V)*
Capital Grille (V)
Captain Linnell Hse./C (V)
Carlo's Cucina (V)
Casablanca*
Casa Mexico*
Chart House (V)
Chatham Bars/C (V)
Chau Chow City*
Cheers*
Cheesecake Factory (V)*
Ciao Bella (V)
Claremont Cafe (V)
Clio (V)*
Coonamessett Inn/C (V)
Copley's Grand (V)
Cottonwood Cafe*
Dakota's*
Davide Rist. (V)
Davio's (V)*
Donatello (V)
Eastern Pier*
East Ocean City*
Epiphany (V)
Euno*
Federalist (V)
FIFTY SEVEN (V)*
Figs (V)
Finale*
Fleming's Prime (V)*
Gallia (V)
Giacomo's (V)
Hamersley's Bistro (V)
Harvest (V)
House of Blues*
House of Siam (V)
Intrigue Cafe (V)
Jacob Wirth*
Jae's (V)
Jer-Ne (V)
Jimmy's Harborside (V)
Joe Tecce's (V)
John Harvard's*
Julien (V)
Kashmir (V)
KingFish Hall*
Lala Rokh (V)
Legal Sea Foods*
L'Espalier (V)
Les Zygomates (V)
Limbo (V)
Locke-Ober (V)
Lucca (V)
Maggiano's (V)
Maison Robert (V)
Mamma Maria (V)
Mantra (V)
Marché*
Masa*
Meritage (V)
Metropolis Cafe (V)
Mistral (V)
Monica's (V)
Morton's of Chicago (V)
News (V)
9 Tastes*
No. 9 Park (V)
Oak Room*
Oceana (V)*
Ocean House/C (V)
Olives (V)
Paddock/C (V)
Palm (V)
Papa Razzi (V)*
Parker's (V)*
Peach Farm*
Penang*
P.F. Chang's (V)
Pho République (V)
Pinang*
Pravda 116 (V)

Special Feature Index

Prezza (V)
Radius (V)
Red Pheasant/C (V)
Rialto*
Rist. Fiore (V)
Rist. Lucia (V)
Rist. Toscano (V)
Ritz-Carlton Din. Rm. (V)
Roadhse. Cafe/C (V)
Rouge (V)
Saffron (V)
Saint (V)
Saraceno*
Seasons (V)
Sel de la Terre (V)
75 Chestnut (V)*
Silks (V)*
Sister Sorel (V)
Skipjack's (V)
Sonsie*
Spinnaker*
Spire (V)
Stephanie's (V)
Tanjore*
Taranta*
Taverna Toscana*
33 Restaurant (V)
Top of the Hub*
Tratt. a Scalinatella (V)
Tratt. Il Panino*
Tremont 647 (V)
29 Newbury*
Typhoon (V)
Union Oyster Hse.*
UpStairs on Square (V)
Vault*
Via Matta (V)
Villa Francesca (V)
Vox Populi (V)

People-Watching

Ambrosia
Aquitaine
Armani Cafe
BARCODE
blu
Blue Room
Boarding House/N
Bomboa
Café Louis
Caffe Umbra
Chart House
Ciao Bella
Clio
Cottonwood Cafe
Cuchi Cuchi
Davio's
Enormous Room
Epiphany
Federalist
Franklin Cafe
Grill 23 & Bar
Kashmir
L'Espalier
Limbo
Lucca
Maison Robert
Mantra
Masa
Mistral
Nightingale
No. 9 Park
Olives
Plaza Garibaldi
Pravda 116
Radius
Red Fez
Redline
Rialto
RooBar/C
Saint
Sonsie
Stephanie's
Summer House/N
Teatro
33 Restaurant
Tremont 647
29 Newbury
21 Federal/N
Via Matta
Vox Populi

Power Scenes

Aujourd'hui
Azure
blu
Bristol Lounge
Federalist
Grill 23 & Bar
Harvest
Julien
L'Espalier
Locke-Ober
Maison Robert
Mantra
Mistral
No. 9 Park
Radius

Special Feature Index

Rialto
Spire
21 Federal/N

Private Rooms
(Restaurants charge less at off times; call for capacity)
Abbicci/C
Abe & Louie's
Addis Red Sea
Aesop's Tables/C
Aigo Bistro
Alberto's Rist./C
Ambrosia
Anam Chara
Andover Inn
Anthony's Pier 4
Aqua Grille/C
Armani Cafe
Arno's/N
Artu
Asgard
Atlantica
Atria/M
Aujourd'hui
Azure
Back Eddy
Bangkok City
Barker Tavern
Barking Crab
Bay Tower
Beach Plum Inn/M
Bee-Hive Tav./C
Belfry Bistro/C
Bella's
Bison County BBQ
Blue Ginger
Blue Room
Bocelli's
Bombay Club
Bonfire
Boston Beer Works
Brant Point Grill/N
Brazilian Grill/C
Bricco
Burren
Cafe Escadrille
Cafe Fleuri
Café Louis
Cafe Marliave
Café Suisse
Caliterra B&G
Cape Sea Grille/C
Capital Grille

Captain Linnell Hse./C
Casa Mexico
Casa Romero
Chanticleer/N
Charley's
Chatham Bars/C
Chau Chow City
Cheers
Chef Chang's Hse.
Chillingsworth/C
China Pearl
Christopher's
Cioppino's/N
Claremont Cafe
Clio
Club Cafe
Coach House/M
Colonial Inn
Coonamessett Inn/C
Copley's Grand
Craigie St. Bistrot
Dakota's
Dalya's
Dan'l Webster Inn/C
Davio's
DeMarco/N
Desmond O'Malley's
Dolphin Seafood
Dom's
Donatello
East Coast Grill
El Coqui
Elephant Walk
El Sarape
Emperor's Garden
Epiphany
Erawan of Siam
Fajitas & 'Ritas
Federalist
FIFTY SEVEN
Fifty-Six Union/N
Figlia
Figs
Filippo Rist.
Finale
Finz
Five North Sq.
Fleming's Prime
flora
Florentine Cafe
Flume/C
Franklin Cape Ann
Fugakyu
Gallia

228 subscribe to zagat.com

Special Feature Index

Giuseppe's
Glenn's Rest.
Golden Temple
Good Life
Grapevine
Grill 23 & Bar
Gusto
Hartwell House
Harvest
Helmand
Henrietta's Table
Hilltop Steak
House of Blues
House of Siam
House of Zen
Hungry i
Il Capriccio
Indian Club
India Pavilion
Intrigue Cafe
Ithaki
James's Gate
Jared's/N
Jasper White's
Jimmy's Harborside
Joe's American B&G
Joe Tecce's
John Harvard's
José's
J's at Nashoba
Julien
Kashmir
Kaya
KingFish Hall
Kowloon
La Groceria
Lala Rokh
Lambert's Cove/M
Landing
La Summa
Laurel
Legal Sea Foods
Le Languedoc/N
Le Lyonnais
Le Soir
L'Espalier
Limbo
Lobster Pot/C
Locke-Ober
Lola's/M
Lucca
Lucy's
Lyceum B&G
Maggiano's

Maison Robert
Mamma Maria
Mantra
Marché
Marino Rist.
Martin House/C
Massimino's
McCormick & Schmick's
Misaki/C
Mistral
Morton's of Chicago
Mother Anna's
Mr. Sushi
News
Oak Room
O'Fado
Oga
Olé, Mexican
Olives
Opus/M
Òran Mór/N
Paddock/C
Palm
Papa Razzi
Pearl/N
Penguins Sea Grill/C
Phoenicia
Pho Pasteur
Piccola Venezia
Piccolo Nido
Plaza Garibaldi
Plaza III
Polcari's
Pravda 116
Radius
Raffael's
Red Inn/C
Redline
Red Raven
Red Rock Bistro
Red Sauce
Regatta of Cotuit/C
Rest. Cesaria
Rialto
Rist. Barolo/C
Rist. Fiore
Rist. Lucia
Rist. Marcellino
Rist. Toscano
Roadhse. Cafe/C
RooBar/C
Royal East
Rustic Kit.
Saint
Sal's Place/C

get updates at zagat.com 229

Special Feature Index

Sandrine's
S&S
Sapporo
Saraceno
Seasons
Serafina Rist.
Sherborn Inn
Sichuan Garden
Silks
Silvertone B&G
Skellig
Soya's
Spire
Stellina
Stephanie's
Stir Crazy/C
Stockyard
Sultan's Kitchen
Sunset Grill
Sweet Life Cafe/M
Tangierino
Tantawan
Tasca
Thai Basil
33 Restaurant
Tokyo
Top of the Hub
Topper's/N
Torch
Tosca
Truc
Tullio's Rest.
21 Federal/N
Typhoon
Vault
Victoria
Viet's Café
Villa Francesca
Vinny's at Night
Vox Populi
Wayside Inn
West Creek Cafe/N
West Street Grille
White Rainbow
White Star Tavern
Woodbox/N
Woodman's
WuChon
Yama
Yangtze River
Yanks

Quiet Conversation
Aspasia
Atria/M
Aujourd'hui
Bay Tower
Beach Plum Inn/M
blu
Cafe Barada
Carmen
Casa Romero
Centro
Clio
Daedalus
Davide Rist.
Edwardian Tea Rm.
Fugakyu
Hamersley's Bistro
Hungry i
Icarus
Il Capriccio
Inaho/C
Jasmine Bistro
Julien
Khao Sarn
Lala Rokh
Le Languedoc/N
Le Soir
L'Espalier
Maison Robert
New Ginza
Oga
Pigalle
Prezza
Rialto
Rist. Barolo/C
Ritz-Carlton Din. Rm.
Sandrine's
Seasons
Sfoglia/N
Straight Wharf/N
Sweet Life Cafe/M
Top of the Hub
Troquet
Truc
Tsunami
Turner Fisheries
Twenty-Eight Atlantic/C
Vault
Zen 320

Raw Bars
Atlantic Fish Co.
Back Eddy
Betty's Wok
blu
Brant Point Grill/N
Café Suisse

Special Feature Index

Captain's Wharf
Central Kitchen
Chatham Squire/C
Dancing Lobster/C
East Coast Grill
Epiphany
Finz
Fireplace
Flume/C
Jimmy's Harborside
KingFish Hall
Legal Sea Foods
Naked Oyster/C
News
Oceana
Parker's
Red Inn/C
Riva
Ross' Grill/C
SeaGrille/N
Skipjack's
Turner Fisheries
Union Oyster Hse.
Woodman's

Reserve Ahead

Ambrosia
American Seasons/N
Anthony's Pier 4
Aujourd'hui
Azure
Belfry Bistro/C
blu
Blue Ginger
Brant Point Grill/N
Cafe Moxie/M
Cafe St. Petersburg
Chanticleer/N
Chatham Bars/C
Chester/C
Chillingsworth/C
Clio
Company of Cauldron/N
Coriander
Fifty-Six Union/N
Five Bays Bistro/C
flora
Galley on Cliffside/N
Gargoyles on Sq.
Grapevine
Grill 23 & Bar
Hamersley's Bistro
Hungry i
Il Capriccio
Julien
Lambert's Cove/M
Le Languedoc/N
Le Soir
L'Espalier
L'Etoile/M
Locke-Ober
Lumière
Maison Robert
Mamma Maria
Martin House/C
Meritage
Mistral
Morton's of Chicago
No. 9 Park
Oak Room
Oleana
Olio
Opus/M
Òran Mór/N
Pearl/N
Pigalle
Prezza
Radius
Red Pheasant/C
Red Raven
Regatta of Cotuit/C
Rialto
Ritz-Carlton Din. Rm.
Sage
Salts
Sandrine's
Scutra
Seasons
Sel de la Terre
Serafina Rist.
Sherborn Inn
Silks
Sonsie
Sosumi Asian/C
Spinnaker
Spire
Square Café
Stellina
Stone Soup
Straight Wharf/N
Summer House/N
Sweet Life Cafe/M
Ten Tables
Theo's/M
33 Restaurant
Topper's/N
Tosca
Tratt. a Scalinatella

Special Feature Index

Troquet
21 Federal/N
UpStairs on Square
Villa Francesca
West Creek Cafe/N
Woodbox/N
Zabaglione
Zephrus/M

Romantic Places
Argana
Ariadne
Aspasia
Atasca
Azafran
Bay Tower
Beach Plum Inn/M
Belfry Bistro/C
Carmen
Casa Romero
Chillingsworth/C
Clio
Coriander
Craigie St. Bistrot
Daedalus
Dalí
Davide Rist.
Euno
Fireplace
Five North Sq.
Grapevine
Hungry i
Icarus
Julien
Lala Rokh
Le Languedoc/N
L'Espalier
L'Etoile/M
Maison Robert
Oak Room
Paolo's Tratt.
Pigalle
Ritz-Carlton Din. Rm.
Salts
Sandrine's
Scutra
Seasons
75 Chestnut
Sol Azteca
Straight Wharf/N
Sweet Life Cafe/M
Tangierino
Tapeo
Tasca

Top of the Hub
Torch
Tosca
Tratt. a Scalinatella
Tratt. Pulcinella
Troquet
Truc
Twenty-Eight Atlantic/C
UpStairs on Square
White Rainbow

Singles Scenes
Aqua
BARCODE
Blue Cat Cafe
Border Cafe
B-Side Lounge
Cactus Club
Elbow Room
Enormous Room
Independent
Joe's American B&G
John Harvard's
Miracle of Science
Mistral
Pho République
Red Fez
Redline
Saint
Sonsie
Sunset Grill
Temple Bar
33 Restaurant
Trio
West Street Grille

Sleepers
(Good to excellent food, but little known)
Abbondanza
Alloro
Antonia's
Artichokes Rist.
Bangkok City
Bangkok Cuisine
Bombay Classic
Brenden Crocker's
Buteco
Casa Portugal
Cassis
Centre Street Bistro/N
Cioppino's/N
Copley's Grand
Craigie St. Bistrot
Davide Rist.

Special Feature Index

DeMarco/N
Dom's
Dong Khanh
Eastern Pier
Eclectic Cafe/C
El Cafetal
Enormous Room
Esther's/C
Glenn's Rest.
Great Thai Chef
Il Moro
Imperial Seafood
Indian Cafe
Indian Club
Indigo
Intrigue Cafe
J's at Nashoba
King Fung
La Summa
Le Lyonnais
Misaki/C
Neighborhood Rest.
New Jang Su
Oceana
O'Fado
Opus/M
Outermost Inn/M
Park Corner/M
Passage to India
Piccolo Nido
Pit Stop BBQ
Ponte Vecchio
Red Raven
Sabur
Saigon
Sapporo
Sconset Café/N
Second St. Cafe
Sfoglia/N
Shalimar of India
Sichuan Garden
Sidney's Grille
Sosumi Asian/C
South St. Diner
Square Café
Stir Crazy/C
Stone Soup
Suishaya
Sunset Cafe
Sushi by Yoshi/N
Tacos Lupita
Tantawan
Taverna Toscana
Theo's/M
Tokyo
Trio
Twenty-Eight Atlantic/C
Viet Hong
Village Sushi
Vin & Eddie's
V. Majestic
White Rainbow
Woodbox/N
WuChon
Zabaglione

Tasting Menus

American Seasons/N
Balance/M
Blue Ginger
Chillingsworth/C
Clio
Club Car/N
Coriander
Davide Rist.
DeMarco/N
eat
EVOO
Federalist
Fifty-Six Union/N
Gargoyles on Sq.
Harvest
L'Etoile/M
Meritage
No. 9 Park
Radius
Ten Tables
Top of the Hub
Topper's/N
Torch
Tratt. a Scalinatella
Tremont 647
Trio
Troquet

Theme Restaurants

Bisuteki
Border Cafe
Bugaboo Creek
Cheers
Fire & Ice
House of Blues
Johnny's Lunch.
Kowloon
Maggiano's
Union Oyster Hse.

Views

Adrian's/C
Anthony's Pier 4

get updates at zagat.com 233

Special Feature Index

Aqua Grille/C
Aujourd'hui
Back Eddy
Barking Crab
Bay Tower
Beach Plum Inn/M
Black Dog Tav./M
Brant Point Grill/N
Bridgeman's
Chatham Bars/C
Clancy's/C
Coach House/M
Coonamessett Inn/C
Daggett House/M
Davio's
Finz
Fishmonger's Cafe/C
Galley on Cliffside/N
Home Port/M
Ipanema/M
Jimmy's Harborside
Landing
Lobster Pot/C
Martin House/C
Meritage
Mews/C
Ocean House/C
Opus/M
Outermost Inn/M
Red Inn/C
Red Rock Bistro
Ross' Grill/C
Siros
Spinnaker
Straight Wharf/N
Top of the Hub
Topper's/N
Twenty-Eight Atlantic/C

Waterside

Anthony's Pier 4
Aqua Grille/C
Atlantica
Barking Crab
Beach Plum Inn/M
Black Cow
Black Dog Tav./M
Brant Point Grill/N
Bubala's/C
Cape Sea Grille/C
Chart House
Chart Room/C
Chatham Bars/C
Clancy's/C
Coach House/M
Daggett House/M
Daily Catch
Dancing Lobster/C
Eastern Pier
Finz
Fishmonger's Cafe/C
Galley on Cliffside/N
Martin House/C
Outermost Inn/M
Red Inn/C
Red Rock Bistro
Siros
Straight Wharf/N
Tom Shea's
Topper's/N

Winning Wine Lists

American Seasons/N
Angelo's
Atria/M
Aujourd'hui
Azafran
blu
Blue Room
Café Louis
Caffe Bella
Chanticleer/N
Chester/C
Federalist
Grapevine
Grill 23 & Bar
Hamersley's Bistro
Harvest
Il Capriccio
La Campania
L'Espalier
Les Zygomates
Lucca
Lumière
Maison Robert
Mamma Maria
Mantra
Meritage
Mistral
No. 9 Park
Paddock/C
Prezza
Radius
Salts
Sel de la Terre
Silks
Taberna de Haro
Tratt. a Scalinatella

Special Feature Index

Tratt. Pulcinella
Troquet
Truc
21 Federal/N
UpStairs on Square
Vault

Worth a Trip

Andover
  Cassis
Beverly Farms
  Yanks
Canton
  Olio
Cape Cod
  Abba
  Chester
  Chillingsworth
  Regatta of Cotuit
  Twenty-Eight Atlantic
Hingham
  Tosca
Hull
  Saporito's

Martha's Vineyard
  Atria
  L'Etoile
  Sweet Life Cafe
Nantucket
  Chanticleer
  Òran Mór
  Pearl
  Topper's
Natick
  Oga
Randolph
  Caffe Bella
Salem
  Grapevine
Scituate
  Barker Tavern
Tyngsboro
  Silks
Wellesley
  Blue Ginger
Westport
  Back Eddy

Wine Vintage Chart

This chart is designed to help you select wine to go with your meal. It is based on the same 0 to 30 scale used throughout this *Survey*. The ratings (prepared by our friend **Howard Stravitz**, a professor at the University of South Carolina) reflect both the quality of the vintage and the wine's readiness for present consumption. Thus, if a wine is not fully mature or is over the hill, its rating has been reduced. We do not include 1987, 1991–1993 vintages because they are not especially recommended for most areas.

	'85	'86	'88	'89	'90	'94	'95	'96	'97	'98	'99	'00	'01
WHITES													
French:													
Alsace	24	18	22	28	28	26	25	23	23	25	23	25	26
Burgundy	26	25	17	25	24	15	29	28	25	24	25	22	20
Loire Valley	–	–	–	–	25	23	24	26	24	23	24	25	23
Champagne	28	25	24	26	29	–	26	27	24	24	25	25	–
Sauternes	21	28	29	25	27	–	20	23	27	22	22	22	28
California (Napa, Sonoma, Mendocino):													
Chardonnay	–	–	–	–	–	22	27	23	27	25	25	23	26
Sauvignon Blanc/Semillon	–	–	–	–	–	–	–	–	24	24	25	22	26
REDS													
French:													
Bordeaux	25	26	24	27	29	22	26	25	23	24	23	25	23
Burgundy	23	–	21	25	28	–	26	27	25	22	27	22	20
Rhône	25	19	27	29	29	24	25	23	25	28	26	27	24
Beaujolais	–	–	–	–	–	–	–	–	23	22	25	25	18
California (Napa, Sonoma, Mendocino):													
Cab./Merlot	26	26	–	21	28	29	27	25	28	23	26	23	26
Pinot Noir	–	–	–	–	–	27	24	24	26	25	26	25	27
Zinfandel	–	–	–	–	–	25	22	23	21	22	24	19	24
Italian:													
Tuscany	26	–	24	–	26	22	25	20	28	24	27	26	25
Piedmont	26	–	26	28	29	–	23	26	28	26	25	24	22

Is that a Zagat in your pocket?

INTRODUCING
ZAGAT TO GO℠
2003 Restaurant and Nightlife Guide
FOR POCKET PC & PALM OS® DEVICES

- **Extensive Coverage:** Includes over 20,000 establishments in 45+ cities
- **Search:** Find the perfect spot by locale, price, cuisine and more
- **Free Updates:** Stay current with new content downloads throughout the year
- **One-Touch Scheduling:** Add your plans directly to your Date Book or Calendar

Available wherever books and software are sold

or for download at www.zagat.com/software